THE SOVIETS IN INTERNATIONAL
ORGANIZATIONS

The Soviets
in International
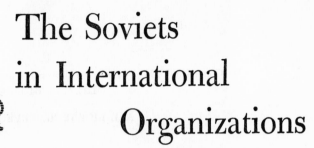
Organizations

Changing Policy Toward
Developing Countries, 1953-1963

BY ALVIN Z. RUBINSTEIN
with a Foreword by Philip E. Jacob

PRINCETON UNIVERSITY PRESS
PRINCETON, NEW JERSEY
1964

Printed in the United States of America
by THE WILLIAM BYRD PRESS, INC.

To Frankie

Foreword

THE STUDY of international relations, especially in contemporary American scholarship, has shown a remarkable propensity for didactic generalizations based upon a priori assumptions concerning the determinants of national political behavior.

This propensity has characterized both the so-called "utopian" and "realist" approaches to international relations. It is not so obvious in the case of the latter, because the realists profess devotion to seeing things as they are. But in fact, the methodology customarily applied by utopians and realists alike in the analysis of foreign policy has not been sufficiently rigorous to sustain a genuinely empirical inquiry. In default of empirically verified findings, scholars and statesmen have both set forth and subscribed to propositions which *seemed* cogent to them. In other words, they have made "guesstimates" of the objectives and determinants of policy and accepted their own judgments as the end truth, indeed, as a factual basis for policy recommendations and decisions.

The scholar's propensity for the didactic has been abetted by the strong manipulative disposition of many governments, especially in the conduct of their foreign relations, and by the mantle of secrecy which has consequently enshrouded the records of policy decision-making. Knowing that some governments are not above the use of deception in furthering their policies, the student of international relations would be naïve to take at face value the publicized professions of any government; yet the inaccessibility of documentary and other forms of evidence of the actual decisional process leaves the analyst with inadequate points of reference to determine when a particular government is playing hide-and-seek or is acting in bonafides.

Eager at all costs to avoid the charge of naïveté, many a scholar has sought to establish his sophistication by interpreting the actions and words of a government's policy officials in terms of either a set of principles or "laws" which he holds to characterize the international actions of states in general— or a dialectic which he holds to govern the actions of a particular state. Such analyses not only suffer from a lack of empirical referents but actually tend to compound the possibility of error, because they presume an omniscience which is not warranted. Instead of reading *from* the facts of national behavior, they read *into* these facts implications which reflect assumptions, biases, and judgments formed to a large extent outside the verified experience of those who have had a hand in shaping policy.

It is such self-contained interpretations of foreign policy which block the development of anything which might properly be called a scientific approach to the analysis of international relations. The problem is peculiarly acute in reference to Soviet foreign policy. On the one hand, the confining line of Communist doctrine inhibits trustworthy indigenous scholarship. On the other, the reliability of much non-Communist commentary is impaired by almost equally rigid and doctrinal convictions concerning the systematic imperatives dictating Soviet behavior. And, of course, the kinds of primary data needed to check the validity of either set of analyses are pathetically sparse.

This has forced responsible scholars to rely on Soviet actions as the principal indicator of the Soviet decisional process and to use these actions as the major test of the adequacy of their interpretations of the determinants of Soviet policy. But this approach is also vulnerable, because action is not at all identical with policy. Action provides at most a clue to factors which influence policy; it is not a direct and sure guide to policy determinants. Action is the result of decisions, usually a complex of decisions. When we try to look back through action to identify the nature and sources of policy, we confront the dilemma that the same action may reflect quite different sets of objectives and motivations. How can one tell what it was that really prompted policy-makers to take the particular step they did?

The risk of mistaking the character of policy behind action is heightened in the case of western studies of Soviet behavior, because the cultural and political context of policy-making differs radically from circumstances with which most analysts are personally familiar.

Against this background, Dr. Rubinstein's study makes a methodological contribution of special significance, quite apart from its substantive insights concerning the conduct and development of Soviet policy in international organizations. It demonstrates a procedure of inquiry whereby the determinants of policy may be explored empirically without benefit of access to authentic records of policy formation. In effect, the analyst "triangulates" the policy process from several independent points of reference. He secures a "fix" by coordinating and comparing various bodies of evidence.

In this work, the author has systematically examined and compared expressions of Soviet policy toward underdeveloped countries at four different points of impact: (1) in debates on issues arising in organs of the United Nations and Specialized Agencies, (2) in relationships with members of the international Secretariats concerned with these issues, (3) in communications with officials of underdeveloped countries, who constitute a major target of Soviet policy, and (4) in internal Soviet professional and scholarly commentary. By using each source as a check against the others, it has been possible to identify certain features of Soviet policy rationalization which are so consistent, regardless of audience or circumstance, as to indicate what may be basic motivational pivots of those responsible for policy decisions.

On the other hand, detection of contradictions among the four sources of evidence, or of sharp differences of emphasis, helps to identify the priorities which Soviet policy-makers have adopted in choosing among competing values and to indicate areas where Soviet action is shaped primarily by manipulative considerations.

One of the principal results of this method of analyzing Soviet political behavior, at least in this study, is to shed the sensationalism that so often characterizes current critiques of Communist strategy. When the dramatic and strident ideological tones of the Communists' public discourse are heard alongside their cool, often reserved communications off the podium, the pragmatism of post-Stalin Soviet policy becomes sharp and clear. Dr. Rubinstein shows how flexible the Soviets have been on issues affecting the underdeveloped countries, guided apparently by considerations of effectiveness in winning respect and confidence in these areas.

Furthermore, within the framework of the international institutions on which Dr. Rubinstein has focussed his attention, Soviet conduct does not exhibit the monolithic integration often attributed to it. Actions on similar issues vary so greatly from forum to forum as to suggest a serious lack of coordination between different organizational levels and divisions of the Soviet bureaucracy.

It also becomes abundantly evident from this study that the Soviets in general give a low priority to international organizations as vehicles of policy. But even in this respect they are not bound to a rigidly set pattern of conduct. Their interest has been greater in some institutions like the International Atomic Energy Agency; and it has been greater at some times than at others. Here again, Dr. Rubinstein has uncovered an empirical variable which is a helpful indicator of basic influences at work in the formulation of Soviet policy. Soviet preoccupation with an international institution apparently reflects the importance attached, not to the functions with which the institution is concerned, but to the areas of the world where the institution may have an impact.

This may in part explain the predominantly negative role of the Soviet Union in even the economic and social international organizations in which it has participated. Dr. Rubinstein discerns a sense of rivalry on the part of the Soviets whenever an international institution becomes effective and acquires support from the uncommitted nations of the world. Their policy is then directed, both within and outside the organization, toward limiting its impact and interposing Soviet influence. In the more sophisticated strategy of the post-Stalin period, this policy usually avoids outright obstructionism but, behind a facade of cooperation, strives to constrict the full-scale development of international operational programs.

In terms of its contribution to the general field of international behavioral analysis, Dr. Rubinstein's work is not an isolated effort. It has been undertaken within a broad program of comparative research on the influence of social values in the determination of public policy. This program was initiated by an interdisciplinary group at the University of Pennsylvania with which Dr. Rubinstein is associated, and is being developed jointly with social scientists at other American institutions and abroad. Its principal aim is to identify and contrast the values and beliefs which enter into decision-making at different levels of government and in various countries—in other words to clarify and weigh the ideological components of public policy. These studies hopefully will lead toward a common conceptual and methodological framework which will facilitate comparability across cultural lines of data on the interaction of social values and the political process.

Dr. Rubinstein's meticulous study, devoting close attention as it does to ideological factors, is an important example of one approach to this type of motivationally oriented policy research at the international level. Both the techniques of inquiry and the findings will increase in significance as similar studies are completed on other countries and aspects of public policy.

PHILIP E. JACOB

Preface

ON JULY 15, 1953, a startled assemblage of delegates to the Sixteenth Session of the UN Economic and Social Council heard the Soviet delegate, A. A. Arutiunian, announce that the Soviet Union was henceforth prepared to participate in the United Nations Expanded Program of Technical Assistance for underdeveloped countries. Arutiunian's announcement ushered in a new Soviet approach both to the underdeveloped countries and to the international organizations concerned with aiding them. Within a few years, Soviet bilateral programs of economic and technical aid helped Moscow attain unaccustomed heights of prestige, respectability, and influence among neutralist countries of the underdeveloped world. The process of shifting from a continental-centered to a global-oriented strategy, and of politically courting neutralist countries, was facilitated by, and initially reflected in, the change in Soviet policy toward the technical assistance activities of international organizations.

This study is concerned with changing post-Stalinist policies and behavior in the Specialized Agencies and regional economic commissions of the United Nations. Those organizations most preoccupied with problems of interest to underdeveloped countries will be analyzed, particular effort being devoted to isolating the determinants that brought about the changes and to elucidating the distinctive aspects of Soviet behavior. An attempt will be made to relate Soviet policy in international organizations to over-all Soviet foreign policy interests and activities, of which it represents a minor part; the vast amount of primary source data available, and as yet insufficiently investigated, commends it for this analysis. It is hoped that this case study of one phase of Soviet foreign policy may add to the existing body of knowledge on the relationship between the Soviet Union and the neutralist countries of the underdeveloped world and on the nature and scope of Soviet objectives in international organizations.

I have proceeded along three broad, interrelated lines of inquiry. First, a thorough examination was made of the summary records and documents of the Economic and Social Council, the Technical Assistance Committee, the International Labor Organization, the International Atomic Energy Agency, and the Economic Commission for Asia and the Far East, as well as their subsidiaries, for whatever clues they could supply to an understanding of Soviet policy and motivation. Second, the writings of Soviet scholars on the activities of UN organizations concerned with helping underdeveloped countries were analyzed, on the assumption that the changing interpretations of Soviet scholars would reflect changes in the policies and attitudes of the Soviet leadership. Third, to gain an added insight into the conduct of Soviet representatives at meetings of international organizations and into the behavior of Soviet nationals who are employed in international Secretariats, extensive interviewing was undertaken in New York, Geneva, New Delhi, Bangkok, Tokyo, and Vienna. Those interviewed have had extensive experience negotiating with Soviet officials and observing their behavior in international organizations and were therefore uniquely qualified to offer first-hand information and interpretations. Every care has been taken to minimize the dangers involved in interviewing those of different institutional, national, and political backgrounds. Out of this composite effort an attempt has been made to present the rationale behind Soviet policy and behavior in international organizations, assess the impact of ideology upon Soviet behavior, and relate these specific findings to the broader policy lines of Soviet interest in underdeveloped countries.

The study completed, there remains only the genuine

pleasure of expressing my deep appreciation to the persons and institutions who have contributed so greatly to the completion of this book, and who, it must be noted, bear no responsibility for its shortcomings. My debts are many and here gratefully acknowledged. To the career officials of international Secretariats and the foreign service personnel of various countries who gave generously of their information, experience, and interpretations, I express my deepest gratitude and respect. For understandable reasons, they have requested the protective and politic cloak of anonymity. But whatever modest contribution this study may make toward greater understanding of Soviet policy and behavior in international organizations is due, in large measure, to their willingness to talk candidly, to share information and insights that are not to be found in the written public records. The Rockefeller Foundation very generously made possible an undisturbed year of research and writing and interviewing in Europe, Southern Asia, Japan, and the Soviet Union. The American Philosophical Society provided two summer grants at preliminary stages of my investigation. The Committee for Advancement of Research of the University of Pennsylvania made available a grant-in-aid.

I am deeply indebted to my teacher and colleague, Dr. Philip E. Jacob, for his stimulus, counsel, and constant encouragement. I have benefited from the pioneer work done in this general area of Soviet policy by Professor Alexander Dallin of Columbia University and Professor Harold K. Jacobson of the University of Michigan, who also made valuable suggestions for improving this study. A number of others gave generously of their time in reading sections of the manuscript: Dr. Sydney D. Bailey; Dr. Benjamin Barg; Professor Frederick C. Barghoorn of Yale University; Professor George A. Codding, Jr. of the University of Colorado; Professor Leland M. Goodrich of Columbia University; Dr. John Melby of the University of Pennsylvania; Professor Walter R. Sharp of Yale University;

Professor John G. Stoessinger of Hunter College; Ambassador James J. Wadsworth; Professor David Wightman of Birmingham University; and Professor J. K. Zawodny of Washington University. I am grateful for the assistance of Dr. Lawrence S. Finkelstein and Dr. John Goormaghtigh of the Carnegie Endowment for International Peace. The editors of *International Organization, Survey,* and *The Proceedings of the American Philosophical Society* kindly granted their permission to use parts of my articles which had appeared in these publications. The library staffs of many international organizations were most helpful; I would like to mention, in particular, the assistance of Mrs. Edith Javor and Mrs. Elizabeth Ruckenbauer of the International Atomic Energy Agency. Mrs. George Kimmelman contributed greatly to the shaping of the final product. Mrs. Eve Hanle of Princeton University Press ably helped with the editing of the manuscript. Charles F. Marker managed to complete the typing under the strain of frequent changes. Finally, to my wife, who was a constant source of encouragement and a wonderful companion, I can only express my heartfelt sense of good fortune.

Philadelphia, Pennsylvania   Alvin Z. Rubinstein
July 1963

Contents

Glossary

ACABQ	Advisory Committee on Administrative and Budgetary Questions
ASA	Association for Southeast Asia
BTAO	Bureau of Technical Assistance Operations
ECA	Economic Commission for Africa
ECAFE	Economic Commission for Asia and the Far East
ECE	Economic Commission for Europe
ECOSOC	Economic and Social Council
EPTA	Expanded Program of Technical Assistance
FAO	Food and Agriculture Organization
IAEA	International Atomic Energy Agency
IBRD	International Bank for Reconstruction and Development
IDA	International Development Association
IFC	International Finance Corporation
ILO	International Labor Organization
IMF	International Monetary Fund
IRO	International Refugee Organization
ITO	International Trade Organization
ITU	International Telecommunication Union
OAEC	Organization for Asian Economic Cooperation
ONUC	United Nations Military Operation in the Congo
OPEX	Operational, Executive, and Administrative Personnel Program
RESREP	Resident Representative
SUNFED	Special United Nations Fund for Economic Development
TAA	Technical Assistance Administration
TAB	Technical Assistance Board
TAC	Technical Assistance Committee
UNEF	United Nations Emergency Force in the Middle East
UNESCO	United Nations Educational, Scientific and Cultural Organization
UPU	Universal Postal Union
WFTU	World Federation of Trade Unions
WFUNA	World Federation of Associations for the United Nations
WHO	World Health Organization

THE SOVIETS IN INTERNATIONAL
ORGANIZATIONS

List of UN Symbols Used in Footnotes*

A	General Assembly document
A/C.2	Second Committee, or Economic and Financial Committee
A/C.3	Third Committee, or Social, Humanitarian, and Cultural Committee
A/C.5	Fifth Committee, or Administrative and Budgetary Committee
E	Economic and Social Council document
E/AC.6	Economic Committee
E/AC.49	AD HOC Committee of Eight
E/CN.1	Economic and Employment Commission
E/CN.1/SUB.2	Sub-commission on Employment and Economic Stability
E/CN.1/SUB.3	Sub-commission on Economic Development
E/CN.11	Economic Commission for Asia and the Far East
E/CN.11/I & T	ECAFE Committee on Industry and Trade
E/TAC	Technical Assistance Committee
GC	General Conference (of the International Atomic Energy Agency)
GC/COM.1	Program, Technical and Budget Committee
GC/COM.2	Administrative and Legal Committee
GOV	Board of Governors of International Atomic Energy Agency
SF	United Nations Special Fund

* See also *Glossary*, p. xx.

I ⟡

Background: The Stalin Era,
1945-1953

THE UNITED NATIONS was created in 1945 out of the Western
Powers' belief that international organization offered the best
prospect for preserving the peace and preventing a third
World War. They assumed that through the United Nations
the wartime allies would act in concert to restrain any would-
be aggressor, and that the five Great Powers—China, France,
Great Britain, the Soviet Union, and the United States—would
cooperate to maintain the peace as they had to win the war.

The Soviet Union, on the other hand, joined the UN as an act
of accommodation, not conviction.[1] Stalin had no ideals or
illusions concerning the nature of the UN, its capacity to
safeguard Soviet security, or its domination by the Western
Powers. Aware that the UN was ideologically and institu-
tionally a creation of the capitalist West, Stalin agreed to membership only when the right to veto any moves inimical to
Soviet interests was made a cornerstone of the new organization. The veto was a precondition for Soviet participation.
Indeed, it is likely that the Western Powers, too, would not
have ratified the Charter without the veto, which guaranteed
that national interests would not be overridden by voting

[1] There have been few comprehensive studies of Soviet policy in the
United Nations, though the periodical literature of specific aspects of that
policy is considerable. For information on early Soviet assumptions,
attitudes, and policies toward the United Nations and its affiliated organi-
zations see: Alexander Dallin, *The Soviet Union at the United Nations*
(New York: Frederick A. Praeger, 1962); Irene Blumenthal, "The Soviet
Union and the United Nations" (MS); a forthcoming study by Harold
K. Jacobson on "The Soviet Union and the United Nations Economic
and Social Work"; and Richard F. Rosser, "The Soviet Union and the
Underdeveloped Countries in the United Nations" (MS).

majorities either in the Security Council or in the General Assembly. To all the Great Powers, the political and security functions of the UN were of paramount importance, an understandable emphasis in view of their narrow margin of victory.

But among many of the Western architects of the UN there was also shared the conviction that backwardness, ignorance, and instability provided fertile ground for demagoguery and dictators; that, in great measure, the roots of war emanate from the diverted quest of the downtrodden and despairing for economic, social, and political equality and progress; and that the UN must provide a positive program to eliminate these ills if international stability and orderly change were to prove realizable goals. Accordingly, they incorporated in the UN Charter provisions calling for the promotion of "higher standards of living, full employment, and conditions of economic and social progress and development." These were regarded as ancillary but by no means subordinate functions. They committed the UN and its affiliated Specialized Agencies to permanent struggle against poverty, illiteracy, and disease. The wealthy nations were to aid the poor nations, and the developed were to extend their knowledge of science and technology to the less developed in order to help raise international standards of living.

These attitudes and aspirations were not shared by the Soviet leaders who viewed the UN with mistrust and failed to appreciate the ways in which it could be used to promote Soviet interests. Stalin's xenophobia, his insistence upon unquestioning obedience, and his political objectives in Eastern Europe reinforced the already deep-rooted Soviet antipathy toward international organizations. Moscow's past, brief experience with collective security through the League of Nations had ended acrimoniously. Soviet leaders saw no reason to alter their fundamental conception of international organizations, a conception born in revolution, rooted in ideology, and reinforced by bitter interwar experiences. Ideologically, Moscow believed the UN was controlled by capitalist countries and dedicated to the preservation of Western influence. Soviet participation and the existence of the veto would at least minimize the likelihood of its being converted into a militant anti-Soviet coalition. Politically, Moscow thought that Soviet security could best be attained by extending Soviet control over Eastern Europe and keeping Germany divided and weak. Economically, the USSR was preoccupied with its own recovery and reconstruction; it had emerged from the war victorious but impoverished, and economic rebuilding was given top priority. When it became apparent, as early as mid-1945, that no significant economic assistance could be expected from the United States, the sole creditor nation with the capacity for making large-scale loans, Moscow undertook to rebuild its economy by accelerating the sovietization of Eastern Europe and keeping the Soviet people at a subsistence level.

Convinced ideologically that fundamental economic and social changes could not be accomplished through a patchwork of piecemeal, "reformist," policies, Moscow was against providing the UN with responsibilities in the economic and social fields. Its opposition was consonant with the basic Soviet approach to international relations, conditioned as it was by past experience with "capitalist" efforts to interfere in Soviet domestic affairs, by its ideological conception of the inevitable hostility of the non-Communist world (the wartime alliance being regarded only as an instance in which the Soviet Union had taken advantage of the split in the capitalist camp to defend its interests by temporary cooperation with one group of capitalists against another), and by its a priori assumption that capitalism is doomed historically and cannot forestall the advent of communism. However, in the diplomatic bargaining that accompanied the drafting of the UN Charter, Moscow acceded to President Roosevelt's insistence that the Economic and Social Council be included as one of the integral bodies of the UN.

5

As a signatory of the Charter, the Soviet Union assumed responsibilities devolving upon member states to promote welfare activities set forth in Article X. But it did little to promote these ends. Nor, during the Stalin period, did it even join most of the Specialized Agencies which constitute a major portion of the total UN activity in the economic and social spheres. The insignificance which these activities assumed in Moscow's early thinking can be seen in the failure of Soviet Foreign Minister V. M. Molotov even to mention them in his address at the founding conference of the UN in San Francisco in April 1945.

Once the Economic and Social Council (ECOSOC) commenced deliberations, Moscow sought to limit its operations, always on the ground of upholding the inviolability of national sovereignty. The anomaly of the Soviet Government, the Marxist-Leninist progenitor of world revolution, protesting alleged UN interference in the domestic affairs of other countries was not completely lost on underdeveloped countries. But, paradoxically, Moscow managed to derive from this position a measure of stature among them because of their sensitivity regarding threats to their independence and political status in the international community. After an early realization that ECOSOC could not provide tangible economic assistance to it or any other country, Moscow used ECOSOC primarily as a propaganda forum for criticizing Western policies and for lauding the superiority of the Soviet system. Its main concern was to keep ECOSOC activities minimal and to ensure that they would not be used to enhance the influence of the Western Powers nor promote the stability of the capitalist world.

In the United States, European economic recovery was felt to be a major political responsibility. The realization that massive aid was necessary to strengthen Western Europe against the twin threats of Soviet expansionism and indigenous Communist subversion led Secretary of State Marshall, on

June 5, 1947, to set forth the outline of an American proposal which subsequently became known as the Marshall Plan. For a fleeting few weeks, hopes soared among those who advocated the strengthening of the UN that the United States would agree to direct its economic aid through international channels. They argued that such an approach would greatly reduce the Cold War implications of American aid, perhaps arrest the accelerating cleavage of Europe into two hostile camps, and also vitalize the operational arms of international organizations. The newly established UN Economic Commission for Europe, then headed by the distinguished Swedish economist, Gunnar Myrdal, was considered the logical organization to administer American aid and coordinate all-European recovery efforts.

However, the Cold War had become too pervasive a blight on the international landscape for the American Congress to appropriate funds which might in part be destined to rebuild the Soviet Union. The potentialities for aid administered through the UN were perhaps never greater than in 1947, but the increased sovietization of Eastern Europe and the widespread fears of Communist takeovers in Italy and France, gave rise to the political decisions which doomed, untried, the utopian, and domestically vulnerable, suggestions for channeling aid through the UN.

ECOSOC had been trying to find a focus for its deliberations. As a new organization, overwhelmed with proposals involving funds which it could not hope to raise, and uncertain how best to fulfill its Charter-given mandate, ECOSOC cast its net of interests far and wide. During the 1945-1946 period, relief and refugees were the main issues. As the disruptive aftermath of war gave way to the emergence of postwar normalcy, the emphasis shifted to long-range reconstruction. ECOSOC directed its attention increasingly toward the economic problems of the less developed countries. It anticipated the subsequent interest of the Great Powers in the political significance of these emerging colonial areas, and its extensive

7

discussions brought public attention to the problems of Africa, Asia, and Latin America. During the early ECOSOC consideration of means of stimulating growth in underdeveloped areas, the Soviets showed particular interest in two issues— unemployment and international trade. From the lengthy discussions which surrounded them, emerged the outlines of the Soviet approach to underdeveloped countries during the Stalin period.

The Issue of Unemployment

Unemployment and underemployment are endemic in less developed countries. The situation in any one country bears a disquieting similarity to that in any other: a scarcity of investment capital, a low agricultural productivity, and an inability of the economy to absorb the expanding supply of labor.

One of Moscow's most attractive appeals for underdeveloped countries is its claim that it has eliminated unemployment, and that capitalism (by which it means non-Communist societies) cannot permanently solve this debilitating and degrading societal malaise. Moscow's claims have found general and uncritical acceptance among the elites in underdeveloped countries, where the belief is prevalent that large-scale unemployment is "inevitable" under capitalism.

From the beginning ECOSOC attempted to deal with the unemployment question. On June 21, 1946, it established a permanent Economic and Employment Commission to advise the Council on "the promotion of worldwide full employment, the coordination of national full employment policies, and the prevention of economic instability." This was the first of many organizational experiments undertaken to find the most effective way of investigating the bases of backwardness and transmitting twentieth-century technology to less developed areas. Prevailing UN sentiment held that unemployment could best be reduced by increasing industrial and agricultural production and by expanding international trade. Throughout the years, innumerable resolutions were passed and the machinery for translating policy into progress slowly began to take shape.

Though voting for most of the resolutions, Soviet delegates disagreed with the Western approach to economic development and hammered at several political themes: the inevitability of unemployment under capitalism, regardless of any temporary palliatives which the UN might encourage governments to adopt; the relevance of the Soviet experience for underdeveloped countries; and the marginal character of UN efforts. Interspersed were attacks on the United States. Moscow blamed the persistence of unemployment on American policies—the Marshall Plan, the establishment of NATO, the rearming of West Germany, and the attempts to negotiate military pacts with newly independent underdeveloped countries.

Proceeding on the supposition that economic dependence breeds political friction, the Soviet Union turned the spotlight on American-European difficulties. Attacks on United States foreign aid were coupled with defenses of national sovereignty. Dire forecasts were made concerning Europe's imminent loss of independence to America and the reversion of the newly independent Asian countries to their former European masters. Soviet diplomats presented familiar themes in a shopworn ideological mold. Whenever discussions turned to concrete problems or programs, Soviet delegates tried to inject specious political considerations. Failing in this, they lost interest, for they did not then have the voting power to affect the outcome of any proposal, nor the perspective on how voting defeats in international organizations could be made politically useful in enhancing their position with underdeveloped countries.

In all discussions of the unemployment problem, Moscow assumed the role of defender of the working class. It took every opportunity to laud the socially and economically superior Soviet system in contrast with the crisis-ridden capitalist system. Its professed interest in the working class did not, however, induce it to join the International Labor Organization. Instead, Soviet attempts to infiltrate international labor movements were made through the Communist-dominated World Federation of Trade Unions (WFTU). Only in 1954, when the post-Stalinist leadership moved systematically to supplant the barren legacies of Stalin's foreign policy, did the USSR join the ILO. Then, though neither the structure and aims nor the Soviet image of the ILO had changed, political considerations dictated the new approach. Stalin's ideological antagonism to the ILO, which was described by one Soviet diplomat as "a body made up principally of the representatives of monopolies and thus could not be expected to come to an objective decision,"[2] is still shared by his successors, but participation is now regarded as politically useful.

Unemployment still remains a vital concern of UN organizations. In recent years, however, it has been treated not as a separate issue but more as one facet of the broader problem of stimulating economic development and helping underdeveloped countries gain momentum for the self-sustaining growth which, it is hoped, will ultimately absorb their unemployed.

Moscow and the ITO

Moscow supported the preliminary UN efforts to promote international trade and in February 1946 approved ECOSOC's adoption of the American proposal to convene a nineteen-nation Preparatory Conference on Trade and Employment to discuss the establishment of an International Trade Organization. But by the time the conference opened in October, Moscow had changed its position and refused to attend or participate in the deliberations. The proposed ITO was an early casualty of the Cold War. By the late 1946, the ruthless Soviet

[2] Economic and Social Council, *Official Records* (15th Session), p. 50.

approach to internal recovery, the expansionist character of Stalin's objectives in Europe, and his obvious lack of interest in economic cooperation through the UN, when coupled with the recrudescence of ideological militancy, sharpened the lines of political conflict and hastened the self-imposed isolation of the Soviet Union from the non-Communist world. This growing cleavage received formal sanction in the Zhdanov "two-camp thesis" speech of September 23, 1947, which heralded the creation of the Cominform and crystallized Moscow's bipolar conception of international political alignments: between the "camp of socialism" and the "camp of capitalism" there could be no accommodation, and all non-Communist countries, irrespective of their actual policy or preference, were lumped together in the capitalist camp.

This strategy, which was designed essentially for Europe, had disastrous consequences for Soviet foreign policy in underdeveloped areas. Not only did the Zhdanov line prevent Soviet policy-makers from exploiting differences in the non-Communist world and from encouraging underdeveloped countries to pursue an independent line, but its uncritical application by cowed Communist Parties abroad precipitated an alienation between them and mass-supported nationalist movements in Southern Asia and the Middle East. For almost a decade afterwards, Soviet influence in underdeveloped areas was negligible and Soviet professions of support for newly developing countries discredited. In the UN, Soviet isolation was greater than ever.

Moscow regarded the proposed International Trade Organization as American dominated and designed to stabilize the commercial relations of the capitalist countries. It insisted that the authority which was to be vested in the proposed ITO be given to the numerically smaller ECOSOC, in that way seeking to ensure a greater voice for the Soviet bloc. It objected to the orientation of the ITO Charter along the lines of economic liberalism—low tariffs, decreasing import restrictions, and specialization of trade—and specifically protested the proposal to adopt widespread use of the most-favored-nation concept, which provides for a mutual grant of trade concessions. Most-favored-nation provisions in trade agreements stipulate that if any of the contracting parties to a trade agreement should, at some future date, enter into a trade agreement with another country in which a lower tariff was specified for any product or series of products, such lower tariffs would automatically apply to all parties signatory to the M-F-N agreement.

To Moscow, M-F-N provisions were instruments of American imperialism. Eugen Varga, a leading Soviet economist, stated that "the aim of America's economic policy is, by forcing the most-favored-nation principle upon other countries, to ensure greater opportunities for the sale of her goods in the world market and thus to solve, or at least mitigate, the problem of disposing of her products."[3] (Ironically, this criticism of American policy came at the same time that Varga was under attack in Moscow for his view that the capitalist world was entering a period of relative international economic stability.)

While criticizing the United States for seeking to extend M-F-N provisions in the ITO Charter, and opposing the insertion of the M-F-N clause in the pertinent trade sections of the 1946 Peace Treaties with the former enemy states (Hungary, Rumania, Bulgaria), the Soviet Government proceeded to negotiate such provisions elsewhere. Once the Peace Treaties were signed, Moscow concluded bilateral trade agreements with these countries, incorporating that very provision. In this way she forced most-favored-nation treatment from the Eastern European countries, binding them closer to the USSR, pushing ahead with the sovietization of the area, and concomitantly weakening their ties with the West.

Moscow also opposed UN efforts to promote multilateral

[3] E. Varga, "The Prospects for International Cooperation," *New Times* (May 16, 1947), p. 6.

trading arrangements, contending that bilateralism not only ensured equality between the parties to an agreement, but more effectively upheld the principle of national sovereignty. The encouragement of economic nationalism suited Stalin's policy of isolating and dominating Eastern Europe—the major objective of Soviet foreign policy in the years after the war. Bilateralism in foreign trade was the economic counterpart of political isolation in the field of foreign policy. Both were set within a structure of priorities which precluded cooperation with UN economic organizations. UN efforts to promote closer ties between the industrialized nations and the underdeveloped nations of the Middle East and Asia held no interest for Stalin. During the postwar period before the death of Stalin, Soviet policy showed a distinct unbalance between declaration and deed. Soviet delegates spoke of the pressing need to promote the development of countries recently freed from colonial status, but their record belied these assertions and negated the image of interest which they sought to cultivate.

UN Technical Assistance: The Formative Years, 1946-1949

The Soviet attitude toward underdeveloped areas emerged clearly during the early sessions of the Economic and Social Council and was further elaborated at subsequent sessions of pertinent auxiliary bodies. The Soviet Union supported the principle of extending technical assistance and economic aid to underdeveloped areas with, however, the qualification that such assistance must not endanger the sovereignty or independence of the recipient. This qualification was used as an "escape clause" to rationalize nonparticipation and nonsupport for UN programs. A further condition, less explicitly stated, was UN acceptance of the Soviet approach to economic development. Differing as it did with the approach subsequently taken by the UN, Moscow felt justified in opposing the programs which were adopted.

13

The essence of the suggested Soviet approach lies in that aspect of Soviet thought which stresses the primacy of heavy industry. The logic is clear: political and economic independence depend upon military strength, which in turn can be developed only through heavy industry. The sinews of military power emanate from the steel, mining, electrical, and chemical industries of a nation. In their analyses of colonial areas, the Soviets regard the growth of heavy industry as a prerequisite for real as opposed to formal national independence. This approach, confirmed by the developmental experience of the USSR, has been made an unquestioned tenet of the Marxist-Leninist formula for economic development and modernization. Soviet proposals in the UN maintained that economic liberation could proceed only if technical assistance were used to promote the expansion of heavy industry, which alone represents the key to economic development of backward areas. Besides disagreeing with the Western approach which suggested the concentration of initial efforts and resources upon agricultural development and light industry, the Soviet delegates even denied the possibility of extenuating circumstances which might require some modification of their attitude. This unwillingness to argue the specifics of a case reflected Stalin's inflexible insistence upon absolute conformity to ideological orthodoxy.

Western delegates maintained that the Soviet proposals to establish heavy industry in underdeveloped areas were economically unrealistic since they failed to take into account the lack of massive capital investment, physical resources, technical knowledge, and political experience available in these areas—shortcomings which were insurmountable barriers to any projected accelerated expansion of heavy industry. Economic development is a complex process depending upon the growth, not merely of heavy industry, but of several branches of economic life. Various UN surveys have concluded that the necessary combinations for heavy industry are present, even potentially, in only a few countries of Afro-Asia.

However, the underdeveloped countries, particularly those which had only recently gained their independence, found that the Soviet emphasis on heavy industry complemented their aspirations toward rapid economic independence and power. It promised an attractive telescoping of technological development. It also seemed to offer greater promise of solution to the growing problem of unemployment and under-employment. Thus, in effect, the Soviet approach not only served to denounce and deprecate Western policy in an area in which that policy was already faring badly, but it also associated the Soviet Union with ideas welcome to the underdeveloped areas, particularly to broad segments of the influential intellectual elite groups.

Dogmatically and with singular persistence, the Soviets probed Western weaknesses in UN debates, crudely employing distortion and liberal compromises with the truth, and offering a nebulous but glittering idealism. For example, the Soviets cited the failure of the United Kingdom to industrialize Tanganyika as an instance of Western policy that deliberately sought to perpetuate the economic backwardness of a colonial area.[4] The Soviet Government must be presumed to have known the topography and economic resources of Tanganyika; by no twist of the imagination could conditions have been deemed propitious for heavy industry. But ignoring the not inconsiderable British efforts there, the Soviets inflexibly propounded the establishment of heavy industry in *all* underdeveloped areas, for their purpose was propaganda, not progress.

This Soviet tactic did have the effect of keeping Western diplomats continually on the defensive. They felt impelled to respond, partially out of a sensitivity to the manifest shortcomings of Western imperialist rule in colonial areas and partially out of an inflated assessment of the impact of the

[4] E/CN.1/SR. 74, p. 3.

15

Soviet charges on underdeveloped countries. Soviet criticisms found a receptive audience among some Arab and Asian leaders and nurtured the Marxian myth of the uniformly exploitive character of Western colonialism. But the crudeness of the Stalinist ideological conceptualization of Western policies and motivations and the glaring and total absence of any positive Soviet efforts on behalf of underdeveloped countries severely limited the political utility to Moscow of its bitter attacks on the West and its purely vocal support for underdeveloped countries.

These countries, whose pressing needs demanded concrete and immediate assistance, began to regard Soviet obstructionism in UN economic bodies with impatience and irritation. There came a time when lengthy Soviet expositions lost much of their earlier impact, when adopted policies overshadowed professed principles. At one juncture in the discussions of the Economic Committee, the Indian delegate proposed a series of procedural steps for the implementation of a technical assistance program. Most members of the Committee expressed their approval. However, the Soviet bloc, true to its predictable rejection of any specific operational UN program, demurred and suggested a new study of the problem. In an unusually tart reply, rather uncharacteristic of the Indian delegate, Mr. Adarkar criticized the Soviet maneuver, declaring that there had been more than enough discussion of principles and the time had come "to get down to brass tacks."[5] But such rebuffs were the exception rather than the rule.

Soviet obstructionism and nonparticipation came under occasional Asian criticism, but the extent and character of this criticism differed from that directed at Western countries for reasons which are not hard to find. Several hundred years of colonialism and exploitation made the recently freed underdeveloped nations much more wary of Western intentions than of Soviet actions, or inaction. The blame for backward-

[5] E/AC.6/SR. 55, p. 8.

ness could readily be attributed to Western misrule, but the Soviets came with clean hands. Soviet imperialism is not apparent in Afro-Asia and Latin America as it is in Europe, since underdeveloped countries have experienced only Western rule and exploitation.

Soviet officials probed the shortcomings of the Western legacy and availed themselves of every opportunity to place on the West the onus of responsibility for the plight of the underdeveloped areas. That they failed to make tangible headway until after the death of Stalin was the result of his underestimation of the role which these countries could play in promoting Soviet interests and his incapacity, ideologically or politically, to make the marginal adjustments which were to bring so rich a harvest after 1955.

The Problem of International Investment

During the discussions of the Economic and Social Council and the Economic Commission for Europe, Soviet representatives voiced their opposition to all forms of international investment saying that direct investment inevitably led to political interference. Nevertheless, *Soviet* investment in the Eastern European countries was upheld as beneficial; the "evils" inherent in this form of financial development were purely a by-product of the non-Communist world. Soviet attacks on foreign investment were invariably interwoven with criticism of American international economic influence. Private investment came in for particularly heavy fire as the Soviets dinned into the ears of the underdeveloped nations the line that they were "the raw materials appendages" of the Western capitalist countries. Occasionally, much to the discomfiture of the West and the satisfaction of the Soviet bloc, eruptions of voting sentiment would lead to the adoption by UN bodies of resolutions favoring nationalization of basic industries and national resources. This occurred more frequently after 1955-1956 with the doubling of Afro-Asian voting power.

The Soviet Union turned to its advantage the investment history of the West, which during the past 150 years was replete with instances of greed, exploitation, and political aggrandizement. By contrasting this with the economic and social advances of the Soviet Central Asian Republics since the Bolshevik Revolution, and citing alleged accomplishments in Eastern Europe, the Soviet Government sought to validate its credentials as a benevolent power interested in the welfare of all backward and exploited peoples. But Soviet analyses of developments in the non-Communist world were constrained by Stalin's inflexibility and isolationism and by the parochialism of traditionalist Marxist-Leninist thought. They dealt ineptly with the effects of the changing investment pattern, the emergence of former colonial areas as independent nations, and the new evolving pattern of inter-nation relationships. The Soviet preoccupation with casting Western nations as exploiters and villains usually exceeded the bounds of credibility even for those who were prepared to accept demonological theories of Western motivations. The Soviet image of the West was thus largely discounted by policy-making groups in underdeveloped countries, who, however, continued to be open to general Marxian interpretations of Western economic and political behavior.

In principle, the Soviet Union favored a system of loans and credits over that of direct investment, holding that it minimized the likelihood of exploitation and political interference. But it labeled as discriminatory the policies of international lending institutions, e.g. the International Bank for Reconstruction and Development (IBRD) and the International Monetary Fund (IMF), contending that the postwar grant of loans and credits had proved disappointing to recipient countries because the amounts were negligible and because America had exploited its dominant position as the world's creditor. They cited the failure of the Eastern European countries to qualify for loans from the World Bank and openly blamed American policy for this and other impediments to the development of underdeveloped areas. The Soviet Government justified its non-participation in the World Bank and IMF on the grounds of their anti-Soviet, American dominated character. Permeating all the Soviet accusations that the West made economic assistance conditional upon the granting of economic and political privileges was the attempt to relate American grants of aid to the accelerated rearmament of NATO and the increase in international tension.

An interesting aspect of Soviet policy was its ostensible support of the principle of disbursing all loans and credits under the aegis of the UN only. The Soviets maintained that financial assistance should not, under any circumstances, be encouraged between individual governments on a bilateral basis nor subjected to any political conditions. Yet, when confronted with tangible possibilities of implementing programs of international economic aid through the UN, programs which were acceptable to the underdeveloped countries, the Soviet Government withheld its support. It then argued that the amounts involved were inadequate to the task, and that Western domination of the proposals threatened to turn them into an adjunct of Western imperialism. Also, in conducting its own program of technical assistance with the Eastern European countries, the Soviet Union utilized bilateral agreements and made no effort to channel the funds through the UN. Indeed, as postwar developments proved, (and as the Yugoslavs made clear, shortly after the 1948 Tito-Stalin split, in their accounts of discriminatory Soviet trade and loan practices), the sovietization of Eastern Europe was greatly abetted by the establishment of an elaborate system of bilateral trade, technical assistance, and loan agreements. In the classic pattern of Great-Power penetration and domination of small nations, the USSR used bilateral agreements to destroy the tenuous economic links of Eastern Europe with the West, and to recast economic and trade relationships in a way that reinforced

Soviet political and military control over these countries.

These actions contrasted vividly with repeated Soviet statements that "any technical assistance should be given with the participation of the United Nations as the body best fitted to safeguard objectivity."[6] Significantly, these statements favoring active participation by the United Nations were made prior to the establishment of the Technical Assistance Administration (TAA). After 1949, though TAA approximated the type of agency envisaged by Soviet spokesmen, they no longer propounded this view.

The Soviet Government, though emphasizing the "evils" of international investment, especially private investment in the private sector of underdeveloped economies, opposed the drafting of a Code for International Investment.[7] When afforded the opportunity to draw up recommendations specifically designed to mitigate the inherent "evils," the Soviets refused to participate, alleging that piecemeal reforms were ineffectual and superficial and a waste of effort. They also reversed their previous espousal of UN-sponsored agreements and now maintained that bilateral agreements would be more effective in curbing the weaknesses associated with international investment.

Soviet criticisms seldom dealt with concrete proposals. They invariably attacked the West, particularly the United States. After 1954 they became more specific and stressed public, as opposed to private, sector investment; thereby they became more effective, finding supporting sentiment among the elites in neutralist countries. During the Stalin period, Soviet participation in UN plans to aid underdeveloped areas was limited to talk stressing the exploitative role of Western policy. Soviet delegates would, for example, frequently recommend studies to determine the influence of private monopolies in controlling world prices, which they maintained curbed the effective pur-

[6] E/CN.1/Sub. 3/SR. 12, p. 3.
[7] E/CN.1/Sub. 3/SR. 15, p. 4.

chasing power of the underdeveloped countries.[8] They blamed imperialist policies for the present retarded state of the underdeveloped areas and suggested that such studies would help end the economic dependence of these countries. One Soviet delegate suggested the use of bilateral agreements to facilitate the regulation of price relationships, thus ignoring evidence that agreements of this nature, when entered into by a Great Power and a small nation, often accorded the advantage to the more powerful. He expressed concern at the high world prices and declared that the United Nations should recommend measures to reduce these prices to underdeveloped areas.[9] But when the Soviet Union initiated its extensive economic courtship of underdeveloped countries in 1955, the prices which it charged for its goods and which it paid for the products of the underdeveloped countries were rarely less than world market prices. Thus, the Soviet charge of excessive capitalist profits earned on trade with these countries either was exaggerated or one that might as easily be leveled against the USSR.

Soviet proposals for more favorable terms of trade appealed to underdeveloped countries, but Moscow was not prepared to set an example. In negotiating trade agreements with Asian countries, e.g. India, the Soviet Union consistently demanded top prices for its products.[10] During the Stalin period, political prices, i.e. prices considerably lower than those quoted in world markets, were not employed as opening gambits in Moscow's drive for new markets. There was nothing to indicate that the USSR was prepared to subordinate hard business practices to the promotion of economic development of non-Communist, underdeveloped countries, perhaps in part because it did not have the surpluses to spare, nor any interest in establishing closer ties with these countries. In another in-

[8] E/CN.1/Sub. 2/SR. 11, p. 5.
[9] E/CN.1/Sub. 3/SR. 10, p. 2.
[10] *The Hindustan Times,* September 3, 1953.

stance, the Soviets opposed measures proposing to grant ECOSOC the authority to coordinate economic development activities with the approval of member governments. They insisted that ECOSOC's functions were limited to making recommendations.[11] This restrictive interpretation of the Charter's provisions characterized the prevailing Soviet attitude toward attempts to expand the economic competence of the United Nations.

The pattern of Soviet behavior was predictable. Western proposals met with uniform hostility, being regarded as subterfuges for the perpetuation and extension of Western influence. The assumption by the UN of responsibility for operational programs was opposed as a violation of the Charter and as additional evidence of subordination to Western policies. The views of underdeveloped countries were seldom treated to systematic analysis. In discussions of the various UN committees and commissions, the Soviet delegates sought to align their positions with those of the underdeveloped countries, encouraging political and psychological propensities inimical to Western interests. But seldom did Soviet diplomats commit themselves to the specific programs supported by these countries, basing their hesitation on the bogey of imperialist domination. Soviet proposals were made with both eyes toward propaganda and political debate rather than toward their economic utility and feasibility. The result was a dichotomy between Soviet pronouncements and Soviet practices which perpetuated Moscow's estrangement from the non-Communist world.

The attraction of the Soviet Union which persisted in the underdeveloped countries even during the nadir of Soviet diplomatic activity in the 1946-1953 period stems from a series of diverse, yet interrelated elements—*inter alia,* the understandable hypersensitivity of underdeveloped countries to imagined

[11] E/CN.1/Sub. 3/SR. 7, p. 5.

threats to their independence, the absence of any pronounced tradition of intimate cultural and economic relations with the Soviet Union, the differences between Western and neutralist approaches to the problem of containing international communism, and the success of the Soviet experience in industrializing rapidly. This latter factor exerts a strong and continuing influence on groups impatient to convert an essentially feudal, agrarian society into a modern, industrialized one in the shortest possible period.

The Implementation of a Technical Assistance Program

Under stimulus provided by President Truman's 1949 inaugural address, ECOSOC expanded its program of technical assistance. At a meeting in February 1949 it adopted an American proposal for implementing the Point Four concept. During the discussions, which took place throughout the spring and summer, aimed at establishing a new administrative framework for technical assistance, the Soviet delegation argued that the existing machinery of the UN and the Specialized Agencies was adequate for the functioning of the projected program.[12] Despite initial Soviet opposition to the Technical Assistance Administration and to the allied recommendations designed to expand the scope of technical assistance operations, ECOSOC passed a resolution in August 1949 pertaining to the financing of a program of aid which authorized: ". . . the Secretary-General to set up a special account for technical assistance for economic development to which contributions of countries shall be credited and from which transfers shall be made to the participating organizations exclusively for the expanded technical assistance programme to be carried out in the light of the observations and guiding principles . . . connected therewith."

[12] Economic and Social Council, *Official Records* (9th Session), p. 397.

23

On November 16, 1949, the General Assembly unanimously approved a program of expanded technical assistance to underdeveloped areas. To maintain the consistency of its ideological position—supporting underdeveloped countries—the Soviet Government voted for the program. The provisions were consonant with the mandate established at the third session of the General Assembly in December 1948 which held that:

The technical assistance furnished shall:
- (i) not be a means of foreign economic and political interference in the internal affairs of the country concerned and shall not be accompanied by any consideration of a political nature;
- (ii) be given only to or through governments;
- (iii) be designed to meet the needs of the country concerned;
- (iv) be provided, as far as possible, in the form which that country desires.[13]

Analysis of these provisions suggests that the General Assembly had been sensitive to Soviet reservations, had taken them under serious advisement, and had, indeed, incorporated many of them in its final resolution. Previous Soviet statements had demanded that any program of technical assistance promote the development of underdeveloped countries and not be accompanied by encumbering conditions of an economic, political, or military character.[14] Conceivably, the safeguards adopted should have satisfied the Soviet Government, but they did not. The Soviets refused to participate in any of the technical assistance projects or to contribute to the Expanded Program of Technical Assistance (EPTA). However, they accepted membership on the Technical Assistance Committee (TAC), the policy-making body responsible for the implementation of ECOSOC resolutions on technical assistance.

[13] E/1174, p. 15.
[14] Economic and Social Council, *Official Records* (8th Session), p. 435.

Estranged by choice, the Soviets remained apart, criticizing the UN technical assistance program, but continuing to assert their adherence to the principles on which it was founded. They explained their refusal to help the financing of EPTA by claiming that American domination of the program perpetuated colonial conditions in underdeveloped countries and that "the methods followed in the implementation of the programme were based less on the Charter of the United Nations than on the Point Four Programme of President Truman."[15] Similarly, they explained their nonparticipation in most of the Specialized Agencies on the basis of these organizations "being guided more by the policies of Washington than the principles of the Charter."[16]

But the proof of the pudding is in the eating. Soviet forebodings did not discourage underdeveloped countries from seeking the benefits of technical assistance. Quite the contrary; requests for aid greatly exceeded available appropriations, and expectations soared. Underdeveloped countries saw no threat to their independence in the program and looked hopefully to the UN for the investment capital and technical knowhow that they needed for economic development. Attention to the possibility of channeling aid through UN organizations, so widespread and enthusiastic during the early years of EPTA, waned when it became apparent that the UN could not obtain the amounts necessary to satisfy the needs of the clients. The implementation of technical assistance programs proceeded, limited only by the availability of financial resources. But that limitation was, in a short time, to lead underdeveloped countries to appreciate and turn to advantage their strategic geographic and political importance in the global competition between the Soviet and Western blocs.

Soviet abstention from UN technical assistance programs also meant that no Eastern European country submitted requests

[15] E/TAC/SR. 15, p. 21.
[16] E/TAC/SR. 1, p. 2.

for aid, despite Soviet and satellite statements defining Eastern Europe as underdeveloped and in need of aid. For several reasons, the Soviets made no attempt to seek help from EPTA. First, the USSR, involved in the systematic Stalinization of the area, opposed the operation of UN commissions in Eastern Europe. This was consistent with Soviet policy of eliminating all Western influence from the area and preventing any direct contact between UN officials and the various peoples of Eastern Europe, whose isolation was a necessary step in the establishment of Soviet hegemony. Second, the fetish of secrecy, traditionally a hallmark of Czarist and now Soviet society, was pursued with fanatic intensity in occupied Eastern Europe. The xenophobia of Stalin, the imprimatur of orthodoxy and conformity which stamped all of Soviet society and empire, and the crude exploitation of Eastern Europe dictated not only the direction, but also the style, of Soviet diplomacy. Third, aside from having no desire to see the technical assistance programs accomplish anything which might strengthen the non-Communist world, the Soviet Government held the view that there was really nothing to be gained materially from participation. UN resources were too small to be meaningful. Against this evaluation of the economic factors, the pressing political considerations clearly dominated.

The Logic of Stalinist Policy

During the Stalinist postwar period, the Soviet Union did not contribute "one red ruble" to UN efforts to promote the economic development of underdeveloped areas, nor did it manifest any willingness to become involved in EPTA's operational activities. It accompanied its refusal to participate in the actual undertakings of the UN with severe criticism of the work that was being done. These facts were emphasized many times by the Western Powers in UN deliberations and placed the Soviets in an unusually exposed and sensitive position. To divert attention from their policy of indifference and neglect, they depreciated the modest achievements of EPTA and raised the spectre of capitalist expansion in underdeveloped areas;[17] for example, their abstention from the International Refugee Organization (IRO) was explained as a reaction to the IRO having "been transformed into an office for providing cheap labor for United States planters and colonizers."

The continued disparity between Soviet declarations and deeds raises the question of the motivation behind Stalin's policy in international organizations dealing with underdeveloped areas. Why did the Soviet Union, avowedly a staunch advocate of the principle of technical assistance, refuse every proffered opportunity to cultivate the friendship of the underdeveloped countries which hold so pivotal a position in Soviet doctrine? This was no oversight; it was intentional and tailored to the cut of over-all Stalinist foreign policy.

Soviet thought has long maintained that the key to a Communist victory in Europe rests on the ability to alienate the industrial West from the markets and raw materials of the underdeveloped areas. But with the exception of China in the mid-1920's and early 1930's, and Turkey during the Allied intervention in Russia between 1919 and 1921, most underdeveloped areas had been in no position to affect the international position of the Soviet Union. Nor were they, as colonies or dependencies of the European Powers, able to act contrary to fundamental Western policies. They could, therefore, be politically ignored in the formulation of policy. To adapt ideology tightly to the security needs of the Soviet state, the role of proletarian internationalism was subordinated to the defense of Soviet national interest.

Stalin's assertion in August 1927, that internationalism required proletarians of all countries to support the Soviet Union, since an internationalist is one who "unhesitatingly, uncondi-

---

[17] G. Slavianov, "Ekonomicheskiye voprosy na 13 sessii ekonomicheskogo i sotsial'novo soveta O.O.N.," *Planovoye khoziaistvo* (November-December 1951), p. 84.

tionally, without vacillation, is ready to defend the USSR because the USSR is the basis of the world revolutionary movement, and it is impossible to defend and to advance [this movement] unless the USSR is defended," meant, in practice, that Soviet security was the number one concern of all Communists. If the interests of underdeveloped countries were subordinated to Moscow's immediate objective, or if Soviet diplomatic neglect seemed to contrast with doctrinal pronouncements, the burden for understanding and obedience rested with foreign Communist Parties. Prior to World War II, Soviet leaders were deeply involved with problems close to home. Interest in underdeveloped areas remained secondary to the paramount problem of ensuring Soviet security. The revolutionary instrument of early Bolshevik leaders—the Communist International—was transformed by Stalin into a docile, pliable instrument for the dissemination of propaganda and for the purging of anti-Stalin factions in foreign Communist Parties. By 1929 it lost whatever revolutionary dynamism it had once had.

But in 1945, Moscow felt that world capitalism had been seriously weakened, that European empires were tottering, and that the developing Arab-Asian revolutionary movements were a force which might accelerate the decline of Europe. Accordingly, it resurrected the Leninist theory of imperialism applied to underdeveloped areas, i.e. that the capitalist countries in their quest for raw materials, cheap labor, and potential markets have seized the underdeveloped areas, thus forestalling their own inevitable decay and disintegration. The twin themes of national self-determination and progress through communism were sedulously elaborated.

Though these views were repeated for the benefit of underdeveloped countries many times in UN meetings, Stalin's primary interest was still Europe, not Asia or Africa or the Middle East per se. His bipolar view of international politics suited a strategy intended for Europe, not Asia. Both its faulty interpretation by Communist Parties long accustomed to unquestioning subservience to Moscow's fiat and Moscow's failure to prevent its uncritical application with subsequent harmful consequences to underdeveloped countries led to the squandering of Soviet prestige and the alienation of indigenous Communist Parties from the mainstream of nationalist movements in underdeveloped countries. Underestimation of the importance of underdeveloped areas led Moscow to make a number of grievous errors from which these Parties have not yet recovered.

Stalin's primary concern was the attainment of political and strategic objectives in Eastern Europe, and he displayed a singlemindedness of purpose in achieving them. Despite the attention demanded by the unsuccessful Korean adventure in 1950 and the supple accommodation called for by the Communist conquest of China in 1949, Stalin's main energies were directed toward the elimination of Western influence from East and Southeast Europe, the establishment of Soviet supremacy in that area, and the preservation of a divided Germany. His success in these endeavors is one of the enduring consequences of World War II and remains a major goal of his successors.

Also to be taken into consideration is the Soviet attitude toward international organizations in general, and the UN in particular. Soviet reluctance to join the World Bank and the International Monetary Fund (membership in one was dependent upon membership in the other), UNESCO, the Food and Agriculture Organization (FAO), and the International Labor Organization (ILO), must be seen against the Soviet concept of what international organizations should attempt to do and against Moscow's critical economic posture in the immediate postwar period. Always uppermost in Stalin's mind was the security function of the UN; the economic and social functions were depreciated and basically ignored. The Soviet decision not to join certain international organizations and the subsequent pressure upon the Eastern European nations to quit those they had joined prior to sovietization were conditioned by the growing cleavage between East and West and the general isolationist bent of Soviet foreign policy.

In 1951, during the Korean War, the Soviet government undertook a major reevaluation of its policy toward the UN and the Specialized Agencies. Moscow decided that by walking out of the Security Council in 1950 over the issue of Chinese Communist membership, it had permitted that body to be utilized as an anti-Soviet instrument. Its withdrawal had merely simplified Western domination of the UN and the use of that organization as a weapon in the Cold War. The Soviet Government realized the importance of participating in the Security Council as one way of defending Soviet interests. The logical extension of this policy, i.e. to encompass all international organizations, was not fully appreciated nor implemented until the post-Stalin period. But the potentialities of international organizations for the promotion of Soviet interests appeared in a new light to Soviet policy-makers.

A second consequence of the Korean War was Moscow's initial perception of what is known as the Afro-Arab-Asian bloc—the neutralists of the underdeveloped world—and the current complementary interests shared in many instances between this bloc and the Soviet camp. Emerging as an identifiable group which, though differing politically and economically as a social system from the Communist bloc, was not irrevocably tied to the West on all issues, the Afro-Asian bloc could not be uncritically lumped with the capitalist camp. Moscow recognized that these countries were not part of the Western anti-Soviet coalition and that they had "objective" reasons for not wishing to be tied too closely to the West. The role played by some of the Arab-Asian diplomats in the behind-the-scene negotiations that led to serious Korean armistice talks, helped convince many top echelon Soviet officials of the political importance of the underdeveloped countries: of the convenient use that they might serve in transmitting Soviet views to the West and in influencing the West to adopt a more conciliatory policy toward the USSR. At this time, diplomats of several Eastern European satellites, particularly the Poles, also tried to impress upon Moscow the amorphous character of the political alignments in the underdeveloped countries and the advantages in the Cold War which could redound to Soviet policy through skillful and selective cultivation of the leaders of these countries. Thus, the beginning of Soviet recognition of the role which the UN could play in the advancement of foreign policy had its roots in the closing phases of the Korean War and the lessons which the Soviets learned from that experience.

Prior to 1951-1952, Soviet leaders had viewed the UN primarily in a negative light. It was an instrument to be thwarted, not exploited; the exercise of the veto was the monkey wrench to keep the organization from functioning as an anti-Soviet instrument. But after the Korean experience, they realized the positive way in which the international organization could be used, in concert with the neutralist nations, to keep the West on the defensive and to strengthen the international position of the Soviet Union. There were already hints of these impending changes—and a foreshadowing of the Khrushchev courtship of underdeveloped countries—in the Nineteenth Party Congress held in October 1952. At that time Stalin moved toward the formulation of a sophisticated variant of the "two-camp thesis" by declaring that war between the Communist and Western worlds was not inevitable and was less likely than inter-capitalist wars; this Stalin corollary opened the way, ideologically, for Soviet acceptance of diversity in the underdeveloped world. But the more important foreign policy changes came only with the death of Stalin.

II ❧⸺

Moscow and UN Technical Assistance

SOVIET COURTSHIP of the underdeveloped countries began in the United Nations. After the death of Stalin on March 5, 1953, the Presidium of the Communist Party of the Soviet Union (CPSU) agreed to discard certain aspects of Stalin's foreign policy. One of the far-reaching changes, which had been hinted at in the Nineteenth Party Congress of October 1952, was Moscow's approach to underdeveloped areas. As a preliminary to improving relations with the new, independent nations of Africa, the Middle East, and Southern Asia, the Presidium decided to contribute to the UN Expanded Program of Technical Assistance. A high-ranking Soviet diplomat, specializing in UN affairs, told an American scholar that before making this decision the Presidium had asked him only one question: "Is it in the Soviet interest to contribute to EPTA?" Upon receiving an affirmative reply, the Presidium moved quickly.

The Politics and Problems of Participation

On July 15, 1953, at the Sixteenth Session of the Economic and Social Council, the Soviet delegate, Amazasp A. Arutiunian, startled the gathering by announcing the contribution of four million rubles (one million dollars at the old ruble rate) by the Soviet Government to EPTA. Unmindful of the Council's preoccupation with another issue, and ignoring the postwar Soviet record of non-participation and financial non-support, Arutiunian declared: "Like many other States Members, the Soviet Union had always supported proposals for the appropriation of specified funds from the United Nations budget for technical assistance to the underdeveloped countries. The Soviet Union delegation wished to announce that the Soviet Union was now prepared to participate also in the provision of technical assistance for the underdeveloped countries under the United Nations Expanded Programme of Technical Assistance. . . . Accordingly, the Soviet Union wished to announce that it was now prepared to take part in the implementation of the United Nations Technical Assistance Programme and to appropriate the sum of four million rubles as its contribution to the Fund for 1953."[1]

Though there had been faint manifestations of change in Soviet behavior in other UN organs, notably the Economic Commission for Europe, the delegates were unprepared for so abrupt a reversal of policy. The announcement was sandwiched between standard Soviet denunciations of Western investment practices in underdeveloped areas and the alleged use of American foreign aid for exacting political and military concessions. Nonetheless, it encouraged the hope of a more conciliatory Soviet approach in the making. Soviet newspapers devoted a few articles to this new development without dwelling on it at length. But in the UN, the move stimulated great interest and much corridor conversation.

Western analysts made the common error of interpreting Soviet foreign policy as if it were designed for its effect on the West. Their attempt to find an immediate and convenient explanation distorted their perspective. They saw the Soviet decision as a blow at America and an attempt to sabotage a functioning and popular program. They did not recognize that it could be the opening wedge in a comprehensive campaign to penetrate the underdeveloped world. True, the timing of the Soviet offer did coincide with the discussion in Congress of the United States' contribution for the coming year. A number of observers were thus led to suggest that Moscow was trying, through a gesture of participation, to

---

[1] Economic and Social Council, *Official Records* (16th Session), p. 142.

intensify the fears of Congressional opponents that EPTA would become a Soviet tool. If U. S. financial support were thus jeopardized as a result of American domestic squabbling, went the reasoning, the greater would be the accolades accorded to Moscow for its support.

In the UN the Soviet spokesman, A. Arutiunian, seized upon the threatened cuts in the U. S. contribution and in the U. S. technical assistance budget to predict that "Point Four had died a natural death" and to caution underdeveloped countries against relying upon substantial help from the United States. The American delegation to the UN was worried about the imminent loss of U. S. prestige. UN officials feared the death-knell of EPTA had been sounded. One official predicted that "to cut the technical assistance program by half would leave the world from Indonesia to Libya strewn with unfinished projects, each of which would be a monument to remind people of the broken promises of the West."[2] Three days after his speech announcing the Soviet readiness to contribute to EPTA, Arutiunian, never one to miss a golden propaganda opportunity, again hit hard at the "selfishness" of American policy:

"The utterance of Congressmen showed that economic assistance to foreign countries was regarded as an instrument of pressure on the internal affairs of recipient countries, and as a means of coercing them into conformity with the United States policies; it was therefore not genuine economic aid in accordance with the UN principles. There was a fundamental divergence between the philosophy which the United States espoused in the Council and the arguments put forward for home consumption.

"The Soviet Union had always held that technical assistance should be made available through the intermediary of the United Nations. By contrast, the United States 'Point Four'

[2] *New York Times,* July 23, 1953.

plan was entirely contrary to United Nations principles, and constituted a weapon of penetration and coercion."[3]

Though retrenchment by the United States would, of course, augment the political value of the Soviet offer, Moscow's decision to contribute rested on compelling reasons which existed independent of anything Congress might do. Soviet officials had known for several years that EPTA was valued by underdeveloped countries. Their diplomats in the UN had reported that nonparticipation was detrimental to Soviet prestige among these countries, but nothing could then be done; Stalin's bipolar conception of world politics circumscribed Moscow's area of maneuver. But in mid-1953, Soviet leaders, desiring to be associated with this popular program, were acting to liquidate at minimal cost this damaging aspect of Stalin's policy by becoming active participants in EPTA. Participation was a necessary first step for dispelling the unflattering image of the Soviet Union which past policies had produced. This, in conjunction with changed directives to foreign Communist Parties, set many of these Parties in underdeveloped countries on the road to political respectability. Participation was also possible now because postwar recovery had been completed; Soviet educational institutions were turning out growing numbers of engineers and technicians who could be spared for assignment abroad as part of the plan for a major cultural-economic offensive. The essentials of Stalin's foreign policy objectives had been attained: consolidation of Soviet power in Eastern Europe; establishment of firm ties with Communist China; and development of a nuclear capability. Kremlin leaders looked beyond the immediate borders of the Soviet world to the "gray" areas between the Soviet and Western spheres of influence. They moved to weaken the Western position there and replace it with Soviet influence. The shift which this entailed from a continental-oriented strategy to a freewheeling global one has

[3] Economic and Social Council, *op. cit.*, p. 183.

been the outstanding development in Soviet foreign policy since 1955. For the first time since its inception in 1917, the Soviet state has the capacity to exploit revolutionary developments in any part of the world.

As Moscow embarked on its foreign aid program, it had to make Soviet assistance respectable and desirable; the suspicions of the underdeveloped countries regarding the nature of Soviet intentions had to be allayed. Specifically, Moscow had to demonstrate that the aid would not be used to subvert existing regimes nor to promote Communist activities within the recipient country. This Moscow hoped to accomplish, in part, by participating in EPTA and in the Specialized Agencies and by publicizing the tangible benefits of Soviet assistance.

The neutralists did not look upon Soviet ideology as a hindrance to the acceptance of Soviet aid. Besides, the "two-camp" thesis, with its uncritical lumping of all underdeveloped countries into the Western camp, was being modified. The "zone of peace" concept, formally enunciated in February 1956 at the Twentieth Congress of the CPSU, effectively shelved the "two-camp" thesis, particularly as it had been applied to underdeveloped areas. It justified ideologically the Soviet courtship of the neutralist nations by emphasizing their political significance and the improved prospects for "socialist" forces coming to power through parliamentary means.

UN officials hailed the Soviet decision to contribute to EPTA as an indication of the growing willingness of the industrially developed countries to aid the less developed ones. The reaction among the neutralists was favorable. But there were no immediate takers for Soviet rubles. An initial hesitancy was reinforced when Moscow tried to set the ground rules for use of its contribution. On November 12, 1953, at the annual pledging session for EPTA and other voluntary programs, the Soviet delegation stipulated that ruble funds could be spent only on projects sponsored by organizations in which the USSR held membership. This meant that they could be used by the Technical Assistance Administration (TAA), but not by most of the Specialized Agencies such as WHO, UNESCO, FAO, and ILO. UN officials refused to accept the Soviet condition, which was too reminiscent of Stalin's obstructionism and attempts to undermine EPTA activities. They stated that UN programs involve coordination among various international organizations, and that any limitation on the use of funds complicated the functioning of the entire program. Further, as one observer noted, "to specifiy how, where, or for what purposes a country's contribution would be used was specifically prohibited by the basic legislation of the program."[4]

In January 1954 Hugh L. Keenleyside, the Director-General of TAA, went to Moscow to discuss the problem with Soviet officials. His mission was successful, for on March 17 the Soviet delegate in the Technical Assistance Committee (TAC) said that "the Soviet delegation regards the funds made available by the Soviet Union to the United Nations Expanded Programme of Technical Assistance to underdeveloped countries as being for the use of the United Nations. The Government of the Soviet Union does not exclude the possibility that, in some instances, part of these funds may be used through the Specialized Agencies that are part of the United Nations system."[5] It was the only remark he made at that TAC session, and he insisted that it be recorded verbatim, an unusual procedure, adopted only when a delegation wishes to stress a particular point. No reasons were given; none were necessary. Henceforth, Moscow dropped its insistence on a direct voice in the allocation of Soviet funds, thus complying with the letter, though, as later became evident, not the spirit, of Gen-

[4] Robert Loring Allen, "United Nations Technical Assistance: Soviet and East European Participation," *International Organization*, Vol. XI, No. 4 (1957), p. 619.

[5] E/TAC/SR. 63.

eral Assembly rules that all contributions be given free of control.

Moscow was now ready for requests for aid, but none were forthcoming. A second and more serious difficulty arose from the unwillingness of any country to request Soviet technicians or equipment because Soviet aid was an unknown quantity and because of the prevailing belief that it might be used to promote Communist activities. The Stalin-sanctioned Communist revolutions of the late 1940's in Burma, India, and Indonesia were well remembered and still rankled in these potential recipients. Less obvious, but equally effective in discouraging requests, were the limitations upon Soviet funds: Soviet contributions to EPTA are made in nonconvertible rubles, which means that they can be used only to purchase Soviet equipment, hire Soviet technicians, or send students and experts from underdeveloped countries to study in the USSR.

The lengthening period of hesitation was a source of embarrassment to both the Soviet Government and the UN officials. However, the combination of intensifying economic problems and assiduous Soviet corridor diplomacy was gradually changing the attitude of the neutralist countries. In all probability, Soviet rubles would have been utilized sooner or later, but the neutralist governments, always attentive observers of Congressional attitudes, certainly moved somewhat sooner because of an inadvertent assist from the United States Congress.

Congressional appropriations for EPTA undergo careful scrutiny and occasionally meet with temporary snags. Before Congress approves the United States contribution, the small, highly vocal, anti-UN minority usually succeed in kindling latent fears among UN diplomats of an impeding American retreat to a "new isolationism." In 1954 the initial impetus that had advanced EPTA quickly into so many operational projects seemed spent. The gap between pledges and contributions broadened. UN agencies had to curtail partially completed projects; grants for fellowships were reduced. Many agencies had to cut back programs by as much as 50 per cent. At the UN, pessimism concerning EPTA's future grew, largely because Congress had tacked a proviso onto its appropriation for the remaining 1954 U. S. contribution to EPTA, which prevented the American UN delegation from making any pledge for 1955 at the annual fund-pledging conference in November, until Congress gave its approval. This approval was not forthcoming until early 1955. Since the United States was then contributing more than 50 per cent of the funds for EPTA, many underdeveloped countries grew restive waiting for Congress to act, wondering whether they would have to abandon or curtail development projects under consideration or construction because of an inability to obtain foreign specialists and equipment. In their search for alternate sources, they looked with new appreciation upon the as yet untapped contributions of the Soviet Union. They believed themselves facing a dilemma: either accept Soviet experts or shelve needed projects. Soviet diplomats, then encouraging requests from underdeveloped countries for bilateral Soviet assistance, discreetly hinted that requests for technicians and equipment through the UN would be welcomed. Long a source of embarrassment to the USSR, the unutilized rubles now became a political asset. For the neutralists prepared to use them, they assumed a promise out of all proportion to their actual amount.

By the time Congress finally approved the appropriation for EPTA's 1955 program, the Soviet Union had already concluded a bilateral agreement lending India $125 million to construct a steel mill at Bhilai. At the same time, India contracted for several Soviet engineers through EPTA. By early 1955 Burma, Ceylon, and Yugoslavia acted to follow India's lead and were investigating the possibility of obtaining Soviet aid bilaterally and through EPTA. Moscow's breakthrough into UN technical assistance operations coincided generally with its launching of a bilateral foreign aid program to neutralist countries. It may be reasonably assumed that, psychologically at least, India's use of Soviet technicians and equipment helped other neutralist countries to overcome their hesitation and led them to accept Soviet aid, bilaterally and through EPTA.

The auspicious inauguration of Moscow's foreign aid program was the result of a convenient concatenation of developments: the difficulty encountered by neutralists in obtaining large sums of investment capital from the United States; Washington's growing emphasis on military pacts (SEATO and the Bagdad Pact) with underdeveloped countries, a policy opposed by neutralist regimes; the disillusionment with the meagerness of UN aid; and the alacrity with which the Soviet Union considered neutralist requests for long-term loans on attractive terms. The neutralists were also quick to sense and exploit the stimulus which Soviet aid afforded their prospects of obtaining more aid from the West. Overnight, their bargaining position had been strengthened; they were now courted, competitively and convincingly, by powerful political antagonists. They could accept aid from East and West, using assistance from each bloc as a lever to pry more from the other. Western economic aid to the neutralists of Southern Asia, for example, has increased noticeably since 1955. One Indian delegate to the UN, commenting on the frequency with which the Soviets publicly credit themselves with having been the catalyst that heightened Western interest in ECAFE neutralists, stated, "If the USSR hadn't entered the field of economic assistance, the Western countries wouldn't have expanded their efforts." This view has been echoed by other neutralist officials.

Spending Soviet Rubles

The bulk of Soviet contributions to EPTA has been utilized

through international organizations operating in India because of that country's readiness to accept Soviet specialists and equipment for large projects. During the 1955-1962 period, more than 70 per cent of Soviet funds were committed to South Asian countries, about 60 per cent to projects in India.

The most ambitious UN-sponsored project in India is the Bombay Institute of Technology. The first Technological Institute had been successfully developed at Kharagpur by the Indian Government, with American and UNESCO assistance. In 1955, in order to take advantage of the accumulating surpluses of rubles and of the bonus then being made available to any country willing to use rubles, UNESCO, in consultation with the Indian and Soviet Governments, undertook to establish near Bombay the second of four higher Institutes of Technology planned for the country. Organized through UNESCO, its heavy reliance upon Soviet experts and equipment has been shrewdly exploited by Soviet propagandists. A preliminary mission of eight UN experts visited Moscow in February 1956 to explore the extent of Moscow's willingness to make men and material available through EPTA. In April 1956 another team, including seven Soviets, visited India for six weeks and drew up a preliminary plan for establishing, equipping, and helping staff the proposed Institute. Based on their recommendations, nineteen posts for experts (including three scientific translators) were established, lists of equipment were compiled, and a fellowship program drawn up. Orders for major equipment were placed in the USSR by the end of the year. The first team of six Soviet experts provided under the UNESCO program arrived in India in January 1957 and was soon joined by two additional teams. Prior to the completion of the Institute, they were assigned temporarily to the Indian Institute of Technology at Kharagpur, the Indian Institute of Science in Bangalore, and the Department of Chemical Engineering of Bombay University. The experts compiled syllabuses, developed teaching materials, and assisted in the training of Indian personnel. The Bombay Institute was officially inaugurated in 1958, and all the buildings are expected to be completed with equipment installed by 1965.

Statements by Soviet officials at TAC meetings showed that Moscow preferred to render its aid in EPTA on an essentially bilateral basis. Once plans for the Bombay project had been approved by the UN, Moscow sought to win over the Committee to the desirability of conducting all further negotiations between the Soviet and Indian Governments bilaterally. The Soviet delegate noted "that the Committee was unnecessarily complicating the problem" and suggested "that direct negotiations between the country carrying out a project and the contributor were a normal phase of the administrative process designed to make possible the optimum use of available funds and did not detract from the multilateral nature of the Expanded Programme of Technical Assistance. Practical administrative measures could not jeopardize the multilateral principle, since all assistance was derived from UN technical assistance funds."[6] Dismissing TAB's interest in preserving the anonymity of the donor and keeping active negotiations between supplying and receiving countries to a minimum, he further suggested that "a certain amount of rivalry between contributing countries was bound to improve the quality of the technical assistance supplied."

Implicit in the Soviet approach was a desire to maximize the political dividends accruing from association with important EPTA projects, while facilitating the use of ruble funds. By "nationalizing" contributions used by EPTA, Moscow was in effect extending the policy of competitive coexistence to the technical assistance operations undertaken through international organizations.

The United States objected, arguing that despite the plausi-

[6] E/TAC/SR. 94, p. 10.

bility of the Soviet claim that "nationalizing" contributions increased the administrative efficiency of an operation, "a definite qualitative difference" existed between using "nationalized" contributions on "a one man technical mission or a small project" and having a major undertaking "manned solely by experts from a single donor country." Acceptance of the Soviet view could pave the way for the practice of securing all staff and supplies from a single country, thereby undermining the multilateral basis of EPTA operations. Dr. Walter Kotschnig, the American delegate, also added that if the United States were to subscribe to the opinion that the experts to be used could come only from the country whose funds financed the project then ". . . 50 per cent rather than 16 per cent of all experts used in UN technical assistance programs would have to be of U. S. nationality, 50 per cent of fellowship holders would have to be trained in the United States, and 50 per cent of the supplies would have to be secured in that country."[7]

UN authorities upheld the American position, but this did not prevent the Soviets from citing the Bombay project as an example of the value of Soviet support for EPTA and the efficacy of Soviet aid for the area. Their propaganda in India cultivated the impression that the Bombay Institute was a Soviet, not a UN, project. The wide acceptance of this view is but one example of the sharp contrast between the effectiveness of Soviet and UN information programs. Subsequent use by the UN of more non-Soviet experts on the project has failed to alter the established public image of it as an essentially Soviet-Indian operation. Among the other types of projects financed out of EPTA funds but claimed as benefits deriving from the Soviet Union are the study missions visiting the USSR. For example, the visit in May 1955 of fifteen senior civil servants of the Indian Government to study Soviet facilities for training Indian personnel in various technological

[7] *Ibid.*

fields was the first of many paid for by EPTA, but for which the Soviet Union sought principal credit.

Of the UN projects in India drawing heavily on ruble funds, the second most important is the Indian Statistical Institute in Calcutta. The UN has supported the project since 1953. In addition to statistical computing equipment, the UN has provided assistance "in the field of demographic statistics, statistical quality control, and in mathematical and economic statistics as related to national plans for economic and social development." Much of the electronic equipment needed has been purchased from the Soviet Union. Other UN projects in India using rubles involve such disparate activities as an ILO engineering training institute, WHO sanitation and health programs, UNESCO work in petroleum geology, and FAO fisheries promotion.

The actual number of Soviet specialists in UN projects in India is small compared to the number engaged in bilateral efforts, for less than 30 Soviet specialists were used in any one year. For example, in 1962, there were 111 foreign specialists serving in India under UN auspices. Of the total, 33 were from Great Britain, 23 from the Soviet Union, and 8 from the United States.[8] Of the Soviet contingent, 19 worked at the Bombay Institute of Technology. Contrast these figures with the more than 800 Soviet technicians involved in the building of the Bhilai steel plant and one gets a perspective on the comparative magnitude of UN and bilateral aid programs in India.

The level of UN assistance to the smaller South Asian countries is much lower. That there is nothing in Burma comparable to the Bombay project is partially a reflection of Burma's more backward condition; it is also a sign of Burma's ultracautious approach to foreign aid. Between 1955 and 1961, about

[8] Technical Assistance Board, "List of Experts and Officials Serving in India Under the UN Expanded Programme of Technical Assistance, Special Fund and Other Experts Administered by UNTAB." List No. 25 of January 1, 1962.

$300,000 in rubles were spent by EPTA in Burma, mainly for technicians. Most UN aid in Burma is designed to help in health and sanitation control, agricultural productivity, and small industry. In a series of interviews in Rangoon in January 1962, Burmese officials particularly lauded the work of the World Health Organization which was active in malaria eradication and anti-TB campaigns, and had performed a valuable service in drawing attention to the heavy incidence of leprosy which affects an estimated 1 per cent of the population. (However, several months after the military coup of March 1962, WHO withdrew its support from the malaria eradication program because the Ne Win regime insisted that the program be run only by Burmese, a condition the World Health Organization would not accept on the ground that it was obligated to ensure the proper use of funds and supplies).

Between 40 and 50 UN experts operated annually in Burma between 1957 and 1961. Prior to 1962, 29 Soviet experts, including 9 interpreters, were used in Burma. Of this total, 7 were there on a short-term basis working in the coal industry, making hydrological surveys, and teaching geophysics at the University of Rangoon. The main Soviet effort to date has been the 7-man team sent in late 1961 to survey the Chindwin River, a major tributary of the Irawaddy River, with a view toward investigating the feasibility of flood control and hydroelectric projects. The Burmese Government is undecided about undertaking so extensive a project, the financial implications of which are enormous for a country with a scarcity of capital and a multitude of unresolved political problems. The UN assuredly cannot pay the bill. Whether the Soviets will offer to finance and construct the project on a bilateral basis depends on their estimate of the significance of the project to their aims in the region, and on whether the Chindwin project has the potential to become to Burma what the Soviet-supported Aswan Dam is to Egypt.[9]

[9] On August 30, 1962, a protocol on Soviet economic and technical

EPTA also uses Soviet rubles to help equip the laboratory of the medical faculty at the University of Kabul in Afghanistan, and WHO is using Soviet physicians and supplies on various projects in India, Ceylon, Indonesia, and Afghanistan.

A detailed breakdown on EPTA ruble expenditures does not give an accurate picture of how much money is actually spent by the Soviet experts in the field, because a Soviet expert may use non-ruble currency to travel to and from and within his assigned country. Also, part of his salary is paid in his own currency in his national bank, while another part may be paid in the currency of the country in which he is serving in order to defray his living expenses. Accepting the difficulty in precisely calculating ruble expenditures, it may be reasonably estimated (from 1962 figures) that EPTA spends about a million dollars or more a year in rubles in Southern Asia, or less than a half of 1 per cent of Soviet bilateral aid for the area. Small though this amount is, an examination of its expenditure, plus the considerable information known about Soviet bilateral aid programs, provided an adequate body of data and experience to present to South Asian officials in order to obtain their evaluation of the relative merits of aid received from the USSR through UN and bilateral channels.

The characteristics of Soviet bilateral programs are well known: the preference for the large, impact projects; the emphasis on heavy industry rather than on infrastructure or pre-capital investment projects; the financing by loans not grants; and the package arrangement, whereby planning, supervision, and staffing is handled by Soviet experts until the project is completed. International organizations, on the other hand, constantly forced to trim extensive requests to

---

assistance to Burma was signed in Rangoon. Under the agreement, the Soviet Union granted a loan of almost $4 million which is to be used to develop an irrigation project in central Burma, a project that could be a forerunner of a more extensive dam construction and irrigation program.

meet available funds, stress technical assistance or the experimental, pilot project. Indeed, EPTA is confined to *technical* aid, while bilateral programs include *capital* assistance.

The differences in type and magnitude between bilateral and UN assistance make comparative evaluation hazardous. Notwithstanding these limitations, much has been written about the advantages of one or the other type of aid. The arguments tend to rest on moral and political judgments, rather than measurable economic criteria or actual experience. So far as I have determined, no attempt has been made to question officials of neutralist countries receiving Soviet aid, bilaterally and through EPTA, about their experiences, attitudes, and evaluations of both types. Though the purpose of all Soviet aid may be the same, namely the enhancement of Soviet prestige and influence, the following section proceeds on the assumption that a tentative comparison should be attempted because some insights may emerge relative to an assessment of the Soviet impact on underdeveloped countries, i.e. the way in which the neutralists perceive Soviet policies and practices.

South Asian Views on Soviet Aid

The attitude of South Asian officials toward UN projects financed by ruble funds is part and parcel of their over-all evaluation of all external aid, whether of a bilateral or international character. These views have been shaped by geography, by political history, and by the personal outlooks of the national leaders. They accord with the leaders' conception of the national interest and are susceptible to change, but always within the narrow framework of foreign policy alternatives.

Officials sum up the situation as follows:[10] South Asian

[10] The bulk of the interviews with South Asian officials took place in India, Burma, Thailand, and Japan (at the 1962 session of ECAFE) during the December 1961 to April 1962 period. Subsequent interviews

countries need investment capital to finance their economic development. Quantitatively, UN sources are meager, and with no foreseeable change in UN prospects, countries must seek elsewhere for funds. The Bombay project is a UN show-case piece, not a prototype possible on a wide scale. The largest project sponsored by EPTA in Asia, it is still less than 1/25 the cost of the Bhilai steel mill, the most ambitious bilateral Soviet aid project in South Asia. Neither EPTA nor the Special Fund (established by the General Assembly in October 1958 to finance the "preinvestment" surveys designed to attract private and/or governmental capital) is equipped to undertake large-scale industrial projects. The UN, which continues to discuss a Capital Development Fund, lacks the wherewithal for integrated, massive projects. The World Bank (IBRD) serves a valuable function, but resembles a commercial lending institution more than an international source of low interest, long-term, easy repayment loans. Its affiliates, the International Finance Corporation (IFC) and the International Development Association (IDA), were established to provide "soft" loans to underdeveloped countries. IFC restricts its lending to investments in private enterprises, whereas IDA extends development capital to governments on much more liberal terms than the World Bank. (The Soviet Union is not a member of any of these international lending institutions, a fact few neutralists ever choose to criticize.) Foreign investors play an important role in some underdeveloped areas, but in many of the neutralist countries which play upon Cold War competition and courtship, private investors are being systematically discouraged and even discredited. The reasons are political, economic, and ideological, and are intensely defended. Only the governments of the major industrial nations have the resources to meet the in-

---

were conducted in Geneva and New York. All the officials had dealt directly with their Soviet counterparts in international organizations and conferences relating to economic development.

vestment requirements of underdeveloped countries. Only they have the capacity to make foreign economic assistance a significant variable in the development equation, to translate plans into projects and hopes into realities.

UN records are replete with speeches by neutralist officials urging the wealthy countries to channel more of their foreign aid through international organizations. The neutralists contend, often with irritating moral overtones, that both the donor and the recipient would benefit. The Great Powers would gain confidence in each other by cooperating through the UN. By sharing in a great enterprise, they would take a bold step toward dissipating mutual suspicion and easing the burden of an expensive competition. The resulting decrease in world tension would permit the Soviet and Western blocs to lessen their arms expenditures. Competitive coexistence would become less intense, less militant, less dangerous, and less expensive. The recipient countries would benefit from the decrease in encumbering political debts which invariably come with bilateral foreign aid, and from the decreased pressure to align with one big bloc or the other. Greater amounts of money would be available for development.

This professed neutralist commitment to the principle of channeling economic aid through the UN, which is frequently and gravely expressed in UN sessions, is in sharp contrast to the views expressed by neutralist officials in private conversations. One eminent, respected neutralist leader acknowledged that his government supported broader participation by international organizations in principle, but regretted that in practice this was not possible. National need made increasing dependence on bilateral aid inevitable. He noted that though political obligations "of a sort" were incurred when accepting bilateral aid, they in no way jeopardized his nation's sovereignty or independence of policy. The obligations were a small drawback when measured against the significance of the aid rendered. Bilateral aid was also "easier and quicker."

49

As long as the donor nations, the Great Powers, preferred to deal directly, and not through international organizations, then the recipient nations could do nothing. He offered the following comment on the role which international organizations play in the thinking of the Great Powers: "The policy of the Great Powers is conditioned by their broad evaluation of their power, the power of their antagonists, and the ways in which their policies in international organizations, as elsewhere, affected their over-all power status. As long as the Cold War existed, national positions in international organizations would be determined by the leaders' calculations of how best to improve their power situation. International organizations cannot function as something apart from national power considerations."

An Indian official drew this telling picture of India's position: "India is poor and needs help. It takes aid where it can. International organizations are not equipped to provide the magnitude of investment capital needed in India, nor are they likely to be in the near future. Four steel mills have already been built in India as a result bilateral aid. This has been a good thing, essential both for economic development and for national security. The political competition among the Great Powers has redounded to India's material benefit."

Another Indian official, a member of the Cabinet, expressed an open preference for bilateral aid, irrespective of the resources available to the UN: "Even if aid through international organizations were available in substantial amounts, it would have the disadvantage to India of giving rise to too many demands for an equal piece of the investment pie. *All* the underdeveloped countries would clamor for equal consideration; they would argue that as political equals they were entitled to equal economic help. Yet, India has more people than all of Africa; its problems are more complex; the types of aid which it requires are more costly. Being at a more advanced stage of economic development, its investment needs are more extensive and expensive. Also, I would be less than candid if I did not admit that, as a result of the Great Power struggle, and India's central political and strategic position, India benefits greatly from the Cold War. If most Soviet and Western aid, currently distributed through bilateral channels, were given through the UN, India would lose much of its preferential treatment." [11]

In the one instance where an international organization—the World Bank—has the resources to finance large projects, South Asians find fault with the method of repayment required. They noted that loans had to be repaid in convertible currencies, which are perennially in short supply. If this mode of repayment is adopted in the future by such international lending and investment institutions as might be established to aid underdeveloped countries, the attractiveness of the aid will be sharply lessened. One of the strong appeals of bilateral aid is the provision that the borrowing country can frequently repay the loan in local currency, with which the creditor may purchase local agricultural commodities, raw materials, or semi-manufactured goods. This not only enables the borrowing nation to husband its precious supply of convertible currency, but also provides it with a market for surpluses of local commodities, which might otherwise not be salable abroad.

[11] That "a pronounced shift from bilateral to multilateral operations is one of the last things the government of India wants" is a theme developed in a study that entailed intensive interviewing in India; see John P. Lewis, *Quiet Crisis in India* (Washington, D. C.: The Brookings Institution, 1962), pp. 263-264. "With respect to United States assistance, Indian leaders are aware that a diversion into international agency channels might reduce the worldwide volume of American assistance. . . . The Indians do not want to be put into the same statistical category with two or three dozen other countries at a lower stage of development readiness; they fear the inappropriate egalitarianism that international politics injects into the parceling out of funds under multilateral operations. The Indian government, moreover, wants to keep its foreign aid bargaining dispersed. Not only may the present arrangement occasionally allow India to play off one benefactor against another; it maximizes the autonomy of Indian development planning."

For underdeveloped countries, bilateral dealings are often more difficult with the West than with the Soviet bloc where all imports and exports are distributed through State corporations. Many underdeveloped countries currently sell their commodities in foreign markets through State corporations, which find it more convenient to deal with other State corporations than to market their goods in the competitive, fragmented, complex trading network existing in the West. Direct dealing with State corporations permits the underdeveloped countries, who are inexperienced and at an economic disadvantage, to avoid the costly and complicated marketing and advertising campaigns needed to attract private buyers in Western markets.

A lack of interest in the proposal to funnel aid primarily through UN channels was evident in discussions with Indians, and to a large extent with Indonesians and Afghans. The Burmese and Ceylonese adhered more closely to their public statements, which support aid administered through international organizations. The number of officials, newspaper editors, and writers interviewed was limited, totaling about 75, but their views, expressed privately and not for attribution, have an inner logic and political cogency that demand close attention. The differences expressed appear to be related to the strategic location, political situation, and economic problems of the respective countries.

India is in a class by itself. Its size and the enormity of its problems impel India to seek help in all quantities and forms wherever it can. Foreign aid is a major item in Indian investment and planning. Any serious curtailment, or significant diversion of investment to military expenditures, would drastically affect India's economic development. To forestall such an eventuality is a major preoccupation of its leaders.

India is strategically situated in South Asia. Its location and unchallenged role as leader of the neutralists give it a pivotal position in world politics. It is courted by East and West. In strategic terms, Moscow understands that if India goes Communist, or can be drawn closer to the Soviet bloc, all of Southern Asia becomes politically untenable terrain for the West; by outflanking the oil-rich Middle East and acquiring naval and trading bases on the Indian Ocean, Moscow would enhance its position in Southern Asia to the point where a dominant political position would be within grasp. Washington, on the other hand, realizes that an India committed to democratic institutions and processes, to the West's efforts to promote economic and social change within a peaceful, orderly political framework, would do much to strengthen the West's case among underdeveloped countries. With China's expansionist tendencies on the rise, Moscow and Washington find friendship with India increasingly important as an aid to improving their power position in Asia, particularly with respect to the containment of Chinese influence.

The unique position which international developments have given Indian leaders makes them confident that continued acceptance of aid from both blocs will not endanger their independence or their role as leader among the other nonaligned nations. This aspect of their policy is a source of envy among the other neutralists, who would like nothing better than to emulate the Indian tightrope act. Indian leaders, however, have learned a lesson from the defeat administered them by the Chinese in late 1962; they are realistic enough to perceive that a further deterioration of relations with Communist China could require them to deemphasize their policy of nonalignment (since 1961, they have tended to eschew the term "neutralism" in describing their foreign policy) and move toward more pronouncedly pro-Western commitments. Hopes that Moscow could restrain Chinese belligerence were largely dashed by the Chinese military attacks of October and November 1962 in the Ladakh and Assam areas of northern India, as were the long-treasured illusions that Moscow would side openly with New Delhi in any direct confrontation between

India and China. Clearly, as long as the Moscow-Peking alliance holds firm, the Soviet Union will not undertake to fill India's growing economic and military needs. Only the West can provide the magnitude of aid that India requires. Though an Indo-Pakistan war over Kashmir—an omnipresent nightmare to Western leaders—could wipe out the careful calculations of Indian planners, it is not now viewed as a danger on a par with the threat from Communist China. For the moment, the Indians are the prime beneficiaries of the Cold War, obtaining more aid from East and West than they could ever hope to get from an affluent UN.

Other neutralists follow in India's footsteps. Indonesia, Egypt, and Afghanistan, for example, avoid entangling alliances and encourage competitive bidding from East and West. The current evolution of the Cold War has contributed to their strategic importance. For these countries, who need vast amounts of foreign assistance to modernize and develop economically, bilateral aid is essential, far overshadowing the possible attraction of aid through international organizations. Though publicly supporting the establishment of new and expanded UN aid programs, i.e. the UN Capital Development Fund, the politically important neutralists regard them as supplements, not substitutes, for the considerable bilateral assistance they currently receive. They realize that if large amounts of aid were suddenly available to the UN, the principal beneficiaries would probably be the countries who are now out of the immediate focus of the Cold War tug-of-influence, countries who, lacking current political or military significance for the Great Powers, must content themselves with bits and scraps of economic aid and inadequate attention to their needs.

There is a paradox in all of this: the countries being courted by the Great Powers gain considerably from the Cold War in terms of their economic development and military buildup, and as long as the Cold War continues, they stand to gain even more. But this Cold War which they help to perpetuate by their acceptance or encouragement of bilateral aid, and exacerbate by their parceling of political favors, threatens their ultimate survival. The neutralists are aware of this paradox, but shrug it aside as if to say, "What can we do to thwart the struggle between the giants."

Burma and Ceylon, also in urgent need of aid, might welcome a shift to UN-administered aid because, politically, they would not be as vulnerable to Great Power pressures and, economically, they might obtain more assistance. At present, though courted by, and accepting aid from, both blocs, they receive proportionately little of the total foreign-aid pie. Both countries have had weak, unstable governments since independence and have experienced chronic economic difficulties; both are afflicted with extremist, divisive, splinter movements which exploit any official move to align closely with either power bloc. Both countries resent and mistrust neighboring India. Intent upon nationalizing key industries and expanding public sector investment, they have steadily discouraged the influx of private institutional capital, preferring to negotiate government-to-government loans. Conceivably, aid from UN sources, by permitting them to steer a more rigidly neutralist course, might minimize the ability of revolutionary-oriented groups to fish in troubled home waters. But before any country places reliance upon a steady flow of aid from international organizations, the UN will have to demonstrate its capacity to raise revenues on a predictable and significant scale. In general, the neutralists are not convinced that any relaxation in the Cold War would be translated into wholehearted Great Power support for a UN economic development fund; they do not believe, for example, that decreased military expenditures, resulting from an arms limitation agreement, would insure a diversion of the savings to the needs of poor countries.

Neutralists also are not convinced that aid from international organizations is clearly preferable to bilateral aid. There

55

is no compelling economic brief proving the superiority of one form of aid over the other. In January 1962, I was told by officials of the Ministry of Foreign Affairs of the Government of India that such an investigation was being considered; no other South Asian country has even given the problem a second thought—nor is there any reason why they should. The amount of aid which they now receive from UN sources is so small as to be of marginal value. Western advocates of channeling foreign aid through the UN generally have not marshalled economic data or undertaken studies in depth to buttress their arguments;[12] instead, they have rested their case upon political and psychological arguments of questionable validity: namely, upon the proposition that aid rendered through the UN is more attractive politically and more effective economically. They have assumed, on the basis of isolated and inconclusive instances, that underdeveloped countries are unhappy over the political strings attached to bilateral aid, and that the critical national needs of these countries drove them to accept this alternative. This assumption is not generally borne out by the experience of these countries, nor by the interviewing conducted by this writer.

Underdeveloped countries accept as the inevitable accompaniments of bilateral aid these annoyances and assorted "strings," which, while not minimized, are not viewed as politically threatening or administratively unbearable. One noted economist writes that, "Fears of strings on aid have subsided markedly as the number of nations and agencies in the aid-dispensing business has increased."[13] The large countries, especially, discount the dangers; the small nations generally have not had reason for concern. A glaring exception

---

[12] A strong case for aid through UN agencies is made by Robert E. Asher in "Multilateral versus Bilateral Aid: An Old Controversy Revisited," *International Organization,* Vol. xvi, No. 4 (Autumn 1962), pp. 697-719.

[13] *Ibid.,* p. 703.

occurred in Guinea in 1961. The Soviet Ambassador's interference in local affairs and attempt to get local Communists placed in key governmental posts brought a sharp crackdown by the Guinea Government. The results: a hasty, conciliatory visit by Anastas Mikoyan, the Kremlin's trouble-shooter; a new Soviet Ambassador; an abrupt reversal of Guinea's drift toward the Soviet bloc, and a new willingness on the part of Sekou Toure to investigate the advantages of closer ties with the West. Similar examples will no doubt develop in the future, but for the present, it must be regarded as atypical.

There is no evidence that Soviet aid has been used directly to finance local Communist Parties. In India, for example, local currency made available to the Soviet Government in partial repayment of Soviet loans has been suspected of finding its way into the coffers of the Communist Party of India (CPI), but evidence is lacking. The amounts involved and the activities which they are thought to be helping have not been such as to elicit repressive government action; they have certainly not been a source of serious friction between the Soviet Union and India.

With the failure of UN aid advocates to establish the economic merits of their argument, neutralist officials have acted on the assumption that "a bird in the hand is worth two in the bush." In fairness to these officials, we must recognize that they are harried, overworked, and immersed in immediate problems. They do not have large research staffs to gather and analyze data and draw up elaborate prognoses. The test is simple: if a program works, keep it. A meeting with a number of Burmese officials produced a consensus which may be described as follows: "The Government of Burma has not evaluated the comparative advantages of bilateral and international aid, but there is no pressing need to do so because of the negligible amount thus far received through UN channels. Both types took time to negotiate; the experts provided under both Soviet and international auspices were policed, by the Soviet Embassy and the UN Resident Representative, respectively; both programs provided able technicians."

"Effectiveness" of aid is a term giving rise to ambiguity. It can be interpreted economically as a function of productivity, or politically as an expression of governmental satisfaction. Until the superior case for aid through UN channels can be demonstrated in terms of either of these criteria, no ground swell toward inducing the Great Powers to change their mode of giving may be expected. Among the underdeveloped countries, the level of satisfaction with the bilateral foreign aid pattern is sufficient to encourage its continuing operation.

Nor does there exist any fundamental dissatisfaction with Soviet aid received through UN organizations. The positive features outweigh the negative. The general assessment of Soviet specialists used on UN projects is favorable: they are competent, hard working, interested in doing a good job, and eager to communicate their knowledge. Soviet experts are adaptable, undemanding of those amenities of everyday living that in underdeveloped areas often seem like luxuries, and prepared to remain as long as they are needed.

There are, however, a few negative features which account for the continued UN difficulty in utilizing Soviet contributions to EPTA. First, there is the language barrier. Soviet experts, used by the UN, though technically as competent as those of Western countries, encounter the reluctance of many countries, even those enjoying friendly relations with the USSR, to accept them as technicians unless they know the working language of the country, which because of the period of colonial rule is usually French or English. Nor does the standing offer of the Soviet Government to provide interpreters at its own expense find a welcome response. Underdeveloped countries contend that the use of interpreters introduces an inefficiency which they prefer to avoid. The preference for senior experts who are mostly in the 40 to 55 age bracket hits the

Soviets in a generation that came to maturity under Stalin, a generation not trained in foreign languages. But this particular problem may disappear within five to ten years because of the much greater language capability evident among the junior grade Soviet experts.

The unwillingness to accept interpreters is prevalent among countries which are not noted for being politically hostile to the USSR, e.g. Indonesia and Burma. These countries argue privately that the use of interpreters makes for political complications. Experts from international organizations generally have a high degree of mobility in traveling around the country in performance of their duties. Should these experts be Soviet nationals with Soviet interpreters, the fear is that political discussions might ensue, and the countries do not want free intermingling of Soviets with people from different strata of society, specifically with local Communists and Communist sympathizers. Ironically, these same countries, which have often criticized the West for its "imperialist" policies, seem quite willing to permit individual experts from "imperialist" countries to travel alone on UN missions.

These criticisms are minor and remediable; they do not preclude the use of Soviet technicians or equipment, nor raise any fundamental questions concerning the utility of what is available. South Asian officials say that the Soviet contribution to EPTA is small but better than nothing. More important, they believe that it acts as a stimulus to continuing and expanding Western efforts. The neutralists frequently repeat what to them is irrefutable: before the Soviets entered the lending and technical assistance fields, both bilateral and international, Western assistance was negligible; since the Soviets began their own aid programs, Western efforts have expanded noticeably. With greater understanding of the political process in the United States, neutralist officials have become increasingly convinced that nothing is more apt to muster Congressional support for a foreign aid project than the threat of Communist subversion. One Nigerian official complained that "America is more prepared to help a country which is likely to fall into the Soviet orbit than a country which is completely independent and not in danger of falling into any orbit."[14]

This evaluation is not easily dismissed. It is based on official American actions and attitudes in the foreign aid field, and on motivating forces in American society as well. Who can deny that Soviet space achievements are the main stimuli for the clinical intensity with which the shortcomings of American education have been examined recently and for the belated realization that achievements in science and military technology are rooted in the classroom and the laboratory? Apparently, even private investors react to the threat of Soviet competition. A drug manufacturer testified before a Senate Committee a few years ago that his company had hesitated to set up a streptomycin plant for the Indian Government because it had doubts concerning the wisdom of governmental (Indian) involvement in drug production. But, he stated, "When we got word that a Soviet team was coming in to put it all in the public sector with Soviet financing, whatever doubts we had were speedily resolved. We quickly concluded arrangements for the streptomycin plant."[15] Such incidents strengthen the view, widely held abroad, that the surest way to obtain more American aid is to leak word that the Soviets are interested in financing the project if the Americans are not.

What the neutralists, by isolating and criticizing the expedient aspects of Western policies, have neglected to consider is the corollary that without Western bilateral aid and Western support for UN technical assistance programs there would in all likelihood not have been any Soviet foreign aid program to begin with. Just as the West has recently accelerated its efforts to aid economically underdeveloped countries, partially out of

[14] *New York Times,* October 16, 1961.
[15] *Ibid.,* February 26, 1959.

concern with Soviet inroads, so, too, have the Soviets been induced to embark on aid programs out of an awareness of the political and economic advantages which accrued to the West as a consequence of its foreign economic activities, and out of the serious limitations which nonparticipation in UN technical assistance programs placed upon Soviet diplomacy prior to 1954. It was, after all, Western initiative, imagination, and interest, culminating in the myriad of current bilateral and international programs, which made it politically necessary for the Soviet Union to make changes and undertake commitments that have benefited the underdeveloped countries. Soviet foreign aid programs have followed in the wake of the Western way.

The Soviet "Style"

The record of Soviet participation in EPTA's operations since 1955 reveals the essentials of what may be termed a Soviet "style," i.e. a recognizable pattern of behavior in UN technical assistance operations. It derives from the nature of the Soviet system of rule and from the Soviet attitude toward international organizations. Many of the characteristics may be found in Soviet bilateral activities as well; divergences may be attributed to the smaller scale and lesser importance of UN programs and to the differences inherent in any country's bilateral as opposed to UN operations.

International civil servants find dealing with Soviet authorities is difficult, time consuming, and frustrating. The barriers to businesslike negotiations are familiar features of Soviet diplomatic practice. They are rooted in the authoritarian heritage of the USSR: the pervasive secrecy, the Kafkaesque anonymity of officials, the ponderous administrative machinery, interlaced as it is with controls and counter-controls at every level, and the evasion of responsibility by lower-level officials. UN personnel seldom have direct correspondence with individuals; they deal with a Ministry or a bureau, with an impenetrable bureaucratic maze which it is impossible to contact by telephone or telegram to gain clarification on minor matters. Since the decision-making centers in Soviet bureaucracies are unknown to outsiders, there is no way of learning which official is in a position to resolve any knotty problem. Problems of major importance are, of course, settled at the top. But in the middle and lower levels of Soviet government the closed and compartmentalized nature of the system impinges on the international official seeking information. He has no way of knowing who is the proper authority, when a Third Secretary might be more helpful than an Ambassador, or when a decision will be taken. The net effect is interminable delay in negotiating minutae.

The initial difficulties of the Technical Assistance Board arose from the paucity of available information relevant to the procedures necessary when doing business with Soviet organizations. For their part, the Soviets, faced for the first time with the need to reach agreements with UN organizations in the field of technical assistance, tended to be suspicious and slow. It takes approximately six to eight months for TAB and the State Committee for Foreign Economic Relations of the USSR Council of Ministers to reach agreement on pertinent matters. This is almost twice the time required to conclude agreements with other countries. But most of the procedural difficulties have been resolved sufficiently to permit Soviet participation in EPTA activities.

Soviet technicians used by EPTA function as a Soviet team, not as UN civil servants. Their collective character is always established and is resistant to modification. For example, the Resident Representative (RESREP) in India requests evaluations from all UN technicians operating in the country in order to eliminate problems encountered in the field and to improve existing programs. Each technician is requested to return a questionnaire to the RESREP in New Delhi. The Soviet technicians never send individual reports; they always submit one report for the group. The suggestions and criticisms are collective, not individual, thereby diminishing their value. Another irritant which UN officials have so far ignored because it has had no serious consequences is the habit of Soviet technicians to report regularly to the Soviet Embassy. This constitutes a breach of UN protocol, since Soviet technicians are ostensibly functioning under EPTA as international civil servants.

Moscow carefully supervises UN application of its rubles. It has made clear its wish that Soviet rubles be spent on technicians, rather than on equipment or short-term fellowships. During a period when TAB was seeking to overcome the resistances operating against utilization of the Soviet contributions, it spent most of the rubles on equipment and supplies not requiring installation or maintenance. Moscow quickly perceived TAB's intentions and insisted that thereafter the bulk of its contributions be used for technicians or equipment requiring accompanying experts. It has denounced Secretariat officials for their explanation that placement of Soviet technicians is complicated because of the language problem, and instead accuses the UN of having Western-dominated Secretariats with ingrained discrimination against Soviet bloc personnel.[16]

---

[16] A. Nekrasov, "Soviet Aid: Past and Present," *International Affairs*, No. 3 (March 1963), p. 83. According to this Soviet analyst, the "Western representatives, who have seized most of the leading posts in the UN technical assistance agency are making every effort to limit the Soviet Union's effective participation in aiding less developed countries through the United Nations. They aim to hamper the use of Soviet contributions under these programmes or at any rate to use them for supplying equipment; they try as far as possible to keep down the number of Soviet experts employed by the UN in this field and also the number of scholarship students sent to the USSR for training. Even at a cursory glance it is obvious that the Technical Assistance Board, the Bureau of Technical Assistance Operations and the functional departments of the UN Secretariat responsible for engaging UN experts are bureaucratic and discriminatory in their attitude toward Soviet specialists nominated for UN vacancies. These bodies either endlessly postpone decisions on the qualifications of Soviet experts over many months or even years or make biased decisions. . . ."

This condemnation is widely disseminated in its propaganda abroad.

Soviet authorities control effectively, though indirectly, the utilization of ruble contributions. Since rubles can be spent only in the USSR, Moscow can veto any request it wishes. It has refused to supply rolling stock, certain kinds of agricultural machinery, medical equipment, and jeeps, on the ground that they were in short supply in the Soviet Union. The unwritten conditions are clearly understood. The UN is limited to using its ruble funds on equipment which the Soviet Government is willing to deliver; as part of the package arrangement, it tacitly agrees to use equipment which invariably needs to be accompanied by Soviet technicians. Once again, the "strings" are obvious and irritating, but not crippling.

Moscow encourages the use of its equipment on readily identifiable projects in its international and bilateral aid programs. Though the UN, because of limited funds, can rarely initiate large-scale undertakings, such as the Bombay project, this is the archetype which the Soviets want international organizations to finance with their ruble accumulations. The Bombay project is blatantly presented by Soviet propagandists as an example of Soviet, not UN, aid.

In bilateral programs, Moscow is able to exploit its contributions even more effectively. First it publicizes its offer of "gifts" to a country. The "gifts" may be a few small tractors, an airplane for the head of State, or some medical equipment. In the meantime, an extensive loan is being negotiated between the Soviet Union and the underdeveloped country. Then in their propaganda the Soviets cannily create the impression that the loans are gifts and thus reap a harvest of good will. This technique was applied in Burma when, shortly after the Bulganin-Khrushchev visit in December 1955, Moscow offered eight "gifts" of a hotel, hospital, technological institute, etc., with the foreknowledge that the Burmese policy of neutralism would not permit it to accept a gift from a Great Power. Moscow had reason to know that Burma would offer in return an equivalent "gift" in rice. Then they constructed the three above-mentioned projects which, though enhancing Soviet prestige, did little for Burma's economic development. They are commonly referred to in Burma as the Soviet "gifts," though Burma paid for them in full. The other five "gifts" of the original offer were dropped in 1958. General Ne Win, who had taken over in March, asked the Soviet Government whether it was prepared to build the five projects without any repayment. When the Soviet Government replied that it was unable to finance the projects on a gift basis, Ne Win cancelled all further discussion of the issue.

Moscow uses EPTA as a place for displaying its wares and stimulating interest in bilateral requests among the neutralists. Participation in a variety of EPTA programs enables the Soviet Union to obtain first-hand information on the needs of individual countries and then to extend bilateral offers of assistance. Soviet help to Ceylon in the field of power and irrigation development was a consequence of initial UN surveys in which Soviet technicians participated. In the same way, Moscow may use the survey drawn up by its experts working in Burma under EPTA as a basis for a bilateral offer to undertake the Chindwin River project. The returns from these enterprises are small, but so is the initial outlay. Considering its contribution to EPTA, the Soviet Union receives a fair dividend.

Soviet Criticisms of UN Technical Assistance Operations

Soviet criticism of EPTA is not a new phenomenon. During the Stalin period, abuse concentrated on EPTA as a tool of Western imperialism, a puppet counterpart of the Truman Point Four Program. With participation, criticism became less virulent and, instead of the broad political attack, it focused on EPTA's alleged waste, diffusion of effort, and discrimination against the Soviet bloc.

UNDERUTILIZATION OF SOVIET RESOURCES

A continuing source of Soviet dissatisfaction is EPTA's limited employment of Soviet experts. In 1955 Moscow expressed annoyance with the small numbers of Soviet specialists used on UN technical assistance missions, protesting that the resulting impression that the USSR was incapable of meeting the technical assistance needs of underdeveloped countries was not only untrue but reflected adversely upon Soviet society and education. The discontented Soviet delegates proposed direct negotiations between the supplier and consumer of experts, but this was subsequently rejected by EPTA as detrimental to its multilateral character and as tending to politicize the aid channeled through international organizations. In recent years TAB has increased its efforts to expand the use of Soviet experts, but has met with limited success.

The Soviets raise this issue regularly at annual meetings of most UN organizations. In a typical instance, at the Twelfth World Health Assembly in May 1959, Soviet delegates took WHO to task for not making adequate use of Soviet health and medical services. They pointed out that only one medical expert had been utilized in the previous year and attributed this to the anti-Soviet bias among the WHO Secretariat: "Among the technical assistance authorities of the United Nations, and in the World Health Organization, there still exists some sort of prejudice or preconceived objection to the use of Soviet specialists as UN experts."[17] At the March 1961 ECAFE session, the Soviet representative went one step further, alleging a calculated policy of discrimination: ". . . the officers of United Nations bodies and agencies were doing everything in their power to prevent Soviet experts from rendering technical

[17] World Health Organization, *Official Records* (12th World Health Assembly, 1959), p. 152.

assistance."[18] The Soviet delegate to the Forty-fifth Session of the ILO stressed that the situation in that organization was particularly bad. He noted that since the Soviet Union resumed its participation in the ILO in 1954, the ILO had sent more than 860 experts to underdeveloped countries "and during all these years the Organization invited only five Soviet experts to go to India, Indonesia, and Yugoslavia, and all of them except one had a three to six month contract only."[19] A similar complaint was made at one session of the Special Fund where the Soviets noted that "of the 370 experts appointed as of 31 March 1962, only eight were nationals of the Soviet Union."[20]

Moscow hits hard at this theme, seeking to convince underdeveloped countries of the West's control of international Secretariats. To strengthen its case, it cites UN statistics that more than half of the experts used annually in UN technical assistance programs are Westerners. It contends that since the Soviet Union contributes about 5 to 6 per cent of EPTA's budget, it should be entitled to at least a proportional share of the experts sent to underdeveloped countries, whereas the actual percentage of Soviet experts used averages only 2 or 3 per cent. Though Soviet references to UN statistics are accurate, they tell only a part of the story. Benjamin Disraeli, the great British Prime Minister of the nineteenth century, once remarked that there were three kinds of lies: "Lies, damn lies, and statistics." What the Soviets choose not to mention is that Western nations contribute more than two-thirds of the total EPTA budget, and should, therefore, by the same logic, be contributing two-thirds of the experts. Further, the total Soviet contribution to EPTA and the Special Fund is approximately 3 to 4 per cent of the combined budget of these programs. On the basis of this figure (a detailed dis-

[18] E/CN.11/566, p. 279.
[19] ILO, *Report of Proceedings* (45th Session—June 1961), p. 565.
[20] SF/SR. 39, p. 8.

cussion appears in Chapter III), the allocation of Soviet experts is not as far out of line with the level of Soviet financial support as Soviet speeches imply. In their frequent references to UN figures, the Soviets seek not only to prove that too few Soviet nationals are utilized, but also that the cause lies in the Secretariats' discrimination against the Soviet Union. To arrive at a balanced picture, it is necessary to probe the reasons behind these figures.

Many UN officials acknowledge that more Soviet experts should be used by EPTA and the Specialized Agencies, and that an anti-Soviet bias does exist among members of some Secretariats. But they contend that the Soviet accusation of discrimination is irrelevant to the issue. The major drawback is that the underdeveloped countries themselves are reluctant, for political and ideological reasons, to accept Soviet experts, especially when Westerners are available. Contributory deterrents are the language barrier and the glacial pace of Soviet replies to UN requests for technicians. UN officials emphasize that only the Soviets express alarm that Western experts will serve the ends of Western "imperialism." If the underdeveloped countries are not concerned over the high proportion of experts coming from Western countries, then it scarcely behooves the Soviet Union to assume the role of self-appointed watchdog. The Soviets discount the relevance of the language-barrier argument (while offering to provide free interpreters) because national prestige is involved. They refuse to admit that their nationals are not as linguistically prepared as Westerners, though the reality of the situation contravenes their stand. In the final analysis, UN officials say, it is the underdeveloped countries themselves who must place the seal of approval upon any experts offered by TAB or the Specialized Agencies.

Arranging for the use of Soviet technicians is a protracted affair which often results in misunderstanding and irritation on both sides. UN organizations try to get personnel into the field as quickly as possible, but the Soviet system does not lend itself to the expeditious assignment of technicians abroad. The lag between UN requests and Soviet responses, coupled with uncertainty and complexity of routine transactions with Soviet officialdom, feeds already-existing attitudes of distrust. One TAB official, criticizing Moscow for its slowness, noted that "in recruiting in the West, for example in the United States or the United Kingdom, TAB ordinarily requires two or three months to get the experts for overseas missions, particularly the short-term ones. Pressure from the recipients is always growing for a further shortening of this period, for a faster placement of experts in the field. Recruiting in the Soviet Union, on the other hand, may, at a minimum, take from four to six months." Another TAB official thought that the Soviets were trying their best to meet UN requests and that their position merited consideration: "Moscow explains that since the Soviet economy is a planned economy, operating at full employment, there are no surplus experts seeking employment. Hence it takes time before Moscow can locate someone who can be relieved temporarily from his post for assignment abroad."

Another Soviet criticism concerns the underutilization of ruble contributions. Since July 1955, at which time only 20 per cent of the rubles had been allocated, the situation has steadily improved. Due to TAB's diligence, ruble funds have not accumulated a backlog equivalent to a one year's contribution, a condition that would entail classifying them as "not readily usable" and require special attention by the Technical Assistance Committee, TAB's parent body. However, the danger of a politically awkward backlog which would embarrass UN officials and embitter the Soviets is ever present. Moscow maintains that nonconvertible currencies can be as "readily usable" as convertible, and that every country should be encouraged to contribute according to its capacity and in whatever currency it chooses. It dismisses as of minor significance the additional administrative difficulties and expenses incurred by TAB in keeping separate accounts for all the different currencies which it receives, and calls upon the UN to devote less discussion to these annoyances and more to new ways of raising funds. In this latter connection, the Secretary-General has been criticized for his unwillingness to accept contributions from the East German Government, as if his refusal were based on the issue of non-convertible currency, and despite his exposition of the principles on which his stand is based.

As a result of the East German Government's offer to contribute 400,000 marks to EPTA, discussions were held in Berlin in January 1956 between TAB and East German representatives. The late Secretary-General, Dag Hammarskjold, rejected the offer six weeks later. He held that contributions could be accepted for EPTA under the mandate and terms of reference of the relevant provision of the Secretariat's rules, which says that contributions may be accepted from "Member States of the United Nations or from countries who are members of the Specialized Agencies" or from private sources, a classification the East German regime had been unwilling to accept. The Soviets took exception to the Secretary-General's interpretation; they insisted that he was empowered by the general principles guiding EPTA's use of funds to accept voluntary contributions from nations which were not members of the UN or its Specialized Agencies if these contributions were "consistent with the policies, aims, and activities of the Organization." [21] The Soviets considered his position a violation of the principle of universality of contribution and participation, which purportedly guides EPTA policy, and a cause of needless deprivation for underdeveloped countries. It was inconceivable, and an act of gross irresponsibility, they argued, at a time when the needs of underdeveloped countries for technical assistance were so great, to refuse legitimate offers of aid.[22]

[21] E/TAC/SR. 98, p. 15.
[22] Cf. E/TAC/SR. 185, p. 11; E/TAC/SR. 210, p. 11.

In diplomacy, a pattern of minor accommodation may beget major policy changes. The associated issues of contributions and convertibility are, in this instance, a backwash of the German question. Moscow seeks legitimacy and international acceptance for East Germany. Acceptance by EPTA of the East German offer would be a short, first step in the direction of East German participation in UN technical assistance activities, which could be the jumping off spot for admission to some of the Specialized Agencies. However, for the present, no further action by the UN is necessary: though desiring recognition for East Germany, the Soviets are not willing to allow the Pankow Government to contribute in convertible marks since that would weaken their case for nonconvertible contributions; nor are the East Germans interested in contributing as a private party, for what they seek is recognition as a Government. If the East German contribution were accepted, as it would be if given in convertible currency and as coming from a private source, the East Germans could make a case for receiving observer status to UN meetings concerned with underdeveloped countries. (Note: West Germany participates in EPTA and is a member of TAC.)

For the UN, nonconvertible currencies are a perennial administrative headache. They require that programs be increasingly tailored to fit what is available rather than what is needed. Fellowships and study missions must be organized in the donor country; its control over experts, equipment, and supplies must be accepted. The net effect of nonconvertible currencies is the "nationalizing" of EPTA activities.

To the American delegation's claim that "the result of such practices (making contributions in nonconvertible currencies) has been pressure on participating organizations to develop projects for which the contributions of certain countries could alone be used, which in turn entailed endless consultation and the despatch of special negotiating missions,"[23] the Soviets

[23] E/TAC/SR. 109, p. 9.

reply that these exaggerations and the endless debates which they engender are out of place, and that all contributions should be accepted; to place conditions of convertibility upon contributions would discourage those who can give very little and lead, in fact, to a situation where only the wealthy would contribute to EPTA.

Though discounting the difficulties involved in using non-convertible currencies, Moscow, in July 1956, as a result of TAB's inability to spend its accumulated rubles and the growing Western criticism, agreed to make 25 per cent of its annual contribution available in convertible currency. However, it stipulated that this sum could be used only in conjunction with services or equipment provided by the Soviet Union. This concession mollified the United States and quieted UN officials' fears that the United States might restrict its contribution by insisting that American funds not be used to defray the expenses of Soviet technicians working on EPTA projects.

The Soviets have never explained their refusal to make their voluntary contributions to EPTA and the Special Fund in convertible currency. Though there is the possibility that Moscow suffers from a chronic shortage of hard currency, this would not appear to be the controlling consideration in view of the small amount involved (between $3 and 4 million a year). Rather, an explanation should be sought in the political factors involved. Moscow understandably desires to have its technicians and equipment used widely in underdeveloped countries in order to establish their quality and win friends for the Soviet Union. However, in view of its repeated assertion that UN bodies are dominated by Western cliques, and its belief that anti-Soviet discrimination is already being practiced by organizations conducting UN technical assistance operations, Moscow may be proceeding on the assumption that, were its contribution made fully convertible, Soviet experts and equipment would likely be bypassed in favor of Western ones. Hence only by contributing in nonconvertible currency can it ensure, at this stage of the UN's development, that its offerings will be used abroad. Also, Soviet leaders have often maintained that the ruble is as strong a currency as any other (if not stronger). Considerations of prestige require that they act as if it were. Finally, seeing that many poor countries prefer to give their token contributions in nonconvertible currencies, Moscow may seek to bolster their position, while serving its own interests.

The issues concerning currency convertibility and the utilization of Soviet technicians continue to occupy the attention of delegates to UN meetings. Moscow continues to criticize, and the UN officials manage to increase the number of Soviet experts and rubles used and to satisfy a few more of the requests from underdeveloped countries. When friends disagree, a satisfactory resolution is usually not hard to find; but between enemies, even minor matters resist solution. Were the Cold War to end, these issues might be only the subject of passing comments in UN deliberations; but on today's international stage they occupy a fixed place as a constant reminder of the pervasive character of East-West hostility.

UN RESIDENT REPRESENTATIVE (R E S R E P)

UN innovations in the field of technical assistance invariably give rise to bitter Soviet opposition and ominous warnings of impending infringements on the national sovereignty of the underdeveloped countries. The Soviet Union, though unable to forestall changes, can, if it arouses the national sensitivities of the neutralists, effect modifications which waterdown the proposed innovations, making them susceptible to further alteration and subsequent erosion. A case in point is the office of the UN Resident Representative (RESREP), established in 1951. The RESREP is responsible for expediting negotiations between the country requesting aid and the international organization supplying it, and for coordinating the diversified UN activities to keep duplication and inefficiency to a minimum.[24]

From the very beginning, the Soviet Government contended that coordination of the activities of international organizations should be the responsibility of the recipients themselves and not that of a UN-appointed intermediary; and the supervisory function should be exercised by the host government. Administratively, the RESREP would confuse, not clarify, the planning and implementation of programs by unnecessary interference; and, politically, he would tend to act as an agent for the Western powers, against the best interests of the underdeveloped countries.

A forceful defense of the RESREP was made by David Owen, the director of TAB, at the July 1953 meeting of ECOSOC: "The resident representative had been appointed in pursuance of the Council's own instructions concerning the need for coordination between the various agencies at the country level. They were, in fact, just what the Soviet Union representative had said they should be, experts in the provision of technical assistance. They acted as intermediaries between the operators of the program and the country requesting assistance. In view of the very complicated machinery and the need to deal with so many different agencies, technical assistance had been in some danger of becoming a burden for the recipient countries, and it was precisely to help them in tackling the administrative problems involved that the system of resident representative had been instituted. He emphasized that resident representatives were never sent to a country unless they were specifically asked for, and that the country concerned negotiated with the representative appointed regarding his terms of reference and other questions connected with the appointment."[25]

[24] For a detailed account of the functions and activities of the Resident Representative see UN Documents E/AC.49/3; A/5138; and E/3625.
[25] E/TAC/SR. 42, p. 13.

After the post was established, the Soviet position shifted to an insistence that the RESREP be a national of the country in which he served as a safeguard against his using the office to help restore imperialist (Western) influence under a new guise. UN officials fought against adoption of the Soviet view, noting that in order to ensure objectivity and prevent undue exposure to political pressures from the host government, the RESREP should not be a national of the country, lest he be pressured into upholding national rather than UN policies to the detriment of the entire EPTA operation.

Over the years, the RESREP has proved his value and become an integral figure in UN technical assistance operations. But in their search for increased control over UN programs, some underveloped countries, encouraged by the Soviets, have sought to gain acceptance for the view that the Deputy RESREP should be a citizen of the country in which he serves. The junior staff positions of RESREP field offices are staffed 80 per cent by nationals of the host countries, but opponents are not satisfied, insisting that the top positions be "nationalized." Recruitment on the basis of national origin would weaken the institution of RESREP and with it the general concept of the international civil servant as an agent responsible to the UN and capable of withstanding narrow national pressures. By pushing for the "nationalization" of the Deputy RESREP, Moscow gave notice of its intention to launch anew —a frontal assault on the entire institution.

A common way to weaken programs which one opposes but cannot forestall through direct action is to strike for financial curtailment as part of a drive for greater administrative efficiency. At the July 1960 meetings of the Technical Assistance Committee, the Soviet delegate suggested that the RESREP's functions be assigned to national committees in order to reduce the financial burden of the underdeveloped countries, a change that would complete the "nationalizing" process favored by the Soviet Government. In concluding his case, the Soviet delegate said, "he need hardly add that he had nothing against the system of the Resident Representative as such, who at a certain stage of development had a definite role to play. But the situation was changing, and the national coordinating committees were rapidly acquiring experience; in many countries they might already be capable of providing the necessary link between TAB and their governments."[26]

As Moscow sees it, the RESREP is a Western convenience. Since most RESREP's are Westerners, the first Soviet national having been appointed Resident Representative to Ceylon only in August 1962, the Soviet Government has taken advantage of nationalist and neutralist sentiments to attract underdeveloped countries to its views. In times of strain between the Western and neutralist countries, it exploits ultranationalism as a dependable ally, using it to "politicize" UN discussions and "nationalize" the multilateral bases of UN operations.

But the Soviet voice is not a controlling or even a prominent one in determining the direction of the RESREP. One comment at this point may help to promote balance and perspective in assaying judgments on UN activities and their relation to Great Power politics; it should also discourage the tranquilizing but specious belief that if it weren't for Soviet hindrances all would go well in international organizations. The RESREP faces his supreme challenge in dealing with Secretariats of international organizations, not with the Soviet Union. The determination of what the RESREP's functions are and, indeed, whether there is to be such an institution, is made by the General Assembly, ECOSOC, and its subordinate bodies. In these bodies the Soviet Union can throw its full weight around; however, once agreement is reached, the RESREP then operates within his defined powers in areas where he has few dealings with Soviet authorities. His prin-

[26] E/TAC/SR. 210, p. 10.

cipal task is to work with the various international organizations, each of which is jealous of its reputation, prerogatives, and organizational independence. As one RESREP in South Asia confided: "Among UN organizations, as among national governments, there exists a compartmentalized, petty, timid approach to regional and global problems which militates against the development of a strong UN-concept. Each organization seems more zealous in defense of its status than in promotion of technical assistance. Absurdities are commonplace. For example, letterheads on stationery do not just say 'United Nations'; they identify the specific organization or committee issuing the correspondence and invariably overshadow the lettering of 'United Nations.' The cost in terms of dollars is in the thousands; in terms of weakening the UN concept, is incalculable."

Dag Hammarskjold tried to strengthen the RESREP. He strongly believed that the mushrooming of UN organizations and activities resulted in overbureaucratization and fragmentation which not only curtailed UN operational effectiveness, but, more significant, seriously weakened the ability of the UN to establish itself as both an ideal and an institution which could draw grass-roots support from among the world's peoples. The alphabetizing of international institutions dismayed him; it spelled confusion. Specialists may know what the ILO, IAEA, IBRD, WHO, IMO, etc. represent; the layman does not; to him it is political activity signifying nothing. More than inefficiency and waste, this diffusion of efforts reflects the purposelessness, the internal inertia, the narrowness of outlook which can be found in many international organizations.[27]

---

[27] A blunt and searing critique of the entire complex of inter-governmental economic organizations comes from Dr. Gunnar Myrdal, the distinguished Swedish social scientist and former Executive-Secretary of the UN Economic Commission for Europe. A few of his pungent observations may be noted:

"The Economic and Social Council and the General Assembly . . . have made hardly any substantial progress in terms of action in the direc-

Hammarskjold's attempt to promote amalgamation was just getting underway when he died tragically in the Congo on September 18, 1961. He had, for example, merged the heads of the UN Information Centers in New Delhi, Mexico City, and Colombo with the position of RESREP, a trend that has been continued.

Under the protective banner of defending their "constitutional responsibilities," some of the Specialized Agencies expend as much energy on organizational matters as they do on constructive operational activities. According to officials and observers in the field, one prime offender is the International Labor Organization. The ILO is sensitive to any attempt to supervise its activities because its very *raison d'être* is under heavy attack. The cry is heard increasingly that the ILO has outlived its usefulness. The implications, rarely expressed, are: disband the organization or reduce its activities to a fraction of its present level. The tripartite structure of the ILO was established in 1919 and mirrored nineteenth-century institutional and ideational attitudes, resting on the assumption no longer dominant in the world that free enterprise economies are the

---

tion of the main purposes, accorded them by the Charter, of both initiating and coordinating international action on a broad scale in the economic and social field. In recent years the Council in particular has sunk to a level of unimportance which must appear almost scandalous in view of these declared purposes."

The attempts of the regional economic commissions "to approach major economic issues have mostly been frustrated."

"The International Labor Organization was already outmoded a generation ago. . . its basic approach . . . really reflects the situations as they were conceived, and the problems as they were formulated, in Bismarck's Germany and Lloyd George's Britain. . . ."

Dr. Myrdal takes the Western Powers to task for their belated and perfunctory support for an international agency to distribute capital aid, for their inadequate attention to the unsettling effects of fluctuating international commodity prices, and their reluctance to grapple with the stifling practices of international cartels. Gunnar Myrdal, *Beyond the Welfare State* (New Haven: Yale University Press, 1960), pp. 270-274, excerpts.

highest form of human organization. The trend toward state planning, centralization, and expansion of the public sector has rendered anachronistic the tripartite division of the ILO into labor, management, and government, and the assumptions upon which it was based. In most underdeveloped countries, labor and management do not function freely as independent institutional agents, but as government-controlled institutions. The views which shaped ILO affairs for so long are without appeal in the underdeveloped countries. To justify their continued existence, ILO officials are trying to reorient their activities away from the traditional concerns and conventions of labor and management to the technical assistance and training fields where they can contribute to the technical needs of backward countries. Each year the ILO Secretariat undertakes a study of some pressing social-economic problem, e.g. the problem of aged persons, the effect of automation on unemployment, etc. These reports are informative and comprehensive, but they are scarcely sufficient reason for so large an organization.

One long-time ILO official observed: "The ILO was created for another age. It is an anomaly to talk about promoting free labor movements, as they are understood in the West, in underdeveloped countries where the trend is unmistakeably toward authoritarian control from the center, toward a subordination of labor and management to the policies of the state. 'Free' labor leaders there are often in jail or underground, while 'free' employers are handmaidens of government. To survive, the ILO is departing from its primary purposes, as stated in its constitution, of promoting free labor and employer contacts and movements, and strengthening labor-industrial standards throughout the world; the ILO is becoming more and more a service organization, establishing and conducting training institutes, and assisting technical assistance projects concerned with increasing productivity in industry. By becoming less political, and more technical-oriented, it hopes to retain its organizational identity."

Agency particularism is also strong in the World Health Organization and UNESCO. WHO, for example, has been reluctant to work closely with the RESREP's, and opposes any threat to its operational independence because it considers itself several professional notches above other international organizations. Its personnel are mostly medically trained and regard themselves as essentially apolitical professionals. WHO is a professional organization, seeking selfless ends, yet it, too, is not without its insularity.

The resistance of entrenched bureaucrats to threats against their empires is age old. That it should be so prevalent in international organizations is regrettable. There are, however, encouraging indications that agency particularism may be diminishing.[28] In addition to the integrative impact of the Special Fund, a number of steps have been taken which could result in significant improvements in the coordination and functioning of technical assistance activities. The Advisory Committee on Administrative and Budgetary Questions (ACABQ) of the General Assembly has repeatedly urged the consolidation of premises and services of the UN and Specialized Agencies in foreign countries. In August 1961 the Economic and Social Council established, under Resolution 851 (xxxii), an *ad hoc* Committee of Eight (subsequently expanded to ten members) ". . . to explore ways and means

---

[28] In his outstanding study, *Field Administration in the United Nations System* (New York: Frederick A. Praeger, 1961), Walter R. Sharp concludes that "while the field picture remains spotty, varying markedly from country to country, agency particularism has noticeably declined during the past few years" (p. 386).

Professor Sharp believes that the RESREP's are gaining acceptance among the Specialized Agencies and that their influence on programming is on the rise. His analysis of the administration and operation of UN field programs is a major contribution to our knowledge of the functioning of international organizations.

of bringing about in developing countries a closer relationship within the United Nations family of agencies, giving special attention to the potential role of the Resident Representative, to provide more concerted advice to countries that request it on the technical preparation and implementation of country programmes and on the technical aspects of individual parts of such programmes." The Committee has issued several preliminary reports, setting forth the principal areas requiring detailed examination.[29] So wide is the spectrum of views, however, that there is little likelihood of any early or drastic alteration in the existing pattern of organizational relationships.

OPEX

On May 30, 1956, in an address at McGill University, Dag Hammarskjold said, "Fundamentally, man is the key to our problems, not money. Funds are valuable only when used by trained, experienced and devoted men and women." Endorsing proposals made by Lester B. Pearson, former Canadian Secretary of State for External Affairs and present Prime Minister, he called for the creation of an International Administrative Service composed of qualified personnel "who were prepared to devote a significant part of their lives to work in the less-developed countries of the world as public officials integrated in the national administrations of these countries while maintaining their international status." He had in mind particularly the emerging African states, many of which were thought unlikely, for political reasons, to retain former colonial officials as government advisers.

After considerable discussion in the United Nations, a compromise program was adopted. In late 1958, the General Assembly appropriated $200,000 to establish OPEX (Operational, Executive, and Administrative Personnel) on an ex-

[29] UN Documents E/3639 of May 21, 1962 and E/3750 of April 18, 1963.

perimental basis. In 1961 OPEX was placed on a continuing basis with an annual budget of $850,000. The program operates as follows: when the UN receives a request from a member government, OPEX undertakes to appoint, and partially finance, experts to perform duties specified by the requesting government. The experts remain only as long as they are wanted; they help train local staff to carry on the work for which they have been temporarily responsible. Underdeveloped countries, particularly the new African states, welcomed OPEX and immediately sought its assistance in developing administrative cadres.

Critical from the beginning, the Soviet Union opposed the establishment of OPEX, but, because it was supported by the African states and Asian neutralists, Moscow abstained on the final resolution. Moscow deplored the possibility that OPEX experts might, in performance of their operational or executive function, come into conflict with national authorities, thereby jeopardizing that nation's sovereignty. To preclude this eventuality, the Soviets pressed for the formation of national administrative cadres, overlooking the fact that OPEX's express purpose is to train national personnel to handle their own administrative affairs; and that OPEX appointees are members of the national service or institution to which they are assigned. Moscow suggested that the expertise could best be transmitted "in the form of seminars, working groups, and the establishment of regional and national training centers for persons from these countries,"[30] and not by foreign experts working and training local staff concomitantly, i.e. on-the-job-training. It questioned the need for new machinery, holding that OPEX's services could be provided through TAA and the Specialized Agencies, and argued that by substituting for the administrative authority wielded by OPEX officials an EPTA-type relationship in which experts

[30] E/TAC/SR. 163, p. 4; E/AC.49/SR. 25, p. 5.

function solely in an advisory capacity, UN interference in domestic affairs would be virtually eliminated.

Apprehension that OPEX officials would advance Western interests was implicit in Soviet statements.[31] Believing that the Western Powers control the recruitment machinery of international Secretariats and seek to restore their former influence, the Soviets warned prospective applicants that OPEX would place Western agents in key governmental posts in underdeveloped countries, that under the guise of training native personnel, OPEX would penetrate the administration of weak countries and prepare the way for their recolonization. In the Soviet view, "if the developing countries desired the assistance of experts having executive functions, they should request them, not through the United Nations, but from other sources on a bilateral basis."[32] Finally, Moscow objected to financing OPEX out of the regular UN budget and preferred that "all technical assistance programs should be financed exclusively from voluntary contributions."[33]

Other delegations, e.g. the Ethiopian, French, and Mexican, shared some of the reservations of the Soviet Government, and their objections to initial proposals led to important modifications. Thus, instead of maintaining a permanent core, OPEX recruits personnel as requests come in, and appointments are short-term rather than long, with few experts serving beyond one or two years. In such changes, Soviet lobbying and natural neutralist suspicions are discernible. The results have given rise to some disappointment. In recent reports, the Secretary-General has noted that arrangements for the training of local successors have not been generally satisfactory and the recruitment of OPEX personnel has been slow.

Like RESREP, OPEX also elicited opposition from some

[31] E/TAC/SR. 192, p. 12.
[32] E/AC.49/SR. 25, p. 6.
[33] Ibid.

international Secretariats. Hammarskjold indicated that the heads of several Specialized Agencies had expressed serious reservations to the proposed International Administrative Service because of its possible effects "on the legitimate interests of their respective agencies." It remained, however, for a freer political agent to strike at the root of the discord. Mr. C. Shurmann, the delegate of the Netherlands, castigated the Secretariats for their uninspired reliance on a "fixed framework of rules" to the exclusion of "the constantly growing body of unwritten adaptations of changing circumstances which alone prevented the rules from becoming obsolete and kept them abreast of significant movements of human thought and aspiration." To resist, in the realm of economic and social development, "the creative urge towards integration of effort and abolition of particularism" was to doom, in the political and administrative spheres, the capacity of organizations for effective service.[34]

Current UN discussions aimed at improving the coordination and functioning of technical assistance activities have produced a variety of opinions concerning OPEX's future role and ways of making the program "more responsive to the needs of Governments."[35] Though OPEX has employed only a small number of experts—during the 1959-1963 period, it supplied approximately 100 experts to Governments of 38 countries—UN officials note that they receive three times as many requests as they can fill. Whether OPEX is maintained as a separate program depends upon the demonstrated willingness of the Governments of underdeveloped countries to act in accordance with the recommendations of the experts, who have only an advisory capacity. The eventual scope and character of all the programs depend upon the outcome of the deliberations of the Committee of Ten.

[34] Economic and Social Council, *Official Records* (24th Session), p. 94.

[35] Cf. E/3750, pp. 19-20.

Observations

Linked to the Soviet position on these specific issues is the controversial and broader question of the strengthening of the regional economic commissions by a transfer of responsibility for technical assistance operations from UN headquarters to regional centers.[36] The United States agrees with the Secretary-General "that the regional commissions should have a significantly larger part in the economic and social activities of the United Nations, particularly at the planning and programming stages."[37] However, it generally counsels a cautious approach, seriously questioning the utility of having regional economic commissions enmesh themselves in technical assistance responsibilities and operational programs already carried on by the Specialized Agencies. Above all, the United States does not consider "that decentralization should involve increasing the staff of the regional economic commissions at the expense of Headquarters," nor does it favor any weakening of the "supervisory and coordinating" role of the Economic and Social Council.[38]

The Soviet Union, sensing an opportunity to weaken the Western hold on the Secretariat, supports the decentralizing effort, which implies a reversal from the previous trend toward making international organizations universal in composition and function.[39] By elevating regionalism over internationalism, Moscow wants to give free rein to the nationalists aims of underdeveloped countries; weakening the center and strengthening the regional organizations will afford greater maneuver-

[36] See UN Document E/3522 on "Decentralization of the United Nations economic and social activities and strengthening of the regional economic commissions"; also, ECOSOC resolution 793 (xxx); A/4911; General Assembly resolutions 1518 (xv) and 1709 (xvi); E/CN.14/227.

[37] Economic and Social Council, *Official Records* (32nd Session), p. 27.

[38] *Ibid.*

[39] *Ibid.*, p. 93.

ability for Soviet diplomacy. At the Thirty-fourth Session of the Economic and Social Council, the Soviet delegate observed that, "decentralization should ensure a fuller utilization of the technical and scientific knowledge of personnel from all countries, including socialist countries. That was far from being the case, however, owing to the bureaucratic approach adopted by Headquarters and some of the Specialized Agencies. . . . Similarly, a transfer of posts from TAB, the Special Fund and the Department of Economic Affairs at headquarters to the regional commissions would ensure that the staff actually responsible for providing assistance would be associated more closely with the recipient countries."[40] Moscow's position is also determined by its desire to diminish the centralizing and supervisory role of ECOSOC. It has frequently criticized the failure "to implement the resolutions on decentralization"[41] and, in opposition to the American stand, has urged that "the regional economic commissions should concern themselves with all questions relating to the execution of regional projects, including control over technical assistance experts and over the execution of projects under the regular programme, the Expanded Programme and the Special Fund."[42]

The controlling element in the Soviet position may be the attractiveness of decentralization for the underdeveloped countries. To these countries it promises more administrative posts for their nationals, increased autonomy and authority in the planning and conduct of technical assistance, decreased control from the center, and recognition of nationalist interests. It also offers the prospect of concentration on a few major projects in contrast to EPTA's diffusion of efforts. One Ethiopian delegate said he believed that decentralization would lead to simplification of technical assistance procedures:

[40] E/SR. 1211, pp. 13-14.
[41] E/AC.49/SR. 20, p. 6.
[42] E/AC.49/SR. 22, pp. 12-13.

"There was a growing feeling among the African Governments that the United Nations agencies responsible for carrying out assistance programs had become too cumbersome and complicated and that the United Nations was trying to do too much at once with too little money. The United Nations efforts were, it was believed, thinly spread over a wide range of objectives. There was no selection of clearcut aims, no concentration of efforts, and no mobilization of resources. Further, recipient countries were faced with serious administrative difficulties in their dealings with the United Nations."[43]

The degree of decentralization is of paramount importance to the Specialized Agencies, for the strengthening of regionalist trends inevitably involves some diminution of authority by the central organs of the Agencies. To retain their current prerogatives, while accommodating to the demands of underdeveloped countries for greater representation and responsibility, some Specialized Agencies, e.g. ILO, WHO, UNESCO, have established regional conferences and institutes. WHO, which maintains six regional organizations, each comprising a regional inter-governmental committee and a regional office, has moved the farthest in the direction of effective decentralization. But, for most of the Agencies, the steps taken are few and halting, and it is too early to tell how effective they may be.

Moscow has suggested that regionalism be extended beyond administrative and technical assistance operations to include foreign trade, where fear of the Common Market is growing among the underdeveloped countries as they see themselves forced out of traditional markets and faced with a glaring inability to compete and earn adequate foreign exchange for imports. The Soviet Union, in its open and virulent attacks on the Common Market, has suggested since 1955 the establishment of an International Trade Organization or re-

[43] Economic and Social Council, *Official Records* (32nd Session), p. 32.

gional trading organizations for underdeveloped countries to improve their bargaining position. In May 1962 Khrushchev called upon the UN to review the entire question of the impact on less developed countries of the Common Market, which he termed a "union of capitalist monopolies," and urged the creation of an "international trading organization embracing all regions and all countries without discrimination." Growing apprehension on the part of the underdeveloped, economically weak countries about being edged out of traditional markets by the Common Market led to support for Moscow's proposal to convene a UN-sponsored international trade conference in early 1964.

Participation in EPTA has not changed Soviet attitudes toward international organizations, economic development, or the nature of Western objectives. On the contrary, it appears to have confirmed Moscow's belittling assessment of the economic efforts and capacities of international organizations and its disdain for the gradualist Western approach to industrialization. Moscow sees the Western Powers' acceptance of the formal independence of their former colonies as a necessary adaptation to changed political conditions; but the Western aim remains, as Leninist theory has long proclaimed, the perpetuation of the economic dependence of the underdeveloped countries and the continuation of their role as suppliers of raw materials. The feebleness of UN efforts and the buckshot character of EPTA's activities merely reinforce Soviet conviction that only through concentration on heavy industry, reliance upon internal rather than foreign financing of industrialization, and extensive planning, resource allocation, and public sector investment can underdeveloped countries achieve an appreciable economic breakthrough.

Financially, participation in EPTA is a negligible item; politically, it has produced an impressive harvest and offers opportunities for new yields. It provides Moscow with closer contact with neutralist countries and facilitates bilateral economic and cultural efforts. The skill of Soviet technicians and the utility of Soviet equipment have received favorable publicity. At little expense and effort, Soviet wares have reached a wide market. Good public relations in EPTA have helped Moscow in every area of its contact with underdeveloped countries.

Moscow has had a noticeable impact on EPTA. Serving as constant critics and gadflies of the West, the Soviets introduced an urgency into technical assistance discussions. By stressing the need for heavy industrialization, they sharpened the impatience of the underdeveloped countries. EPTA's inadequacy and the stalemated potential of international organizations resulted in part from the politicization of technical assistance discussions, a development which is an outgrowth of the Cold War dialogue. Finally, underdeveloped countries look upon the Soviets as a constant spur to the West's greater interest and support.

Moscow, in turn, has not been unaffected by its participation in EPTA, though the changes are more in temper than in substance. In courting the neutralists, Moscow has grown more conscious of occasions when its own behavior is irritating, and more receptive to the criticisms from these countries. Moscow has been educated to the realization that it can support modifications and accept compromises in international organizations without jeopardizing its basic objectives. In the act of accommodating to neutralist positions, Moscow need relinquish nothing that is fundamental; the very act of accommodating redounds to its advantage.

III ◊⁂⊱━

Genealogy of Four Soviet Positions in International Organizations

SOVIET BEHAVIOR in international organizations can be observed, and changes in official attitudes can be traced. But the "why" of their position on any particular issue eludes fathoming. The decision-making process is a zealously guarded secret, and Soviet officials give no explanations for foreign policy actions, no justifications for reversals. Nor do Soviet publications offer speculations, examine official positions critically, or place changes in perspective. They merely incorporate the new official line into their analyses. Occasionally, fragmentary information on the positions of opposing factions within the Party hierarchy are made public, but more for reasons of internecine power jockeying than for the public's edification of the country's foreign policy. Political writing in the Soviet Union is not informative or independent; instead, it is tendentious, selective, and tailored to the immediate purposes of the rulers.

The observer of the Soviet scene has no way of knowing whether a change in position is the result of internal or external political or economic pressures, is a new perspective on the "alignment of forces" in the outside world, or is merely a new tactic being used to achieve old objectives. A close review of four different issues raised in international organizations may illumine some determinants of Soviet behavior in these specific issues and perhaps in broader questions of their policy in international organizations. The issues were selected primarily because of the intense interaction between the Soviet Union and the leading neutralists of the underdeveloped world. In studying the anatomy of the Soviet attitude during the most critical stage of each issue, several considerations will be kept in mind: a) was there any indication in Soviet statements or actions which could have led one to anticipate the shifts; b) what justification, if any, was offered for the change; c) where did shifts occur and what reasons can be adduced for them; d) did ideology enter into the final decision; e) was national prestige an important factor?

The SUNFED Affair

The substantial sums of investment capital required by underdeveloped countries for economic development can be obtained at present only from the two competing Great Power blocs. As long as the Cold War lasts, underdeveloped countries, neutralist and committed alike, stand to benefit. If neutralists, they can seek aid from both sides, playing on the unwillingness of either to be put at a political, economic, or propaganda disadvantage by the foreign aid and support of the other. Courted countries such as Ghana, Egypt, and Indonesia can flirt with the Soviets and the West and still obtain assistance from both. Because the Great Powers regard them as vital battlegrounds for ideological, political, and cultural conflict, intensive interest by one bloc arouses fear in the other that it will be outmaneuvered, the result being counter-manifestations of largesse and support. Committed countries can expect continued assistance from their benefactors as long as they retain strategic and political importance. Thus, while Afghanistan is at odds with Pakistan, an ally of the United States, it can count on generous Soviet assistance; so can Cuba, as long as it is an embarrassing and thorny problem for the United States. Concomitantly, Pakistan, Iran, and South Vietnam can rely upon extensive American aid for their survival and stability as long as they seek assistance against Soviet and/or Chinese expansionism. As the Cold War and competitive coexistence over the underdeveloped countries intensifies, the ante is raised. Higher stakes bring increased commitments.

To all underdeveloped countries, neutralist and committed,

bilateral assistance has been, and will continue to be, far more important than aid provided through the UN. Needy countries cannot obtain adequate investment capital from indigent international organizations. Even those who allegedly prefer aid from international sources must seek aid from the blocs or else do without it. Only the Great Powers have the capacity to provide sustained and significant infusions of capital on which economic development depends, and for them, bilateral aid offers more tangible political dividends. The SUNFED issue should be viewed against this background.

EARLY GREAT POWER ATTITUDES

The idea for a Special United Nations Fund for Economic Development (SUNFED) crystallized in 1951 at the Sixth General Assembly as a result of a series of proposals by the Burmese, Cuban, and Yugoslav delegations. SUNFED was intended to provide investment capital in the form of grants-in-aid to underdeveloped countries for infrastructure-type projects—projects vital for economic growth but unable to earn a profit or pay for themselves, such as road building, sanitation systems, railroads, and power stations. Both the United States and the Soviet Union initially opposed its establishment, though for different reasons. Dominating the politics of both countries were the Korean War, the remilitarization in Europe, and the burgeoning costs of modern military weapons systems. Rearmament was in the saddle, and in this atmosphere, the needs of underdeveloped countries assumed a low priority.

The United States delegation openly stated that, given the burden of fighting a war in Korea, the Congress was not prepared to support financially the creation of a fund for economic development. It opposed the resolution because "in existing circumstances, the draft resolution, even in its modified form was likely to mislead the underdeveloped countries and to be the cause of further disappointment, since it would engage the Economic and Social Council laying out blueprints and principles which could not be given life under present circumstances."[1] Against a background of war and worsening East-West relations, the West would not undertake additional commitments for underdeveloped countries.

The Soviet Government, preoccupied with Eastern European and Far Eastern problems, and imbued with Stalin's antipathy toward all UN programs extending aid to underdeveloped countries, denigrated the plan. The Soviet delegate, A. A. Arutiunian, held that proposals such as SUNFED overestimated the significance of foreign capital for economic development and tended "to encourage intervention in domestic affairs through the channels of foreign capital and to perpetuate the economic subordination of the underdeveloped countries." He branded the proposal a new gambit whereby American imperialism would be spread under the guise of international assistance and remarked that "it was clear that all the talk about financing through grants-in-aid and long-term loans was merely altruistic phraseology with no solid foundation."[2] It was a new form of American imperialism.

Notwithstanding the opposition of the Great Powers, the General Assembly, in an assertion of independence, passed a modified resolution (520 [vi]) requesting: ". . . the Economic and Social Council to submit to the General Assembly at its seventh regular session a detailed plan for establishing as soon as circumstances permit, a special fund for grants-in-aid and for low-interest, long-term loans to underdeveloped countries for the purpose of helping them, at their request, to accelerate their economic development and to finance non-self-liquidating projects which are basic to their economic development." Succeeding debates in ECOSOC met with a chilly response from both the United States and the Soviet Union, and without support from these nations who were expected to finance the operations of SUNFED, nothing could be done.

[1] UN, General Assembly, Second Committee, *Official Records* (6th Session), p. 123.

[2] *Ibid.*, pp. 115-116.

In July 1953 Moscow decided to liquidate that aspect of the Stalinist legacy which had placed the USSR in perennial opposition to concrete measures for aiding underdeveloped countries and announced its readiness to contribute to EPTA. But it still opposed SUNFED. During the discussion in ECOSOC of SUNFED, a major article had appeared in *Pravda,* which noted that such aid would aggravate the financial straits of recipient countries. But in the subsequent few months, in keeping with the general tenor of Soviet speeches in UN organizations, Soviet criticisms became less heavy-handed and were no longer characterized by dire warnings of Western imperialist domination and disdain of SUNFED's potential. By the fall session of the General Assembly, the Soviet position had altered sufficiently for support to be given to a resolution calling for the establishment of SUNFED. However, Moscow continued to express serious reservations, and at the Eighteenth Session of ECOSOC in July 1954 the Soviet delegate, Mr. Kumykin, pointed out that: "The documents before the Council did not provide enough information about the projects that would be assisted by SUNFED, the order of their priority, the methods by which the contributions of the various states would be assessed or what say the underdeveloped countries would have in deciding how the Fund would be distributed."[3] He acknowledged the advantages that SUNFED had over private capital, but cautioned against exaggerated expectation of what could be accomplished and called first for a thorough exploration into the potential sources of domestic capital before anything definite was done.

Both the United States and the Soviet Union continued to argue that "an attempt to establish SUNFED immediately would result only in disillusionment and frustration for the underdeveloped countries."[4] But there was a difference: the United States continued to oppose the SUNFED proposal, both

[3] Economic and Social Council, *Official Records* (18th Session), p. 156.
[4] *Ibid.,* pp. 156-158.

by declaration and by its vote in various UN bodies, whereas, at the close of the 1953 session, Moscow voted for the adopted resolution calling for further investigation of the SUNFED proposal. Moving beyond its lukewarm acceptance of the 1953 resolution, the USSR soon aligned itself with the developing nations which it was then starting to court in earnest. A sharpened awareness of the importance of underdeveloped countries as targets in the new phase of the Cold War—competitive coexistence—and a readiness to espouse causes favored by neutralist nations made Moscow an advocate of SUNFED, though it was also evident that Moscow was undecided how far it should go in pushing the proposal.

Subsequent developments pressed Moscow to unqualified support of SUNFED. On December 6, 1954, the Economic and Financial Committee of the General Assembly approved a resolution calling for the creation of an International Finance Corporation when in a reversal of attitude Washington agreed to put up half of the initial subscription. In 1956 the IFC commenced operations. By its financial support of productive private enterprises in underdeveloped countries, it seeks to nurture confidence in, and attract foreign and domestic private capital for, local ventures. Membership is restricted to members of the World Bank, a stipulation effectively barring Soviet bloc countries. Though obviously not a substitute for SUNFED, IFC proponents hoped that it would ease, at least temporarily, neutralist pressure for SUNFED. For Moscow, IFC's exclusive concern with private enterprises and its integral tie to the World Bank relegate it to the status of another American-dominated international lending institution.

THE CURRENT SOVIET VIEW OF SUNFED

At the July 1955 session of ECOSOC, Mr. Kumykin again took the floor to discuss SUNFED, this time as a full-fledged supporter. All previous reservations were dropped. He stated that "his Government was ready to consider participating in

SUNFED" and recommended several revisions of the proposal before the Council. First, he opposed the view, favored by underdeveloped countries, that aid should be given primarily in the form of grants, noting that the problem "could not be solved by the creation of a charitable society: what was required was an organization capable of development, which could renew and expand it resources."[5] Aid should be given in the form of long-term, low-interest loans. This proposed modification served notice on the underdeveloped countries that Moscow would not give outright gifts but was willing to grant loans, and was intended as a slap at the World Bank for its policy of lending at commercial rates of interest. It also substantiates the view that Soviet foreign aid is predicated on the assumption that gifts are neither sound politics nor sound economics. Second, Kumykin proposed that SUNFED loans should be repayable in national currencies; third, contributions could be in the form of equipment and machinery; fourth, SUNFED should not be placed under the IBRD but should be constituted as an independent lending authority— one of the few times that Moscow has advocated the creation of new UN machinery; fifth, the underdeveloped countries should "have their due say in its management, the allocation of its funds and the execution of its operations."[6] By this, the Soviets apparently meant that the Executive Council of SUNFED should be composed equally of contributing and recipient countries. Finally, so urgent were the needs that the creation of SUNFED should not, he maintained, be contingent upon any prior agreement on disarmament—a tie-in insisted upon by the United States. The American position is that the funds saved from a disarmament agreement could be applied to SUNFED, since disarmament would enable a reduction in the budget of those countries which are to finance SUNFED.

On December 9, 1955, the General Assembly passed a reso-

[5] Economic and Social Council, *Official Records* (20th Session), p. 167.
[6] *Ibid.*

lution (923[x]) requesting the Secretary-General "to invite the States Members of the United Nations and members of the Specialized Agencies in the economic and social sphere, to transmit to him, not later than March 31, 1956, their views, as definitely as possible, relating to the establishment, role, structure, and operations of a Special United Nations Fund for Economic Development." Despite United States disapproval, the General Assembly, composed increasingly of underdeveloped countries, pushed the issue. As more and more nations came out in favor of SUNFED, they sought to bring pressure on the USA, since as the most prominent prospective contributor its agreement was essential, but Washington remained unyielding.

The Soviet reply to the Secretary-General shed light on Moscow's attitude not only toward SUNFED but toward foreign aid in general. Moscow favored the financing of SUNFED through voluntary contributions, rather than regular assessments; contributions should take the form of local currencies, in convertible and nonconvertible currencies; it opposed any provision that would make contributions in convertible currencies mandatory; the actual amounts and utilization of contributions in local currencies would be determined by mutual agreement between SUNFED, the donor, and the recipient country; contributions would also be permitted in the form of goods and services (though a number of neutralists, e.g. Burma, Cambodia, Ethiopia, and Egypt, opposed contributions in kind); SUNFED could start with an initial sum of $100 million, considerably less than the $250 million minimum recommended by the *Ad Hoc* Committee of Experts, and an early start was favored, provided all major industrial states agreed. Moscow was not prepared to commit itself to any arrangement which would require it in advance to pledge increasing amounts to the Fund but agreed that when progress was made in disarmament, greater contributions should be forthcoming. It strenuously opposed the disbursement of resources in the form of grants-in-aid, insisting that SUNFED should extend only loans. All loans were to be long term, low interest, and repayable in local currencies. Furthermore, repayment should be in the form of products of the debtor country, since that would help promote international trade. These same operational principles currently guide bilateral Soviet foreign aid policy.

By the fall of 1957, Washington became concerned over the awkwardness of its position. Though it could forestall the creation of SUNFED, it could not prevent the proposal from being widely discussed or the Soviets from capitalizing on America's resistance to a measure enjoying wide popularity among underdeveloped countries. At the November 18 meeting of the General Assembly's Second Committee, the American delegate, Congressman Walter E. Judd, reiterated U.S. opposition to the establishment of a multilateral fund which could not command sufficient support to permit it to carry out its intended functions. In words as strong as any ever used by the United States in the Committee, he made it clear "that the United States would not only vote against any resolution submitted at the current session that contemplated the immediate establishment of such a Fund but would also refuse to participate in the work of any preparatory commission which might be appointed to draft the regulations of the Fund."[7]

To temper the disappointment of the underdeveloped countries, he offered a consolation loaf. He noted that economic development required a "concentrated, systematic, and sustained effort" in such basic and associated fields as the survey of natural resources, industrial research, and the training of manpower. Accordingly, he proposed "a substantial increase in the Expanded Programme, in the form of a rise in the total annual contribution from 30 million to 100 million dollars and the establishment as an integral part of the program, of a

[7] UN, General Assembly, Second Committee, *Official Records* (12th Session), p. 215.

Special Projects Fund, earmarked for systematic and sustained assistance in the fields which he had just mentioned." Although Mr. Judd later declared "that the United States proposal was not a substitute for SUNFED, an alternative to SUNFED, or an attempt to exclude the future development of SUNFED," few interpreted it as anything but an attempt to divert attention from SUNFED by offering a less expensive type of fund.

While the United States emphasized that the Special Fund was intended as a supplement to EPTA, the Soviet bloc offered a contrary interpretation. The Czech delegate accused the USA of suborning SUNFED; he dismissed American arguments as neither convincing nor valid, especially the one linking creation of SUNFED with an agreement on disarmament because, he maintained, the initial capital required to start the Fund was a mere fraction of the world's total arms expenditures: "The real reason for the opposition of the United Kingdom and the United States was only too apparent; it was their desire to preserve bilateral assistance as an economic weapon for bringing political pressure to bear on certain underdeveloped countries." The Soviet delegate took an equivocating tack. Agreeing with the Indian delegate, he said that SUNFED could begin operations with an initial capital of $100 million, an amount that could be increased as sums were released from arms budgets, but qualified his support by adding that operations should begin only after "contributions had been announced by not less than thirty states which, in his delegation's opinion, should include the major industrialized countries as the main contributors."[8] Moreover, the Soviets never specified how much they were prepared to contribute to the Fund and repeatedly stressed that contributions should be voluntary, not assessed. They were unwilling to translate political support into a financial impetus that might have en-

[8] A/C.2/SR. 431, p. 231; Cf. A/C.2/SR. 500, p. 252.

couraged the underdeveloped countries to push ahead and went along with the proposal for the Special Fund.

On December 14, 1957, the General Assembly adopted resolution 1219 (xii) which called for the establishment "as an expansion of the existing technical assistance and development activities of the United Nations and the Specialized Agencies of a separate Special Fund which would provide systematic and sustained assistance in fields essential to the integrated technical, economic and social development of the less developed countries." The Special Fund commenced operations on January 1, 1959.

THE SOVIET RATIONALE

The SUNFED dialogue has been part of UN deliberations for more than a decade. It crops up under new pseudonyms, most recently the UN Capital Development Fund, but the essentials of the original proposals remain very much in the political thinking of the majority of UN members. Since late 1953, the Soviet Union has made of SUNFED a repeated example of its sympathy with underdeveloped countries. That it succeeds without serious challenge is symptomatic of the deep-rooted dilemma which permeates UN affairs: that while the greatest champion and benefactor of the UN and its manifold activities is the United States, the ability of American leaders to commit resources to UN projects is outdistanced by the desires of the underdeveloped countries. The resulting disenchantment among the beneficiaries of American support creates a climate suited to Soviet diplomacy, to advocacy of whatever is popular, with minimum concern for fulfillment.

During the summer and early fall of 1953, Soviet leaders reached the decision that support for SUNFED would be politically beneficial and would cost little, even if it should be adopted. However, Soviet journals have paid scant attention to SUNFED. Only in the UN are lengthy supportive speeches made. Support for SUNFED was a natural concomitant of Moscow's participation in EPTA: in each case, the Soviet Government clearly established its determination to have control over its degree of commitment and to maintain it at a minimum level consonant with its over-all approach to international organizations. At a time when Moscow was undertaking to improve relations with underdeveloped countries, Soviet support for a proposal enjoying enormous appeal among these countries made good politics, particularly in the light of American opposition. By pushing SUNFED, and contrasting it with the inadequacy of the International Finance Corporation or the Special Fund, Moscow hoped to engender disillusionment with American efforts through the UN and enhance the attraction of Soviet bilateral assistance.

In recent years, however, Soviet exploitation of the SUNFED issue has been blunted because of the availability of new and alternate forms of capital and because of Moscow's refusal to state exactly how much it is prepared to contribute to a Capital Development Fund. As one Western diplomat expressed it, "Had the Soviets made a concrete offer of 10 to 15 million dollars, SUNFED would have been approved by the General Assembly, and the United States would have found itself in a politically impossible position and been forced to go along." Moscow's failure to act generously at the critical juncture in the discussions has led neutralist nations to treat its subsequent statements on SUNFED with considerable reserve.

Support for SUNFED served a Soviet purpose at a particular period: it lent credibility to Moscow's championing the cause of rapid heavy industrial development for underdeveloped countries; and it helped dispel the widespread skepticism among them that had been the lingering consequence of Stalin's lack of interest in UN aid programs. The shift to support for SUNFED, as to participation in EPTA, was a change which did not require any basic modification of objective or attitude, though it did portend the subsequent reappraisal of the importance of underdeveloped countries for Soviet foreign policy and the way in which the interests of the Soviet Union could coalesce and complement those of these countries.

The USSR and the World Health Organization: The International Health and Medical Year

The Specialized Agencies of the United Nations operate under separate constitutions which afford them maximum independence in conducting their programs. Though their professional activities are supposedly nonpolitical, the Specialized Agencies are not devoid of politics. On the contrary, in recent years they have become an important arena in the Soviet-Western struggle for the support of the less developed countries. The degree of politicization varies: it is intensive in the International Atomic Energy Agency and the International Labor Organization; negligible in the Universal Postal Union and the International Telecommunications Union, although even the least political of the Agencies are occasionally subjected to Cold War byplays.

BACKGROUND TO SOVIET PARTICIPATION

The World Health Organization was formally established on April 7, 1948, when the requisite 26 acceptances of its Constitution were received from UN members. The objective of the Organization is "the attainment by all people of the highest possible level of health." Though WHO activities seldom receive public attention, they affect the well-being of hundreds of millions of people in less developed countries. The creed of Hippocrates knows no ideological or political distinctions; it is beyond personal prejudices and partisan politics. But man is a political animal, and even the medical profession functions in a milieu of national and international political pressures.

Soviet participation in WHO confronts the analyst with a mixed record. For a number of years during the Stalin era, the Soviet Union withdrew from the activities of the Organization, charging that WHO was not providing the USSR or the countries of Eastern Europe, which had suffered most from the war, with adequate assistance; that it was diffusing its limited sources in the financing of technical missions which were of questionable value; and that it discriminated against Soviet personnel in the staffing of the WHO Secretariat. Efforts by the Director-General to heal this breach failed, for Stalin had no real interest in the Organization. Moscow forced the Eastern European countries to become inactive, as part of its policy of isolating them from any contact with the non-Communist world.

The changed attitude of Moscow toward the economic and social organizations of the UN led the Soviet Union to re-activitate its membership in WHO in 1957. At the Twentieth Session of the Economic and Social Council in July 1955, the Soviet delegate noted that WHO was doing constructive work and indicated that his Government was prepared to enter actively into its work.[9] The Director-General and the USSR Ministry of Health shortly thereafter opened discussions aimed at bringing the Soviet bloc back into the Organization. The problem of the annual assessments, which had been unpaid during the inactive period of the USSR, was satisfactorily resolved with the proviso that "States resuming active membership should pay in full their arrears of contributions for years in which they participated actively, that a token payment of five per cent should be accepted in full settlement of their financial obligations for the years in which they had been inactive and that such payments could be made in equal annual installments over a period up to ten years."[10] Albania, Bulgaria, and Poland resumed active membership in January

[9] Economic and Social Council, *Official Records* (20th Session), p. 76.
[10] *The First Ten Years of the World Health Organization* (Geneva: WHO, 1958), p. 80. Whether a legal curiosity or an example of the legal acumen of the framers of the WHO Constitution, no member may withdraw from the Organization; he can only become inactive.

1957, and the USSR followed in April; Rumania returned in May 1957 and Czechoslovakia in January 1958. However, for reasons known only to the Kremlin, the Ukrainian and Belorussian Republics have not yet activated their membership. Renewed participation was one phase of the Soviet quest for respectability among the underdeveloped countries, and it was to affect the climate of the World Health Organization, as well as that of the other Specialized Agencies and regional economic commissions which had been neglected by Moscow during the Stalin period.

THE INTERNATIONAL HEALTH AND MEDICAL YEAR

The most important item for discussion at the Twelfth World Health Assembly of May 1959 was the proposal to conduct an International Health and Medical Research Year. The purpose of such a year was to stimulate research and to promote international cooperation in various areas of health and medical research, to bring dramatically to human consciousness the ills of mankind. As with the International Geophysical Year, the International Health and Medical Research Year was to be conducted primarily on a national basis.

The American proposal, which had initially been submitted for WHO consideration on November 8, 1958, was discussed on May 22, 1959, in the ninth Meeting of the Committee on Programme and Budget. The Director-General of WHO, Dr. Candau, stressed the significance of the projected International Health Year and suggested that it start in May 1961 and end in December 1962. The American delegation then outlined its proposal in detail. A challenge came immediately from the Soviet delegate, Dr. S. A. Sarkisov. Noting that Article 55 of the UN Charter called for promotion of solutions to international economic, social, and health problems, he stated that, "it was in accordance with those aims that the General Assembly at its thirteenth session (fall 1958) had unanimously approved a proposal by the delegation of the Ukrainian S.S.R.

for the holding in 1961 of an International Health and Medical Research Year."[11] He declared that the Soviet Union was in full accord with the proposed Health Year, believing in the principal objective of WHO, "the attainment by all peoples of the highest possible level of health." Dr. Sarkisov dwelt on the past work of WHO, the importance of the Health Year, and expressed the willingness of his Government to assist underdeveloped countries who were short on funds and experts. He stated that the Soviets would contribute to the success of this worthy international enterprise "by forming and equipping teams of specialists for malaria and smallpox control, providing consultants to help organize centers for health education, maternal and child health, and industrial health, and supplying insecticides and smallpox vaccine."[12] He offered Soviet money, drugs, equipment, and experts to help make the International Health Year a success.

This lengthy aside served to establish Soviet interest in the project and to elaborate the extent to which the USSR was prepared to offer concrete support. It also dramatized the impact of what was to come. Sarkisov continued: "The Soviet delegation considered all its suggestions so far as preliminary proposals. It had certain objections to make to that section of the document before the meeting which dealt with the history of the question, and which was not in accordance with the documentary evidence." Sarkisov maintained that the question of holding an International Health and Medical Research Year had initially been raised by the Ukrainian delegation in the General Assembly on September 17, 1958. On November 6, 1958, the Ukrainian delegation had published a draft resolution. The next day the head of the delegation had delivered a detailed statement on this proposal in the Third Committee of the General Assembly. On December 8, 1958, the General

[11] World Health Organization, Committee on Programme and Budget, *Official Records* (12th World Health Assembly), p. 263.

[12] *Ibid.*, p. 265.

Assembly had then adopted unanimously the proposal and invited WHO, in a letter dated December 11, 1958, to undertake the organization of the International Health Year. The Soviet delegate noted that the American proposal had first been made on November 8, 1958, that is to say, subsequent to the proposal by the Ukrainian delegation. He therefore insisted that "the necessary corrections be made in the document" being considered by the Committee.

A review of the origins of the idea for an International Health Year suggests that considerations of national prestige were the principal motivations behind the Soviet position. The idea for the International Health Year had been first expressed by President Eisenhower in his State of the Union Message on January 10, 1958. He urged the Soviet Union to join the United States in a major effort to eradicate disease. Support from Premier Khrushchev came on January 26, during a speech in Minsk. At the Eleventh World Health Assembly in May, both the American and Soviet delegates indicated a growing interest in the project.

On June 8, 1958, Adlai E. Stevenson, speaking at Michigan State University, proposed the convening of an International Medical Research and Health Year to spur cooperation among the Great Powers. The year of 1958 was the period in which the concept of peaceful competition was acquiring political vogue. The United States and the Soviet Union stepped up their courtship of underdeveloped countries and moved ahead with plans for a nuclear test ban and major disarmament negotiations. On August 18 the United States Senate approved a resolution submitted by Senator Hubert H. Humphrey calling upon President Eisenhower to take immediate steps to initiate an International Health Year.

Dr. Candau, a dedicated international civil servant, sought to heal this potentially serious breach. In a moving plea for tolerance and accommodation, he noted that "history was very difficult to write." Presenting the sequence of events as they had come to his attention, he declared that history, so far as WHO was concerned, had occurred as stated in the American proposal.[13] The American proposal, dated November 8, 1958, had been received on that date by WHO. At the time, the Ukrainian proposal had been placed before the General Assembly, and not WHO. Only after the Ukrainian proposal had been adopted by the General Assembly on December 8, 1958, had it been brought to the attention of WHO in a letter dated December 11, 1958. The Executive Board of WHO had included the Ukrainian proposal in the supplementary agenda, an agenda already containing the United States proposal. He noted that no change was possible at this late date in the document before the Assembly. Thus, as far as the World Health Organization was concerned, the American proposal was the first one which had been received by the Organization and was the one which was controlling the present situation. Attempts were made to clarify some of the difficulties of sponsorship of the proposal, but these failed as the Soviet delegate insisted that an appropriate amendment, acknowledging the original initiative of the Ukrainian delegation, be inserted in the proposal for an International Health and Medical Research Year. The Cold War was about to chill prospects for a concerted attack on disease.

The Chairman requested the Soviet delegate to submit his amendment in writing. Dr. Sarkisov noted that time was needed to word the amendment and asked for a postponement until the next meeting. The Chairman, after stating that he had been instructed to complete discussion of this item of the agenda at the current meeting, reversed his position and agreed to a one-day delay when it became clear that the Soviet delegation would otherwise not support the proposal before the Committee for an International Health Year.

The next day, at the tenth meeting of the Committee on

[13] *Ibid.*, p. 268.

Programme and Budget, the Soviet delegate submitted a resolution which was virtually identical to the American proposal. The only difference lay in which nation would receive credit for being the main sponsor of the International Health and Medical Research Year. There was every indication that so committed were both the United States and the USSR to the idea of an International Health Year, that they would have sponsored a joint resolution if time and circumstances had allowed.

However, before the Soviet resolution could be discussed, the Pakistani delegate offered a resolution proposing that "owing to the existing heavy commitment of national and international effort in the field of health and medical research, the holding of an International Health and Medical Research Year be postponed for the present." The Iranian and UAR delegates promptly supported the Pakistani resolution. The Soviet delegate meanwhile indicated that "he would be prepared to discuss the matter [of differences in resolution] with the United States delegation in the hope of reaching agreement on a consolidated text." The Director-General, anxious to keep alive this prospect, urged that "time might perhaps be allowed for such informal discussions and for consideration of drafting changes to the Pakistani draft resolution, the vote being postponed until the following meeting." In his eagerness and quest for time, he failed to realize or sought to ignore that the Pakistani resolution was diametrically opposed to the Soviet and American resolutions. This, however, was not lost on the French delegate who immediately raised the point and suggested that a vote be taken on the Pakistani resolution. The UAR, Australia, and Turkey supported the French delegate. Romania, Poland, and the Philippines supported the Director-General. Though both the United States and the Soviet Union voted against the Pakistani resolution, it was adopted by a vote of 36 to 14, with 6 abstentions.

This unexpected development stymied the earnest efforts of

the Director-General and a policy supported by the two Great Powers. It was as unusual as it was unexpected. Rare have been the times when both the United States and the Soviet Union favored the same idea and expressed willingness to compromise differences to permit its implementation, that the idea was subsequently defeated. Even the alignment of forces was unusual in that it did not follow predictable bloc patterns. Several of America's allies voted for postponement, that is to say for rejection in effect, of the United States' proposal.

The immediate reason for the defeat of the International Health Year was the opposition of the underdeveloped countries who believed that, given the limited resources of WHO, too much money and effort would be diverted from the more limited but concrete programs currently in operation; that a comprehensive research program financed from the meager resources available to WHO would detract from programs which tangibly benefited them. In this they showed little political foresight. They failed to see the political wisdom, as well as economic and medical advantage, behind supporting the proposal *just because* it was supported by the United States and the Soviet Union—an error not made by the Yugoslav delegation in its eloquent plea for Assembly approval. Had this proposal been adopted, the Great Powers would have been committed to enlarging the pie that was to be divided among the underdeveloped countries. Politically, these countries who are always calling upon the Powers to work together for world welfare squandered an opportunity to give impetus to their objective.

Among the Western countries opposing the proposal, the tenor of thinking leaned toward the skeptical; they did not see any benefits for themselves and were reluctant about commitment to expensive, ambitious programs. Technical and professional considerations were also involved. Many of the delegates were doctors who did not see how such a year could be organized nor evaluated in view of its brief duration. Also,

109

many in the Assembly were piqued that the resolution had come from the General Assembly and the Great Powers—from political rather than professional circles. They felt that so important a question should first have been studied by medically competent committees.

In seeking to analyze the Soviet attitude toward the International Health Year, a number of questions arise. Why did the Ukrainian delegation submit its proposal of September 17, 1958, for "The Organization of an International Public Health and Medical Research Year" to the General Assembly and not to WHO? Why did the Soviets choose the General Assembly if they were interested in medicine and not propaganda? Why did they choose the Ukraine S.S.R., which was not a member in good standing of WHO, to make the proposal? No authoritative answers to these questions can be given in the absence of official documentation, but the available evidence strongly suggests that propaganda considerations were of primary importance.

In a period of peaceful competition, propaganda assumes increasing importance as an instrument for promoting political ends. It may be that the Soviet Union, realizing that the United States intended to submit its proposal for an International Health Year to the WHO Executive Board, thought to gain a propaganda advantage by introducing such a resolution in the General Assembly, thus anticipating and outmaneuvering the constitutionally correct procedure followed by the United States. That the Ukrainian resolution was offered at the last minute, as a supplementary Agenda item, tends to confirm this interpretation. The Soviet Union had certainly not thought of offering such a resolution earlier in the year, when the Agenda for the September session of the General Assembly had been drawn up. An unusual and thus far unexplained aspect of Moscow's handling of this affair was the decision to introduce the proposal through the delegation of the Ukrainian Republic, which was, and still is, an inactive member of WHO.

From WHO's point of view, not only was the resolution introduced in a constitutionally improper manner, but the Ukrainian Republic was not even a member in good standing. Moscow has never given any reasons for its enigmatic tactics in this affair.[14]

In June 1959, a few weeks after WHO had decided to postpone the International Health Year, the Ukrainian delegate offered a resolution at the Annual Conference of the International Labor Organization calling upon the ILO to support the convening of such a Year. There was considerable opposition to the Ukrainian proposal on the ground that it was improper to anticipate the participation of the ILO in a project which the competent organization had not yet decided to initiate. After lengthy discussion, the Ukrainian delegation succeeded in obtaining adoption of a revised resolution which drew attention to the millions of workers still subject to numerous occupational diseases and called on the Governing Body of the ILO to participate with the World Health Organization "to ensure that in the event of the holding of the International Health and Medical Research Year, programmes designed to protect the life and health of workers shall be developed to the maximum extent possible." The resolution also requested members to ratify ILO conventions, if they had not done so, relating to workers health and medical services and of extending them to all workers under its jurisdiction. Soviet delegates pointedly observed that the Soviet Union was a signatory to these conventions and made available an extensive medical coverage for all its workers.

The Twelfth World Health Assembly requested the Director-General to review the problem and report on his findings at the 1960 Assembly. By then, however, the international

---

[14] A similar situation arose the following year when the Belorussian S.S.R., also an inactive member of WHO, introduced a proposal at the 14th General Assembly, calling for the convening of an International Cancer Year.

situation had deteriorated as a result of the U-2 incident and the breakup of the Paris Summit Conference (1960), and neither the United States nor the Soviet Union showed any interest in an International Health Year.

During the course of these complex, often politically charged discussions, the Soviet press virtually ignored the proceedings. Only four articles in 1958-1959 even alluded to Soviet activities in the World Health Organization. On July 18, 1958, Professor V. Zhdanov, the U.S.S.R. Deputy Minister of Health, wrote an article for *Pravda* in which he reported on the Eleventh World Health Assembly. He noted that "the delegates were greatly impressed by the Soviet Government's generous gift to the World Health Organization of 25,000,000 doses of dry smallpox vaccine." A few weeks later, Professor N. Grashchenkov, the Assistant Director-General of WHO, and a Soviet citizen, wrote a piece in *Izvestiia* on the activities of the Organization. The September 19, 1958 issues of *Pravda* and *Izvestiia* made brief mention of the Ukrainian proposal at the UN General Assembly, on conducting an International Health Year.

No coverage of the developments surrounding the discussion and the subsequent rejection of the idea was accorded by the Soviet press. There was no mention of the other issues raised at the Twelfth World Health Assembly. Nor did the Soviet journals intended primarily for foreign audiences devote any attention to WHO proceedings. The incidents were unknown to the Soviet reading public. This suggests a) that the events at the Twelfth World Health Assembly were not considered newsworthy enough to be journalistically described to the Soviet public; b) that what happens in the World Health Assemblies is of marginal interest to but a few scholars; and c) that the Soviet leadership did not consider the issues worthy of even passing treatment. What we do not know, and what requires constant evaluation in attempts to assess Soviet motives and objectives in international organizations, is the extent to which meager coverage internally can be taken as a lack of interest in the high echelons of decision-making responsibilities.

The Soviet Position on the Use of Volunteer Workers in UN Technical Assistance Programs

The Thirty-second Session of ECOSOC (July 1961) was the scene of controversy over an issue which embodied as much idealism as perhaps any to come before the UN since the Truman Point Four Program of 1949. The discussion, which transcended the usual repetitious melange of speeches and resolutions, referred to the United States proposal to use volunteer workers from all countries in the operational technical assistance programs of UN agencies concerned with underdeveloped countries. The proposal would provide trained, though essentially inexperienced, personnel to work directly with UN teams in the field—in Africa, the Middle East, South Asia—wherever there is a need for skills and training not available locally.

In a memorandum favorable to the American proposal, the Secretary-General observed that volunteers might assist in engineering institutes and schools where there is a shortage of "foremen and other middle-level managerial personnel," in resources development and the allied field of cartography, in economic and statistical surveys which require fact-finding field workers, and "in such capacities as statisticians, supply workers and junior laboratory workers in mass disease control programmes." The UN, he noted, was interested "in the possibility particularly of drawing upon the services of persons of middle-level or associate-expert grade. This is an important category of assistants for whom there is a substantial unfilled need in many underdeveloped countries."[15]

Representatives of the Specialized Agencies all expressed

[15] E/TAC/SR. 251, p. 9.

interest in the proposal. The Food and Agriculture Organization (FAO) and the Bureau of Technical Assistance Operations (BTAO) said they could use several hundred volunteers
a year to assist in community development projects in rural
areas; WHO could use them to help staff health stations in
connection with its Malaria Eradication and Environmental
Sanitation Projects; and UNESCO noted the need for such
help in the fields of education and library sciences.

In its proposal,[16] the United States recognized that the demands of underdeveloped countries for technical assistance
were as great as the funds were limited. Proceeding on the
assumption that "the use of volunteer technical personnel in
groups that are international in character can assist in the
promotion of peaceful relations among nations," it recommended that suitably trained personnel serve as "volunteers"
or "associate" experts in already existing UN programs for
periods of one year or longer. All such volunteers would
receive nominal salaries to be borne by the donor governments, thus relieving the United Nations of any additional
financial burden. To initiate the program, the Secretary-General would "inquire of member governments of the United
Nations and of the Specialized Agencies whether they are
willing to offer and/or to receive volunteer personnel to be
used in approved programmes and projects of technical cooperation." Volunteer experts would then be placed, subject
to the approval of the recipient country and their general
availability, at the disposal of those Specialized Agencies
which had expressed interest. They would work with UN
technical assistance teams, serving under the authority of
full-time experts in whatever capacity the latter might deem
most beneficial for the completion of the project. In this way,
the volunteers would relieve the UN experts of the onerous
drudgeries and complications which beset any executive-ad-
ministrator.

[16] E/TAC/L. 248/Rev.1 of July 27, 1961.

To avoid political taint of any kind, the American proposal clearly stated that "no volunteers shall be sent to a country without prior approval of the receiving country, and that any such volunteers may remain only with the permission of such country." All volunteers would become temporary UN civil servants to ensure their international, nonpartisan character. Since the government providing the volunteers would "be responsible for all identifiable costs as maintenance allowances, insurance, costs of transportation to the place of assignment," there would be no financial drain on the UN, and many nations, including some of the less developed countries which have a reservoir of educated personnel, could contribute some volunteers, thereby broadening the international character of the effort.

Ambassador Philip M. Klutznick, the American delegate, made an impassioned plea for immediate adoption, calling the proposal a unique marriage of "action and idealism" which would promote international understanding and economic development. Discussions were conducted in the Technical Assistance Committee and debate was heated. While supporters lobbied hard for the measure, opponents used every political, propaganda, and parliamentary tactic at their disposal in an effort to destroy, emasculate, or at least delay its adoption.

Opposition came from two directions: the Soviet bloc and several neutralist nations, namely, Afghanistan, Jordan, the Sudan, and the United Arab Republic. The Soviet delegate, Mr. Romanov, illustrated his theme that the West was seeking to extend its systematic spoliation of the underdeveloped countries with an ancedote: "The so-called Peace Corps or the corps of volunteers which the United States proposed should be established under United Nations auspices was reminiscent of the missionaries who had arrived in African and Asian countries during the period of colonial conquest. They had arrived carrying only a cross and a Bible, while at that time the natives had owned the land and its riches; however, after a few years the positions had been reversed and it was the natives who had a Bible in the hand while the colonialists owned the land and its riches."[17]

The bulk of his rebuttal was that the American proposal was a blatant effort to push United States political influence in underdeveloped countries. Labeling it a "new imperialist weapon," Romanov tied it to the equally defamed Peace Corps. He said that both the Peace Corps and the volunteers were political in purpose and designed to restore the initiative in the Cold War to the United States. Under the protective cover of the UN flag, the United States hoped to train para-military cadres in underdeveloped countries and build and maintain roads and communications centers for use in sup-pressing unrest and revolutionary movements in Africa, Asia, and Latin America. To support his views, he cited American tabloid newspapers as reflections of Pentagon thinking. "The United States," he concluded, "is seeking to combat Com-munism under the guise of humanitarianism by attribuing to Communism all the ills of contemporary Capitalism"; just as the United States uses foreign aid as a weapon in the Cold War, so, too, does it seek to exploit UN "volunteers" for selfish purposes. The vehemence of his attack recalled the heyday of the Stalin era. Most members saw it as an open political assault which actually did not deal with the proposal itself.

The other thrust came from U.A.R., Sudanese, and Afghan delegates who put forth a competing resolution. Accepting the principles enunciated in the American resolution, they recommended that its consideration be postponed until the matter had been debated at the next session of the General Assembly. They questioned that there was sufficient informa-tion concerning the reaction of potential recipient countries, the financial burden which might devolve upon UN agencies

[17] E/TAC/SR. 251, p. 9.

and prospective recipients, or the need for such volunteers to warrant action at this session of ECOSOC. In subsequent speeches, the sentiments of the U.A.R. delegate assumed a peculiarly personal and petulant note.[18] Mr. Abdel-Ghani sarcastically noted that he did not consider the U.A.R. objections answered, though the American delegate had "dazzled" the Committee with his eloquence. Before proceeding to his main points, the U.A.R. delegate vented his ire in passing against "the five American assistants who should pay more attention to what was being said." Then, quoting from *Esquire*, implying that it represented informed American opinion, he solemnly asked whether there was not a real danger that the volunteers might not be primarily newly married college graduates searching for an inexpensive honeymoon in faraway places. He also took a sideswipe at "the avalanche of daily attacks by the American press against the U.A.R." Realizing that a frontal assault would have no chance of acceptance, he called for the submission of a lengthy questionnaire to all Member States to determine their views on the American plan, hoping by this procedure to postpone action until it could perhaps be sidetracked in the General Assembly. This delaying tactic has been interpreted as the result of the U.A.R.'s desire to steer a middle course between Great Power pressures and its judgment that there was little that it could hope to gain from the proposal, since the U.A.R. needs investment capital not junior experts.

Given its suspicion of American motives in general and the Peace Corps in particular, Moscow's animosity was not unexpected. According to one American delegate, "The Soviets misinterpreted the proposal from the start, and therefore their action was logical and justifiable. Why did they misunder-

[18] Some UN officials remarked privately that the comments of the U.A.R. delegate may in part have been directed personally against Ambassador Klutznick because of his past record as an effective fundraiser for Israel.

stand? Because they make mistakes, and because comparison with the Peace Corps, from which they drew the worst possible deductions, was inevitable. The Soviets were bound to see American political maneuvers in the proposal." Several members of the Secretariat thought the proposal imaginative and idealistic, but poorly timed. Following on the heels of the Peace Corps, it was, of course, interpreted by the Soviets as an international version of the Kennedy creation. One UN official expressed privately the view that the United States, if it were not interested in gaining fleeting political plaudits, could have improved the likelihood of adoption and kept controversy to a minimum had it requested several neutralist nations to sponsor the proposal, thereby avoiding the Cold War coloration and the automatic opposition of the USSR.

The Soviet delegation had attacked the proposal in April 1961, when it was first added to the agenda. It then brought pressure to bear on Afghanistan, the U.A.R., and other neutralists to oppose the plan. However, they preferred to adopt a critical but uncommitted position, especially after a sounding of general sentiment among other governments had revealed a core of interest in the plan. In this instance, Moscow's initial antagonism so far exceeded the hesitation of most neutralists that it could not subsequently enlist their support for a concerted effort to weaken the proposal.

Prior to the opening of the ECOSOC session, the chief Soviet and American delegates had met several times to determine whether accord could be reached on any of the agenda items. For example, the Soviets were preparing to introduce a resolution on unemployment. The United States delegation inquired whether they were doing so for propaganda purposes or with serious intent. When the latter motivation was established, the two delegations worked out a mutually acceptable resolution. But on the proposal to use volunteers in UN activities, the Soviets did not raise any questions, whereupon the American delegation proceeded to explain the purpose and operating mechanics of the proposal. The Soviet Ambassador remarked that further explanation at that point was useless, since Moscow had flatly decided that no compromise was possible on this proposal.[19]

The position of the Soviet Government was the result of several considerations. First, Moscow viewed the proposal as an attempt to advance American political influence, not to improve economic and social conditions in underdeveloped countries. So similar was it, both in content and timing, to the Peace Corps that no other interpretation made sense. Second, Moscow believed that Western concern for underdeveloped countries is a direct outgrowth of its desire to thwart the advance of Communism. To accomplish this, the West resorts to a variety of tactics, including domination of UN technical assistance programs. Thus, the use of volunteers was intended to further westernize the framework of EPTA. Third, if, as the Americans insisted, the proposal did not intend to introduce vast numbers of volunteers into existing UN programs, why the need for a new formal program? Why not act within the existing technical assistance machinery?[20]

A final point, not mentioned by Soviet officials, needs to be added. Opposition to the proposal may stem from the existence of a different set of values. There is nothing in the values of the Soviet political leadership which would help them understand, or sympathize with, the desire of young people to serve ideals which transcend the national framework and are not linked to the promotion of any particular ideological system.[21] The idea of "volunteers" as used here, is alien to Soviet society.

[19] Interview with a member of the United States delegation in Geneva on August 2, 1961.

[20] E/TAC/SR. 253, p. 4.

[21] *Izvestiia*, on March 15, 1961, ridiculed the idea that hundreds of Americans, "prepared for self-sacrifice," are ready to go to Africa, Asia, and Latin America out of a purely idealistic desire to help the peoples of these areas. See also E/SR. 1182, p. 192.

It presupposes the possibility of transnational mobility and the voluntary proffering of services which are neither accepted nor sanctioned by Soviet leaders. Being a peculiarly Western concept, and tied in this instance to specific, identifiable political purposes, the proposal was bound to encounter their inevitable rejection.

However, on August 1, 1961, the Technical Assistance Committee approved the American proposal by an overwhelming majority: the Soviet bloc voted against the proposal, and Afghanistan, Jordan, the Sudan, and the U.A.R. abstained. The attitude of the Soviet Government was certainly no surprise, given the vehemence of Soviet opposition to the Peace Corps. It may well be that, under current conditions of competitive coexistence, any American proposal for helping developing areas will elicit similar Soviet reactions.

Financing Economic Development

The financial crisis of the United Nations is in large measure an outgrowth of the Soviet conception of what should be the outer limits to political and economic commitments of international organizations. Disavowing financial responsibility for those UN political solutions which it opposes, the Soviet Government has refused to pay its assessed share of the costs for the United Nations Emergency Force in the Middle East (UNEF) and the United Nations Military Operation in the Congo (ONUC). It has also refused support for such welfare programs as the United Nations Relief and Works Agency for Palestine Refugees (UNRWA) and the United Nations High Commissioner for Refugees (UNHCR), which are financed by voluntary contributions rather than regular assessments.

Long an advocate of modest UN budgets, the Soviet Union made use of the uncertainties surrounding the escalation of military operations and expenses in the Congo to demand a ceiling of $50 million on the UN budget (the present level exceeds the $75 million mark), a reorganization of the fiscal system to "make it impossible for some members to embark on political and economic programs at the expense of other member states," and a more efficient utilization of existing staff with a corresponding "end to the swelling of departments, bureaus, and sections."

Mounting UN expenditures (the annual costs for UNEF and ONUC combined are double the regular UN budget) have caused dismay also among many non-Soviet-bloc countries and opposition to any proposal to share the costs in the usual manner, that is on the basis of the regular scale of assessments. Their arguments were founded on three propositions. First, they stated that since the Charter contemplated that peace and security actions should be carried out primarily by the five permanent members of the Security Council, who would furnish their troops without cost to other UN members, then these five members should pay considerably more than their ordinary assessment percentages for peace and security operations such as UNEF and ONUC, especially since in neither case were they furnishing manpower.[22] Second, a number of countries, particularly among the Arab and Soviet bloc, maintained that the "parties of interest" and the "aggressors," who made the UN security operations a necessity, should assume the primary responsibility for the expenses incurred by the UN. Third, many underdeveloped countries were reluctant, regardless of the political merit of UN actions, to commit their meager resources to the financing of costly operations such as UNEF and ONUC. They preferred to utilize their funds for domestic development.

The financial crisis caused by the Congo operation actuated the establishment, in the spring of 1961, of a special fifteen-

[22] Joint Committee Print of the U. S. Senate Committee on Foreign Relations and the House Committee on Foreign Affairs, "Information on the Operations and Financing of the United Nations" (February 6, 1962), 87th Congress, 2d Session, p. 13.

nation UN committee charged with finding a suitable method of raising money. After six months of fruitless discussion, the committee agreed to request an advisory opinion (which is not binding upon member states) from the International Court of Justice on the following question: Does the UN Charter place a legal obligation on members to support financially the military and economic operations of the Organization when ordered by a majority of the states? The gravity of the situation was brought forcefully to the attention of the Fifth Committee (the Administrative and Budgetary Committee) of the General Assembly on December 11, 1961, when the Secretary-General warned that the United Nations faced "imminent bankruptcy, if, in addition to earliest possible payment of current and, particularly, of arrear assessments, effective action is not promptly taken for the purpose of a) enabling outstanding obligations to be settled; b) improving the cash position; and c) providing needed financing for approved continuing activities. . . . In the absence of adequate and assured long-term arrangements looking to the Organization's immediate as well as prospective financial needs the consequence of insolvency will have to be faced seriously and soon."[23]

On July 20, 1962, the Court, in a 9 to 5 vote, expressed the opinion that all members of the United Nations were legally obligated to pay their share of the UN's Middle East and Congo operations. It noted that the Secretary-General had incurred the financial obligations "in accordance with the clear and reiterated authority of both the Security Council and the General Assembly" and with the purpose of fulfilling a prime UN objective—to promote international peace. Accordingly, members were obligated to contribute to the expenses involved in conducting these operations.

Moscow rejects this responsibility in toto. It pays its assess-

---

[23] See UN Document A/C.5/907.

ment for the regular UN budget but will not honor any of the levies for emergency operations in the Gaza Strip or the Congo. Even the total Soviet assessment for the regular budget, which also includes that of Belorussian and Ukrainian S.S.R.'s, and has gradually been increased from 8.0 per cent in 1946 to 17.47 per cent in 1963, is challenged by the USSR as excessive.[24]

UN military operations involve conflicting Great Power interests and raise fundamental political questions concerning the purposes of the UN and the extent to which it can initiate costly operations and still command the support of the great majority of its members. When the vital interests of any country conflict with controversial UN undertakings, perhaps the opposition of that country is to be expected and accepted, at least until such time as UN actions are made binding upon member nations by usage and law. But where national interests are not vitally involved, indeed, where fidelity to UN endeavors is a matter of reiterated public record, offers of only token support throw into question the character of the commitment. Soviet aversion to full-fledged financial support for UN programs for underdeveloped countries contrasts with its avowals of the principles which underlie them. If the Soviet position on fiscal matters is viewed as a continuum and is treated as a discrete policy question, then certain sobering evaluations are inevitable concerning the Soviet view of the extent to which international organizations should help underdeveloped countries, the way in which they should help, and the degree to which Moscow will participate.

The regular UN budget provides approximately 3 per cent

[24] K. Kiselev in his "Unjustified Swelling of the UN Budget," *International Affairs*, No. 10 (October 1962), p. 20 stated that, "A wanton practice has developed in the United Nations: under the pressure of the West, decisions are systematically adopted, increasing the share which the Soviet Union and the other Socialist countries contribute to the UN budget and reducing the share of the United States and the other Western countries."

of the funds spent for aid to underdeveloped countries. The bulk of the financing comes from two sources: first, from EPTA and the Special Fund, both of which depend upon voluntary contributions from UN members; and second, from the Specialized Agencies, each of which operates on its own budget of funds raised by levies against its members. The willingness, therefore, of a Great Power to promote the economic development of underdeveloped countries through international organizations can be adduced from the magnitude and gradient of its voluntary contributions and the comparison which these make with that country's bilateral efforts.

Contributions have risen steadily in recent years but are still pitifully inadequate to satisfy the requests for assistance. A look at the Soviet record is instructive. During the 1954-1960 period, the Soviet contribution to the Expanded Program of Technical Assistance, as indicated in Table 1, never rose above 4.7 per cent and averaged closer to 4 per cent. It was exceeded by the contributions of Canada, France, the United Kingdom, and the United States; during the 1959-1960 years, West Germany and the Netherlands were added to the list of those who contributed more than the Soviet Union. At the Thirtieth Session of ECOSOC, in July 1960, the Soviet Union announced a doubling of its contribution to EPTA, though not to the Special Fund, thereby bringing its percentage of total contributions temporarily to 5.6 per cent, a new high for the USSR.[25] The Soviet contribution to the Special Fund, the other main UN economic development program, is even lower, averaging less than 2.5 per cent, which compares unfavorably

[25] In the General Assembly two months later, Premier Khrushchev denounced Secretary-General Hammarskjold and insisted upon adoption of the troika proposal for a reorganized Secretariat. The denunciations, a by-product of the Soviet rebuff in the Congo, were accompanied by reassurances to the neutralists that the Soviet Union was not contemplating withdrawal from the UN, as some Westerners were speculating, but continued to believe in the UN, as witness its recently doubled contributions to EPTA.

with the larger contributions from smaller, less wealthy countries, such as India, Sweden, and the Netherlands. To the other two UN programs which depend upon voluntary contributions to help poor countries—the UN Children's Fund (UNICEF) and UNRWA—the Soviets have contributed negligible amounts, about 2 per cent to UNICEF's budget since 1955, and nothing to UNRWA. Lack of resources is an unconvincing justification, since the amounts involved in absolute terms during this period represent less than 1 per cent of the more than $3 billion in credits extended by the Soviet Union through its bilateral aid program. What emerges is a picture of deep-rooted antipathy toward UN efforts to help underdeveloped countries.

The Specialized Agencies have their own administrative budgets which are reviewed by the UN Advisory Committee

TABLE 1

United Nations Expanded Program of Technical Assistance
Calendar Years 1954-1963[a]

(Government Contributions in millions of dollars)

	Soviet[b] Contribution	Total Contributions of all Countries	Soviet Contribution as a percentage of the whole
1954	1.175	25.021	4.7
1955	1.175	27.626	4.2
1956	1.175	28.829	4.0
1957	1.175	30.822	3.8
1958	1.175	31.302	3.8
1959	1.175	29.658	3.9
1960	1.175	34.165	3.4
1961	2.35	41.861	5.6
1962	2.35	46.0	5.1
1963	2.35	50.3	4.6

[a] As of March 31, 1963.
[b] Includes the USSR and the Belorussian and Ukrainian S.S.R.'s.

125

on Administrative and Budgetary Questions, with an eye toward avoiding duplication of effort. Their operations in underdeveloped countries are financed through regular budgets. In the agencies, the Soviet Union is assessed a specific percentage of the budget, varying from a low of 4.83 per cent in the Universal Postal Union (UPU) to a high of 15.37 per cent in UNESCO, which must be paid if it is to remain a member in good standing. Though perennially protesting the expense and the high assessments, the Soviet Union is paid up since 1954 in the ILO, WHO, UNESCO, UPU, ITU, IMCO, and IAEA; it has not, however, thus far become a member of the Food and Agriculture Organization (FAO), the International Civil Aviation Organization (ICAO), IMF, or the World Bank.

Moscow believes the UN should, in pursuit of its economic and social ends, ideally advance its advisory rather than its operational function. It acquiesces in token efforts of symbolic and stimulative importance, but does not favor UN-directed major developmental projects. For financing industrialization, it maintains that the underdeveloped countries should rely primarily on their own national resources and not on UN or foreign aid. Its verbal support for the establishment of SUNFED stands as an exception but is as yet untested by actuality. During the speech in which the Soviet delegate first announced Moscow's decision to contribute to EPTA, he also stated that ECOSOC's main task "in the matter of economic development was to draw up recommendations, the implementation of which would assist the underdeveloped countries to develop their own resources in conformity with their national interests."

Moscow's lack of interest in the expansion of UN operational efforts is clearly evident in the endless UN dialogues over fund raising. How can the UN provide more money for economic development? The Soviets have a pat political answer—it doesn't have to. Eliminate the profits of private and foreign enterprises, nationalize industry, institute planning and controls along Soviet lines, and underdeveloped countries will need no assistance from international organizations. In underdeveloped countries, where interest in public sector investment and planning is high, the Soviet prescription is deemed more likely to kill than to cure, for what is lacking is not merely heavy industry but the preconditions for a modern economy.

Specific proposals to augment UN income encounter stubborn Soviet resistance. The Soviets are against increasing the budgets of the UN and Specialized Agencies because this would entail increased assessments. One Soviet delegate agreed that more funds were necessary for underdeveloped countries but insisted that: "An increase in the United Nations budget would not be the right method because such funds were limited and were mainly intended for the execution of the work assigned to the Secretariat by the United Nations, especially by the Economic and Social Council, and any sums that could be spared from the regular budget would hardly suffice to meet the needs of the new countries."[26] Having eliminated the regular UN budget as a source of added funds, he suggested resorting to voluntary contributions, although the years have proved the limitations of such an approach. He concluded with the vague injunction that "all untapped resources should be exploited to the full."

In the Specialized Agencies, where the Soviet Government also voices perennial opposition to proposed budgetary increases, it invariably proclaims that new appropriations represent "an unjustified increase in the administrative and common service costs" of the organization.[27] It agrees that the resources of EPTA and the Special Fund are inadequate but insists that increases be the result of voluntary contributions, not manda-

[26] Economic and Social Council, *Official Records* (30th Session), p. 126.
[27] *New York Times,* December 5, 1958.

tory assessments. Thus, the two main channels for increasing the funds of international organizations—the regular budgets of the UN and Specialized Agencies and the voluntary contributions to EPTA and the Special Fund—meet with persistent Soviet obstructionism.

Moscow constantly calls for reducing UN budgets and simultaneously increasing aid to underdeveloped countries. It contends, as do the United States and other countries, that administrative expenses and inefficiency of UN operations are frequently high. Other delegations have made similar points. The gist of their arguments is that after international organizations hold their growing chain of meetings and conferences, initiate scores of studies, collect data, and publish findings, only small sums are available for specific projects. EPTA and the Special Fund get most of their funds into the field, but inflation has partially erased the real value of steadily rising contributions. Too much money has been spent on marginal activities, particularly by some of the Specialized Agencies; the proliferation of meetings and committees is a heavy drain on money and personnel; too many publications clutter library shelves; there is too little coordination among the Specialized Agencies and the UN, and too much petty squabbling over organizational jurisdictions.

In raising anew these familiar points, Soviet delegates are on firm ground. But, when a recommendation is proffered to alleviate a specific condition, they will retreat from criticism. For example, they rejected the proposal to reduce the number and duration of meetings of the regional economic commissions and the functional commissions. That they were reluctant to cut back on opportunities for contact with neutralist officials and for disseminating Soviet views was never explicitly stated, but it is clear that the political value of frequent meetings outweighed financial considerations. This preference for broad, vague, inconclusive criticisms, encompassing a wide variety of UN organizational shortcomings, is a noticeable feature of Soviet speeches in international organizations. Playing the role of watchdog affords undeniable advantages: it provides wide latitude for forensic forays without putting a premium on performance or reform.

Financing UN activities is complex, cumbersome, and costly. Technical assistance is carried on by the Specialized Agencies and the Bureau of Technical Assistance Operations (BTAO), which was established in 1959 as successor to TAA. There is no centralized control over planning, procurement, or recruitment. The Specialized Agencies, aside from traditional, regulatory and standard-setting functions, collection and dissemination of statistics, research, and reports, allocate part of their budgets to technical assistance;[28] whereas EPTA and the Special Fund deal exclusively with programs related to economic development. Recruiting experts is difficult and time-consuming because of each Secretariat's constant need to be politically sensitive to the question of equitable geographic distribution. Financing is carried on through a multitude of currencies, requiring as many bank accounts. UNESCO, for example, deals in more than fifty currencies. UN officials note that the high overhead of technical assistance operations is due considerably to these expenses. Acceptance of nonconvertible currencies for EPTA had been chosen deliberately, one TAB official observed, "in order to enable as many countries as possible to participate, but it must be recognized that the price of such rich and varied participation had to be paid in the form of higher administrative costs."[29] His thought was clear: if Moscow genuinely seeks greater administrative efficiency in UN technical assistance operations, one major step

[28] Under the definition generally accepted in UN circles, UN regular programs of technical assistance include the regular activities of the UN Bureau of Technical Assistance Operations (BTAO) and the Office for Public Administration in the UN Secretariat, the identifiable technical assistance programs of the ILO, UNESCO, and WHO, and the operational programs of IAEA.

[29] E/TAC/SR. 42, p. 12.

toward attainment of this common objective would be for it, and other Soviet bloc countries, to make their voluntary contributions in convertible currencies.

The Special Fund has been the butt of even more pointed and political Soviet criticisms than those directed against EPTA. Headed by a Governing Council composed of representatives of eighteen states, half from the developed countries, half from the underdeveloped countries, and financed by voluntary contributions, the Special Fund provides "seed money" for projects designed to enlarge the possibilities for public and private investment. The Soviet position is that the Fund's resources should be used "to establish factories, equip them and to train the personnel to operate them—and not to embark upon complex studies and appraisals."[30] One Soviet delegate to ECOSOC contended that the Fund's emphasis on "so-called pre-investment activities" might pave the way for penetration by private investors to the detriment of underdeveloped countries: "indeed it seemed that the Special Fund's machinery was being used for work profiting private credit institutions and commercial undertakings that should be carried out at their own expense rather than at that of the voluntary contributions to the Fund."[31] What was demanded was greater emphasis on experimental pilot projects connected with industrialization. Calling attention to the fact that "virtually none of the projects so far approved by the Governing Council of the Special Fund would directly promote industrialization," the Soviet delegate repeated his Government's support for SUNFED and stated that the Special Fund —the Bulgarian delegate termed it a "Consolation Fund"— "should not be regarded as a permanent institution; in time, it must develop into SUNFED." Soviet delegates have also deplored the Fund's virtual neglect of Soviet experts, the too

[30] SF/SR. 11, p. 7.
[31] Economic and Social Council, *Official Records* (30th Session), p. 145.

extensive powers of the Managing Director, and the slow rate of implementation of Fund projects.[32]

From such statements, and Soviet reluctance to increase its contributions to the Special Fund (currently less than 2 per cent of total contributions, see Table 2), the inference may be drawn that Soviet suffrance of UN economic activities —it has never manifested any enthusiasm—is a necessary act of political accommodation. The same is true of the record

TABLE 2

United Nations Special Fund

(Government contributions in millions of dollars)

	Soviet Contribution	Total Contributions of all Countries	Soviet Contribution as a percentage of the whole
1959	1.175	25.812	4.5
1960	1.175	39.562	2.9
1961	1.175	48.72	2.4
1962	1.175	60.3	1.9
1963	1.175	72.4	1.6

of Soviet financial support for all UN-administered programs aiding underdeveloped countries. In a real sense, the Soviet Union is the Scrooge of international organizations: it gives only when it must and then for heavily political reasons. Its contributions, which are minimal, are inappropriate to its Great Power status and to its level of industry and resources. It has never accompanied vocal support for an increase in activity of a commission or agency with a concrete and generous offer of financial assistance. On the contrary, even in the case of SUNFED, which to all appearances it strongly

[32] SF/SR. 22, p. 11; SF/SR. 25, p. 16; SF/SR. 39, p. 6.

favors, the Soviet Government has never given any indication of how much it would be prepared to contribute. That it would not consent to being assessed at the rate which it currently pays to the regular UN budget seems quite clear from its insistence that SUNFED be financed by voluntary contributions. How much Moscow is willing to give to get SUNFED underway it has never said. Admittedly, Moscow is unhappy with EPTA and the Special Fund because they do not subscribe to Soviet theories about economic development. But there is nothing to indicate that it would be more generous were the UN to undertake heavy-industry projects. Suggestions by various Western and neutralist governments that each country contribute or be assessed an amount equivalent to the percentage it pays the regular UN budget has always encountered unyielding Soviet hostility on the grounds that whatever is suggested is both unnecessary and a violation of the principle of the free will of sovereign nations.[33]

Soviet resistance to increased financial outlays is due to several factors. Moscow contributes to the upkeep and operations of UN organizations to the extent that it believes contributing serves Soviet interests. Contributions are the price Moscow pays to play power politics in international organizations. It participates because the alternative of nonparticipation would, at this time, be a severe liability in the courtship of neutralist countries. The low level of its voluntary contributions reflects its fundamental disdain for the UN approach

[33] At the 1962 Session of the General Assembly, the delegate from the Netherlands pointed out that the contribution of the Soviet Union to the Special Fund and EPTA was "only a fraction of what countries like Sweden and the Netherlands pay." He contrasted the $1 million a year that the Soviet Union contributed to the Special Fund with the $2.6 million contributed annually by his country, and observed that "if the Soviet Union were to pay according to the scale of regular United Nations contributions, its annual share would have to be about 15 million dollars; if it paid at a rate equal to that applied to my country, its annual share would mount to 23 million dollars." A/PV.1147, p. 58.

to economic development and the concomitant belief that only heavy industrialization can improve the intolerable economic lot of the underdeveloped countries. It is also clear that Moscow would under no circumstances be willing to match or even approximate the United States' contributions to UN programs, on the grounds that the USA is still more affluent and can better afford substantial grants to UN agencies, and that the colonial powers have a moral obligation to make restitution "in the form of greater financial assistance, long-term, low-interest or no-interest loans and increased contributions to aid programmes" for their responsibility for "the impoverishment and distress of the countries which now [constitute] the underdeveloped areas."[34]

Moreover, Soviet leaders belittle American assistance to international organizations as inconsequential. In a speech in Moscow on October 20, 1960, Nikita Khrushchev stated: "The imperialists are trying to lend the colonialist policy 'a noble aspect.' They are even not reluctant to speak about rendering assistance to the countries that have freed themselves of colonial oppression. But what kind of 'assistance' is that? Take, for instance, the speech by the President of the United States at the session of the General Assembly. It contained no constructive proposals. The President declared that the United States was prepared to allocate $100 million to the UN program for assistance to the African countries that have gained independence. If this sum is divided among the population of the African countries which has gained independence, it would be 55 cents per person. But, as they say, this would not take you very far. In America, 55 cents would not buy you two packs of cigarettes."

In the final analysis, the compelling conclusion is that the Soviet Union favors keeping programs for underdeveloped countries financially marginal because it is against an indefi-

[34] A/C.2/SR. 762, p. 8.

nite expansion of UN economic activities.[35] Foreign aid has become an integral adjunct of Soviet diplomacy in under-developed countries, and Moscow has no desire to see international organizations preempt or challenge the attraction of Soviet bilateral aid. It assuredly has no intention of contributing to the creation of just such conditions in the area of international economic assistance.

Observations

Certain threads may be identified as common to these four policy positions. First, a detailed review of all published materials revealed that the foreign policy speeches of Soviet leaders and the commentaries of the Soviet press generally did not offer clues to impending changes in international organizations. However, careful examination of Soviet statements and behavior in these organizations could have led to anticipation of the direction, though not the timing, of Soviet policy innovations. Thus, the adoption of a favorable attitude toward SUNFED can be progressively plotted in Soviet speeches in the UN; the reactivation of membership in the World Health Organization proceeded linearly from the decision to join the International Labor Organization and UNESCO in the spring of 1954, just as the opposition to the Volunteer Workers' proposal of the United States followed from Moscow's position

[35] To this writer, there is no question but that the Soviet Government is capable, without straining its capacity to meet its present commitments, of increasing its financial contribution to UN programs aiding underdeveloped countries, if not to the United States level of support, then assuredly to the level of the countries of Western Europe. Accurate figures on Soviet bilateral assistance are difficult to obtain, but it seems clear that the USSR has extended about $6 billion in economic and military assistance to underdeveloped countries during the 1954-1962 period. Soviet commentators acknowledge the granting of more than $3 billion in credits for economic aid during this period. Soviet contributions to EPTA and the Special Fund for this period total a little more than $17 million, or about one-half of 1 per cent of Soviet bilateral economic aid.

on the Peace Corps; and the parsimonious Soviet attitude toward contributing to UN programs for aiding underdeveloped countries has been a consistent feature of Soviet policy. Reinforcing the need for systematic evaluations of all public Soviet statements in the UN, neutralist informants observed that Soviet delegates added little in private to what they argued in public. This means that the diplomat who is in a position to influence policy decisions usually must rest his analysis upon approximately the same information that is available to the scholar.

Soviet press coverage of the four policy positions herein examined was negligible. The bulk of what reporting did take place consisted primarily of excerpts from speeches of Soviet delegates in the involved organization. That financial matters, in particular, were rarely mentioned suggests that Moscow prefers for domestic reasons not to publicize the extent of its financial commitments to foreign aid given through bilateral or international channels.

Second, the Soviets do not explain policy changes. The closest resemblances to what might pass for justifications are usually of two different kinds: a) statements approving the constructive work being accomplished in situations where participation in a UN program has been decided upon; b) vindications of opposition on grounds of a program's intrinsic administrative and operational shortcomings or of alleged Western control.

Third, when changes occurred, there was no evidence that overt external pressures from the United Nations, the United States, or the neutralist nations forced the Soviet positions. Rather, in situations where the Soviet position did shift in the general direction lobbied for by non-Soviet pressure centers, it may be inferred that Soviet decision-makers were *convinced* that positions they held were detrimental to the attainment of their objectives. However, when Soviet policy-formulating circles are in a state of flux, the views of foreign Governments and institutions might be accorded greater consideration, especially if they accord broadly with changing evaluations gaining ascendancy among Soviet leaders. Thus, once having decided that neutralist countries were not "agents of imperialism," and that it was in the Soviet interest to support proposals designed to promote UN programs for developing countries, Moscow then faced the task of deciding which proposals most converged with Soviet preferences. The reversal on SUNFED stemmed partially from the new Soviet awareness of the political significance of neutralist nations and the realization that concessions to neutralist views on matters of peripheral interest to Moscow could bring gratifyingly disproportionate political returns; and partially from the desire to promote an alternative to these international lending institutions which, for various reasons, it deemed unsuitable, e.g. the IFC, and later the Special Fund. Continued neutralist interest in SUN-FED, when combined with American opposition, made that an ideal focus for Soviet backing.

The alacrity with which Moscow supports neutralist proposals that clash with Western preferences is a hallmark of Soviet policy in international organizations; it is also a prime and politic technique for prestige-building. Moscow's constrictive approach to financial matters in international organizations is tempered not only by its extensive program of bilateral aid to neutralist countries, but by the prevalence of this sentiment among many UN members. Similarly, in opposing the Volunteer Workers' proposal, it was not out of alignment with views expressed by a number of neutralists.

Fourth, the operational impact of ideology on any particular decision cannot readily be ascertained. A reasonable assumption is that ideology is adapted by the leadership as their perceptions of the decisive forces of a particular epoch undergo revision, and that in the process it affects the formulation of broad lines of policy but not the adoption of any particular tactic. But the adaptations of the ideology will delineate the spectrum of the most attractive alternatives and predispose the leadership toward a particular choice. Thus, once having decided that the present historical period is dominated by "the national-liberation struggle of the colonial peoples," Soviet leaders moved into more congenial alignment with the neutralists in the struggle against "imperialism" (the West). Participation in EPTA and the Special Fund became acceptable adjuncts of the broader policy of aiding underdeveloped countries, whereas membership in the IFC or support for the Volunteer Workers' proposal did not. This differentiation can be explained in terms of the distinctive objectives and operational features of these programs and the varying degrees of support found among the neutralists.

Finally, Soviet statements were on rare occasions undisguisedly preoccupied with considerations of national prestige, as in the WHO debates dealing with the disagreement over which Government, the Soviet or American, could claim credit for proposing the International Health and Medical Year. The desire for "national prestige" is understandable and universal; the meaning of the term itself is elusive, but most Governments expect that their standing in the international community, and their ability to achieve national objectives, will automatically be enhanced with increases in their national power, diplomatic successes, and capacity to influence peoples in other lands. In the international organizations examined, the Soviet Government appeared only as concerned with improving its standing among the neutralists as did the other Great Powers.

To enlarge our perspective, we turn to an analysis of changing Soviet policy over an extended period in two international organizations that are primarily concerned with underdeveloped countries—the UN Economic Commission for Asia and the Far East and the International Atomic Energy Agency.

IV ◈——

The USSR and ECAFE

ONE SIGNIFICANT ASPECT of post-Stalinist Soviet foreign policy is the determination and skill with which it has been applied in Southern Asia, particularly in nonaligned Afghanistan, Burma, Ceylon, India, and Indonesia. The previous neglect of Southern Asia had been occasioned by Soviet preoccupation with the recovery and reconstruction of its war-devastated economy, the sovietization of Eastern Europe, and the rise of Communist China; also important was Stalin's underestimation of the role which that area and its indigenous Communist Parties, then closely linked to mass supported national-liberation movements, might play in advancing the international position of the Soviet Union. This aspect of Stalinism is now over. Since 1953, Soviet leadership has effectively pushed its interests in Southern Asia, both on a bilateral basis and within the framework of international organizations. Though the bulk of Soviet aid and technical assistance operations is carried on through bilateral channels, Moscow also devotes careful attention to ECAFE because of the presence in it of all the countries of Southern Asia. Soviet behavior in ECAFE, therefore, adds a dimension to the total Soviet effort to extend its influence into this vital region. It affords an excellent opportunity to test performance against promise and to trace, in microcosm, the evolution of a new Soviet policy toward neutralists of Southern Asia.

The UN Economic Commission for Asia and the Far East (ECAFE) was established by the Economic and Social Council on March 28, 1947, for the purpose of encouraging Asian economic reconstruction and development. The decision to establish the Commission was a political one, the result primarily of an alliance between Asians—led by China—and Latin Americans in the General Assembly in December 1946.

Subsequently, UN studies developed in detail the extent of war devastation in Asia, the region's pressing problems and needs, and the most feasible methods of organizing international aid. One early report noted that Asian reconstruction "must be regarded as the first step in a vast readjustment whereby the people of the region, with such assistance as the United Nations can give, would undertake the systematic application of modern technology, adapted as necessary to local needs, as rapidly as may be feasible, to all departments of their economic life."

At the time, the Soviets paid close attention to the structure and operating procedures of the new organization. However, in contrast to their position in the Economic Commission for Europe (ECE), then also commencing operation, they advocated a broad interpretation of ECAFE's terms of reference, holding that the organization should encompass the entire realm of reconstruction and economic development [1]—a position reflecting the views of most of the Asian members. This seeming interest in economic activities was soon eclipsed by the principal Soviet concern, a stress on political issues. Political considerations, often contradictory in character, dominated the Soviet position in ECAFE until 1954. In their highly political approach, the Soviets were not, it may be noted, alone; all the non-Asian powers played a highly political role in these early years, thereby leading the Asians to intensify their struggle to gain control of the organization.

In discussions with several ECAFE officials, they suggested that control began definitely to shift to the Asian members only after the Lahore Convention of 1951 under which the non-Asian powers agreed "to refrain from using their votes in opposition to economic proposals predominantly concerning the region which had the support of a majority of the countries of the region." Much of the credit for this concession was given to P. N. Lokanathan. Lokanathan, an Indian, and

[1] E/CN.11/SR. 6-11.

at the time Executive-Secretary of ECAFE, came into repeated conflict with the Western powers (particularly the United States in 1948-1949) when hopes were still high among EC-AFE members for a Marshall Plan for Asia. Dr. Lokanathan apparently made the same mistake as Dr. Gunnar Myrdal, then head of the Economic Commission for Europe, in expecting that the United States would be willing to channel the bulk of its foreign aid through United Nations organizations; the difference was that Lokanathan made no effort to conceal his disappointment.

The turning point itself, as far as ECAFE's maturity was concerned, occurred in February 1951 at the seventh annual session. The catalytic controversy indirectly involved Communist China. According to several Asian informants, the British delegation leaked word that it was going to recommend that ECAFE seat the delegate from Communist China, a step in the direction of formal representation for the Peking regime. Upon learning of this, the American delegation immediately wired Washington, recommending that pressure be brought to bear on London to forestall such an action at Lahore. Lokanathan learned of these behind-the-scenes maneuverings and became incensed at the situation, for it appeared that ECAFE policy was being determined by powers that were not even members of the region. He fought on this issue and got the non-Asian powers to agree to the principle that the "outside" powers would not vote on matters that were of vital concern to the region's members. The resultant change in the organization has been quiet, unspectacular, but nonetheless real. In recent years, the non-Asian powers have taken a back seat and the main initiative for new programs now comes from the Asians.

The Membership Issue

One of the first political problems to confront the commission was the question of membership for Asian members who were emerging from foreign rule but were not yet independent nations. The controversies which developed in ECAFE as to their status presented the Soviet Union with a golden opportunity to flail Western colonialism and to align itself with India, the actual leader of the agitation for the complete independence of these areas. That Moscow failed to derive much political mileage from its position can be attributed to several factors. First, Stalin's assumption that any non-Communist country would inevitably be pro-Western or Western controlled led to embarrassing contradictions when applied inflexibly to Asia: for though Moscow castigated Western colonialism, it quickly squandered its initial stock of political capital by lumping all non-Communist national-liberation movements together with Western imperialists. The application to Asia of the Zhdanov "two-camp" thesis, a strategy intended for Europe, coupled with the rash of Communist revolts against nationalist governments in Burma, India, Indonesia, and the Philippines, led Asians to view the Soviet Union with increasing suspicion. Though the Soviet position in ECAFE was much closer to Asian sentiments and aspirations than was the West's on issues such as industrialization and economic planning, Asian skepticism of Soviet motives heightened because a) Moscow was unable or unwilling to make tangible offers of aid; b) indiscriminate Soviet attacks on the alleged continuation of Western imperialism (including technical assistance) increasingly offended the national pride of the Asians; and c) Soviet dogmatic prescriptions (a fault shared by the West) irritated rather than illumined. Second, Moscow sought to ensure that no nation entered any international organization through the back door in order to evade the Soviet veto which was waiting at the front,[2] or

[2] For a detailed account of ECAFE membership problems see the sections in A. M. James, "The UN Economic Commission for Asia and the Far East," *The Year Book of World Affairs*, 1959, pp. 161-187. See also David Wightman, *Toward Economic Cooperation in Asia:* The

to escape the bargaining process in the Security Council over membership in which the USSR was interested. Conditioned by its bipolar appraisal of political alignments to assume that new members of ECAFE would be, by definition, anti-Soviet, it found itself adrift in the nationalist tide sweeping the area.

The initial members of ECAFE were Australia, China, France, India, the Netherlands, the Philippines, Thailand, the Soviet Union, the United Kingdom, and the United States. The anomaly of an organization dedicated to Asian problems consisting largely of non-Asian countries was not lost on the Asian leaders. At the twenty-first plenary meeting of the Commission, the Indian delegate noted critically "that not a single Asiatic country was represented on the Economic Commission for Europe, presumably on the ground that Europe was the concern of Europeans . . . if the same principle were applied to ECAFE, the Western Power, now claiming a predominant voice in the deliberations of the Commission, had no justification." Here was an opportunity for the Soviet Union to espouse the Asian cause. But, though agreeing with the Indian delegate's observation, the Soviet delegation did not support the admission to associate status of Asian states which were not members of the UN; it held that such states might be admitted to ECAFE in a consultative capacity on questions of particular concern to them. While the suggestion did not explicitly cover non-self-governing territories, the USSR shortly made it clear that they, too, should be admitted only on these terms. Nor did the USSR (or the United States, for that matter) favor full membership for Asian states which were not members of the UN. It hoped also to minimize Western

United Nations Economic Commission for Asia and the Far East (New Haven: Yale University Press, 1963), pp. 21-36. Dr. Wightman's book, which was published after this study was completed, provides an authoritative account of the diverse economic and organizational activities of ECAFE's first fifteen years.

influence by suggesting the broadening of the geographical
scope of ECAFE to include the Middle Eastern countries
which, however, wanted their own regional economic commission.

Thus, while attacking French imperialism in Indo-China,
the USSR came out against associate membership for Cambodia, Laos, and South Vietnam on the grounds that the
political situation in these areas was too fluid to permit accreditation of any particular delegates,[3] and that their regimes
were not truly representative of their peoples—a view shared
by many Asian Governments, particularly with respect to
South Vietnam. In October 1949 the Commission received
applications from Ho Chi Minh (supported by the Soviet
Union) and Bao Dai (sponsored by France). Both applicants
claimed to represent the same territory. The Commission accepted the latter (with some Asian misgivings) and rejected
the former. However, on the specific question of Indonesia's
request in 1947 for membership, the Soviet Union did side
with India in urging admission as a full member for the
Sukarno regime.[4] Insistence on membership for Indonesia was
designed to promote the quest for power of the Indonesian
Communist Party, then carrying out the revolutionary "united-
front-from-below" policy of the newly formed Cominform and
seeking to capture the entire nationalist movement.

Since late 1949, Communist China has been a perennial
problem for ECAFE. For a number of years, the Soviets insisted at each session that Communist China be given the seat
held by the Nationalists. The neutralists generally sympathized
with the Soviet stand, but grew increasingly restive over
time-consuming Soviet parliamentary obstructionism and
Soviet-Western clashes. Despite consistent and open support
of Soviet motions, by Burma, Indonesia, and India (even after
the Chinese attack of October 1962), the Commission agreed

[3] E/CN.11/SR. 18, p. 4.
[4] E/CN.11/SR. 33, pp. 2-5.

that the issue of Communist China's admission was a political matter to be resolved by the General Assembly.[5]

During the early years, to the frequent annoyance of the neutralists, Soviet delegates demanded roll-call votes which obliged each country to stand up and be counted with one bloc or the other. However, since the advent of Khrushchev's policy of up-grading ECAFE sessions, i.e. by sending larger delegations and devoting more attention to economic problems, a period coincidental with the emergence of noticeable strains in the Sino-Soviet alliance, the Soviets have confined their appeals for Chinese Communist membership to brief remarks which are delivered at the beginning of ECAFE sessions in the course of the opening round of speeches on general Asian economic developments; they mention impressive growth figures for China, deplore her absence from ECAFE, lump the need for her admission with that of the North Korean and North Vietnamese regimes, and then permit the question of Peking's membership to be dropped for another year.

Moscow's recent reluctance to push Peking's case in ECAFE may signify a realistic appraisal of the fact that a regional economic commission is not a proper forum for discussing the political issues involved in the membership of the United Nations, i.e. that it is beyond the competence of ECAFE. Another and admittedly speculative interpretation holds that Moscow's perfunctory espousal of Peking's case is more than a symptom of, or reaction to, deteriorating Sino-Soviet relations; it is a tacit recognition of the fact that many ECAFE countries now share a markedly antipathetical or suspicious attitude toward Peking, though they prefer not to say so publicly. For example, several Indian, Burmese, and Nepalese officials speculated that the Soviet approach has been adopted

[5] See UN General Assembly resolution 396 (v) of December 14, 1950.

with several considerations in mind.[6] First, Moscow may seek to forestall Chinese membership in ECAFE as long as is politically feasible, since, should the Chinese gain widespread Asian acceptance for their model for economic development, Moscow might find its authority and prestige sorely damaged in South Asian countries. Second, in her covert competition with Peking for influence in Southern Asia, Moscow hopes to benefit from the area's great fear of China's territorial ambitions. Not being geographically contiguous to Southern Asia, as China is, they pointed out that the Soviet Union does not arouse this suspicion. From their own standpoint, South Asian neutralists, particularly those with influential Chinese minorities, seek to maintain friendly relations with the Chinese colossus, hoping that the borrowed time will permit them to develop their economies and establish viable political systems, thereby minimizing the danger of internal Communist subversion. Thus, if one assumes that the longer Peking can be kept isolated, the less likely it is to play a leading role in ECAFE activities, one may also infer a present overlapping of aims between Moscow and ECAFE neutralists with respect to China's future in the organization. In informal discussions ECAFE delegates openly acknowledge the complexity of the entire China question for the UN. They are convinced that Communist China will be admitted to ECAFE, also of course to the UN, and are uneasy over Peking's intransigent determination to reconquer Formosa and its insistence that it will enter the UN only when Nationalist China is thrown out. They seem more sympathetic now to an independent Formosa than they were five years ago, the result, no doubt, of recurring Chinese expansionist pressure in Southern Asia and of Formosa's viability as a functioning political entity.

Moscow's subdued approach to the issue of Chinese mem-

[6] These conversations were held in Tokyo in March 1962, at the 18th Session of ECAFE.

bership also reflects the growing maturity of ECAFE. No longer is ECAFE a forum dominated by Cold-War polemics, though these are still occasionally in evidence; rivalry has replaced recrimination. ECAFE is becoming an assembly for the discussion and planning of Asia's economic and social problems. Increasingly high-ranking delegates attend ECAFE sessions. Heavily burdened, pressed for results, eager to modernize, they take a dim view of their time being wasted with Cold War declamatory skirmishing. In recognition of this change in climate, the Soviet Union and the Western Powers concentrate more on matters pertaining to the region's economic development.

The Stalinist Legacy

Throughout the Stalin period, Soviet behavior in ECAFE ran true to the stereotype. Sandwiching denunciations of Western "imperialism" between their glowing declarations of intent, the Soviets repeatedly asserted their readiness to cooperate in Asian economic development but simultaneously shied away from firm bilateral or multilateral commitments. Not only did they fail to contribute to EPTA, but they were conspicuous by their unwillingness to translate offers into aid or to participate in ECAFE's few constructive activities. With few exceptions, their speeches were intended for the press and the public in Asian countries, and not for the promotion of any ECAFE effort. To discredit the West, the Soviets played upon the xenophobic Asian fears of an impending return of Western domination. Though this bogey receives a diminishing response, particularly within the insulated ECAFE framework, from Asian leaders who are concerned with the concrete tasks of economic development and political stability, it still can evoke strong emotions, especially in times of internal stress. Soviet attacks on the West focused on three broad issues: 1) the problem of economic development; 2) the question of trade; and 3) the various programs of technical assistance and foreign aid carried on by the UN and by the United States.

First, on the matter of economic development, the Soviets accused the West of seeking to perpetuate the disadvantageous economic position of the Asian nations. They maintained that development programs should emphasize a rate of heavy industrial growth higher than that envisaged under Western proposals which favored a balanced growth of the various sectors of the economy with particular attention to raising agricultural productivity and expanding cottage and light industries, and which tended to be rather ambiguous on the whole issue of industrialization and as dogmatic in their own ways as those of the USSR. Citing the success of the Soviet Union in overcoming its backward economic condition through concentration on heavy industry, Soviet delegates tried to convince the ECAFE countries that the Soviet experience in state planning, public sector investment, and industrial development could serve as a model for all of Asia. Their speeches singled out the "remarkable" advances being made by Communist China and the Soviet Central Asian Republics. To Asian leaders, eager for short cuts to economic development and influenced by Marxist categories and stereotypes, the Soviet formula held considerable appeal. It reduced complex phenomena to an attractive and easily accepted proposition: heavy industrial growth means political and military power which, in turn, is the only assurance of continued independence. The Soviet explanation for Asian backwardness also had the virtue of simplicity: it blamed Asia's institutionalized economic stagnation and social rigidity on centuries of Western rule.

The Soviet emphasis on nationalization of key industries, heavy public sector investment, and extensive central economic planning found a receptive audience even among Asians opposed to Communism and Soviet policies. The neutralist leaders believed that their countries could not afford the Western

147

luxury of wasteful competition, the latitude of systems which allow private individuals to accumulate great wealth, or the constant siphoning off of scarce resources to satisfy the appetite for consumer goods of a minuscule portion of the population. They also shared the belief that the Western approach to Asian problems was too conservative, too conditioned by Western experience, and too wedded to an essentially *status quo* orientation. These attitudes still dominate South Asian thinking.

Asian apprehensions and distrust of Western motives were further aggravated by the enormous disparity in economic aid given to the Western European nations under the Marshall Plan and related programs as compared with the attention and amount accorded to Asian countries. This irritated Asian sensibilities and lent credence to Soviet charges that the West sought to condemn Asia permanently to the role of supplier of raw materials and "a hewer of wood and a drawer of water." Of the "outside" powers, only the Soviet Union favored elaborating an aid program for Asia. On several occasions, Indian delegates, for example, criticized "the industrially advanced Western countries" for being preoccupied in their approach to the area by political concerns and not by the economic requirements of the ECAFE region;[7] others openly stated that the United States "should be more concerned with what was happening in Asia at present than in Western Europe" and suggested that the solution was a Marshall Plan for Asia.[8]

The impact of these criticisms, however, was somewhat weakened by the conspicuous lack of Soviet efforts to implement their professions of interest in Asian economic development. On infrequent occasions, Soviet delegates suggested studies to promote improvements in Asian working conditions and to raise productivity in agriculture and industry. But these suggestions invariably duplicated activities already under-

[7] E/CN.11/SR. 42, p. 3.
[8] E/CN.11/SR. 49, p. 3.

taken by the Food and Agriculture Organization and the International Labor Organization, respectively—Specialized Agencies in which the Soviets did not seek membership; nor were they ever buttressed by concrete offers of assistance. As a consequence, Asians began to express growing doubts concerning Soviet sincerity.

In discussion of the second major issue receiving Soviet attention, Moscow agreed with the widely recognized need for expansion of the area's trade. Soviet delegates blamed retarded trade levels on "a monocultural development of trade" which limited expansion possibilities and placed ECAFE countries in a position of dependency upon Western importers of raw materials who dictated the prices of the manufactured goods purchased by the Asians.[9] They frequently criticized the Committee on Industry and Trade (established in 1949) for failing to carry out its principal responsibility, that of promoting the expansion of regional trade. The ECAFE Secretariat also shared in the abuse for evasion of the alleged cause of Asia's difficulties: the controlling position of United States and United Kingdom monopolies. The Soviets said that too much time of the Trade Promotion Division was devoted to questions of secondary importance, such as the advertising of foreign concerns, trade conferences, exhibitions, and tourism. They went so far as to argue that the Secretariat's promotion of tourism constituted an unwarranted intervention in the internal affairs of the countries of the region.[10] Though the Soviets showed that they had nothing to offer the Trade Promotion Conferences of 1951 and 1953, they did demonstrate a closer affinity with Asian thinking by supporting the establishment of a Trade Committee at a time when the West opposed such a move and preferred to concentrate, in limited fashion, on trade-promotion studies.

At ECAFE's eighth session (January-February 1952), the

[9] E/CN.11/SR. 64, p. 13.
[10] E/CN.11/I & T/SR. 25, p. 4.

Soviet delegate introduced two modifications, presaging the post-Stalinist orientation—a departure from the uncompromising insistence upon heavy industrial development and an attempt to encourage expanded trade with the Soviet Union. Mr. Migunov declared that ECAFE should assist "the development of cottage and small-scale industries in the region with a view to a greater utilization of local resources and the maintenance of traditional national crafts and of full employment of the population."[11] He also encouraged ECAFE countries to seek innumerable products, industrial equipment, timber, etc., from the Soviet Union, adding that "Soviet foreign trade organizations were ready to discuss with representatives of the business circles of the region, concrete details of the sale and purchase of the above-mentioned goods."[12]

Given the Soviet preoccupation with economic recovery and the shortage of industrial products within the Soviet bloc, it is likely that the offer was never intended to expand trade but was made solely to gain a propaganda advantage from Western rearmament resulting from the Korean War and from the consequent cutback in industrial goods available for export from the United States and Western Europe. The Soviets made no follow-up; no loans were offered, nor was any expansion of trade pushed. Though the suggested trade arrangements were to be conducted on a strictly businesslike basis, the Soviet Government did not respond to the invitations of several Asian Governments, either in ECAFE or in subsequent bilateral discussions, to transform into reality, through the initiation of serious negotiations, these attractive-sounding offers of rapid and reliable deliveries of capital goods and steel. When asked by the Chinese delegate "what amounts of steel his country was prepared to supply the [ECAFE] region," the Soviet delegate refused to answer, either at that time (out of disdain for the Nationalist Chinese regime which it did

11 E/CN.11/344, p. 91.
12 *Ibid.*

not recognize) or subsequently in pertinent discussion sessions. Others also questioned the validity of Soviet offers. The Malayan delegate, for example, cited the dismal experience of his government in trying to obtain industrial goods from the USSR:

"In 1951, the Soviet Union direct purchases from Malaya (mostly rubber) were valued at 73.6 million dollars, while its sales to Malaya amounted to 40 thousand dollars of which 38.5 thousand dollars were for cinematograph films. The ratio of the USSR exports to its purchases was 1 to 1,800.

"At the first ECAFE Conference on Trade Promotion, held in Singapore in 1951, and at the eighth session of ECAFE, held in Rangoon in January-February 1952, the delegation of the USSR had stated that the Soviet Union was a source of supply of capital goods for the countries of the region. The representative of the Soviet Union had made very clear promises, had insisted on the reliability of Soviet goods and on the rapidity of Soviet deliveries. However, the total value of Soviet imports into Malaya in the first eleven months of 1952 was 27.2 thousand dollars, an important part of which was accounted for by canned fish and caviar."[13]

Small wonder that during the latter years of Stalin's rule Moscow's repeated statements of its readiness to supply ECAFE countries with machinery and manufactured goods were ignored or dismissed as propaganda.

There were also obvious contradictions in several aspects of the Soviet critique of Western policy. The Soviets expressed "sympathy" with the plight of ECAFE countries which were either unable to sell their raw materials abroad or else "forced" to do so at deliberately depressed prices. They maintained that this could be avoided by concentrating on heavy industrial development, expanding the use of protective tariffs, and negotiating barter agreements. Also, the Western Powers were

[13] E/CN.11/I & T/78, pp. 99-100.

151

accused of buying excessive quantities of raw materials from the region. All these arguments conveniently, but rather obviously, ignored the fact that the underdeveloped countries could earn the foreign exchange with which to import needed machinery and capital goods only if they sold their raw materials. With Moscow unprepared to make sizeable purchases of what Asia had to sell and unwilling or unable to grant long-term credits for the purchase of Soviet goods, its prescription for Asian economic ills offered little of value to ECAFE countries. The dogmatic bent of Soviet proposals and their frequent irrelevance for the actual conditions of ECAFE countries served to undermine the desired image of the Soviet Union as benefactor and adviser of the weak and the underdeveloped. Indeed, judged by Asian statements and actions in ECAFE, they actually militated against acceptance, or even consideration, of Soviet claims to the validity of their economic experience for Southern Asia.

The Soviet attitude toward UN technical assistance programs and toward all foreign economic aid—the third principal focus of Moscow's attention at ECAFE sessions during the Stalin period—particularly weakened Soviet political influence. President Truman's Point Four Proposal and UN technical assistance activities were described as entering imperialist wedges into the economies of the underdeveloped countries. Soviet condemnations linked the two programs, maintaining that: "The so-called American 'assistance' did not aim at helping the various national economies. It was actually directed toward militarization of the economies of the countries receiving such 'assistance.' The purpose of American 'aid' under Point Four was the political and economic subordination of underdeveloped countries to American monopolies and the increased exploitation of the peoples."[14] Despite Asian delegates' rejection of these charges at the various sessions of ECAFE and its

[14] E/CN.11/363, p. 51.

subsidiary bodies, the Soviets intensified their denunciations and insisted that ECAFE was controlled by Western business-men intent on exploiting backward areas.[15] These unsupported allegations, the Soviet failure to contribute to EPTA, and the unrelenting opposition to all international lending institutions, i.e. the World Bank and the International Monetary Fund, fur-ther disillusioned ECAFE neutralists concerning Soviet inter-est in their development. In addition, until 1954, the Soviets to all practical purposes ignored the work of the purely technical bodies in which much of ECAFE's constructive work is ac-complished patiently and with little publicity, evidencing no interest in their activities and abstaining from discussions of their reports. Soviet comment and attention were reserved for politically exploitable topics in forums commanding wide press coverage.

So far as the Soviet press and Soviet scholarship were con-cerned, ECAFE was itself an "undeveloped" area. On rare oc-casions, ECAFE's annual sessions and major committee meet-ings would receive perfunctory mention in Soviet newspapers, but little else. Soviet scholars ignored ECAFE in their general neglect of the Specialized Agencies and regional economic commissions and the useful exploratory studies being under-taken by them. In 1953 fewer than half a dozen 150-word blurbs appeared in *Pravda* and *Izvestiia* about ECAFE activi-ties. During the entire Stalin period, not one lengthy analysis of ECAFE's problems and achievements appeared in a Soviet journal.

Substantively, this neglect has altered little since 1954, though Soviet newspapers now devote more space to the main sessions of ECAFE and its subsidiaries; and the foreign-trade journal, *Vneshniaia Torgovlia,* carries brief accounts of pertinent ECAFE efforts. The expanded coverage, however, consists exclusively of excerpts from the speeches of Soviet delegates or of delegates critical of Western policy. Nowhere

[15] *Izvestiia,* March 6, 1949.

in Soviet publications is there any balanced presentation of ECAFE sessions. Detailed analyses of ECAFE activities and of Soviet participation in them remain, as will be shown in a later section, an uncharted aspect of Soviet scholarship.

Soviet attacks, stressing the ubiquitous character of Western "imperialism" and "colonialism," did not always get the expected reception, even among those representatives whose governments clearly disapproved of the mushrooming system of Western alliances in Asia and of the Western concentration on containing Communism at the expense of Asian economic and political development. In the course of one speech denouncing the evils of Western technical assistance, the Soviet delegate cited, by way of illustration, an American agreement with Burma which allegedly made the grant of aid conditional upon the United States being given exclusive rights to undertake geological research and "limitless exploitation of all resources."[16] The Burmese representative denied the Soviet assertion and administered an open rebuke: "Burma was not a rich country and looked forward to obtaining foreign aid here, there and everywhere. Whether capital came from the USSR or the United States did not matter, provided the country concerned negotiated successfully with his Government. It might not be technical assistance in exchange for mining concessions, it might just be the love of the particular foreign ideology which would induce his Government to give that concession. He, therefore, asked other countries to try their luck. With reference to the agreement signed with the United States, he regretted that he did not have a copy with him. He did not know that he might be answerable for a subject which had no relevant connection with the item now under consideration. This agreement was an open document and could be seen by anyone. He suggested that when the Soviet representative got away from the crowded and noisy commission meet-

16 E/CN.11/SR. 86, p. 15.

ings, he should take pains to find out that what he said was not correct."[17]

On another occasion, after one particularly violent Soviet outburst at the Ninth Session of ECAFE (February 1953), the Indian delegate, Mr. Karmarkar, undertook one of the most scathing criticisms of Soviet policy ever heard by the Commission:

"He had heard with a pained surprise the speeches of the representative of the Soviet Union. His analysis of the situation could not be considered as objective; his proposals could not be usefully applied to the countries of Asia and the Far East. He had exhibited a tendency to generalization and had spoken of the region as a whole, asserting that progress was insufficient, that there was a tendency toward a decline in agricultural and industrial production. It is true that, owing to certain factors, such as the drought which had struck certain parts of India, there had been in some countries a certain decline in production; however, that could not be considered as indicative of a general trend.

". . . it was extremely unpleasant to hear a representative [referring to the Soviet delegate] say: 'You are dominated by other countries,' and the Indian delegate felt very strongly on that subject.

"The shortage of capital goods was due in part to the fact that industrial production in certain countries was keyed to other purposes. The countries of the region, with their traditionally agricultural economy, also lacked capital. They had been helped by the United Nations, the International Bank for Reconstruction and Development, and the International Monetary Fund and some progressive countries such as the United States.

"Some people said the United States were helping themselves before anyone else. India would certainly not blame the

[17] E/CN.11/SR. 87, p. 12.

United States for promoting their own interests when it was extending its hand to help underdeveloped countries. The United States might be acting out of self-interest when it contributed to the peace and economic progress of the world. It was enlightened self-interest indeed. . . .

"It was malicious to say that the United Nations was dominated by certain national interests. The history of the world organization would be written much later. However, in the last five years, by its participation in the development of underdeveloped countries, the United Nations had already penned a bright chapter of that history.

"Apparently, the representative of the Soviet Union had not had sufficient time to study the real conditions in the area. He might have studied the five year economic plan of India. He would have seen that other people had been aware before him of the importance of agricultural development, that positive planning had been undertaken in the countries of the region, that problems of land reform and of land ownership had not been neglected."[18]

In the waning period of the Stalin era, similarly caustic comments were made by other neutralist delegates. But they had no visible effect upon Soviet attitudes or behavior. As late as April 1953 at the Fifteenth Session of ECOSOC, a Soviet spokesman stated that ECAFE "served as an efficient instrument in carrying out the policy of exploitation which the Colonial Powers had always pursued in Asia and the Far East";[19] it was an organization dominated by the West and incapable of contributing to Asia's economic development. By mid-1953, Soviet influence had plummeted to an all-time low.

Soviet "Discovery" of ECAFE

Stalin's death ushered in an era of amiability which came officially to the UN on July 15, 1953, when the Soviet delegate

[18] E/CN.11/363, pp. 90-92, excerpts.
[19] Economic and Social Council, *Official Records* (15th Session), p. 173.

in ECOSOC announced the willingness of the USSR to contribute to the UN technical assistance program. The "new look" made its first appearance in ECAFE at the Commission's Tenth Session in February 1954 with two innovations: first, a moderated and more balanced critique of the West and of foreign economic aid; second, and of more immediate interest to ECAFE members, a series of apparently serious offers to expand trade and provide technical assistance, loans, and long-term credits. These attracted considerable attention among the ECAFE delegates. Extensive coverage of the session in Soviet newspapers heightened the feeling that something important was in the making. Several of the articles, which were largely lengthy excerpts from the speeches of Soviet delegates, were longer than the entire 1953 coverage of ECAFE in *Pravda* and *Izvestiia*.

Glimmers of change in Soviet policies toward underdeveloped countries inevitably introduced a new line of thinking among ECAFE delegates: a hope that the Cold War would be transformed into a competitive economic struggle between the two power blocs for the friendship of the underdeveloped areas, bringing with it substantial increases in assistance which would help them overcome the unsettling problems of a discouragingly slow rate of economic development, the persistent disequilibrium in the area's international balance of payments, and the omnipresent spectre of economic instability. Soviet statements were therefore scrutinized eagerly but with caution. The prevailing attitude seemed to be: "I'm ready to be convinced, but show me."

The Soviets directed their offers principally toward the non-aligned nations of Southern Asia—Afghanistan, Burma, Ceylon, India, and Indonesia. Mr. Menshikov, a former Ambassador to the United States, then stationed in New Delhi, showed a shrewd sensitivity to their needs, both economic and psychological. No extensive program of grants was proposed, nor was the Soviet Union about to embark on any extensive aid or give-away program for Asia. Rather, Mr. Menshikov indicated the willingness of the Soviet Union "to consider the conclusion of long-term contracts with countries of the region for locally produced goods in exchange for goods from the Soviet Union, paying particular attention to the question of negotiating stable prices over a long-term period and to the possibility of payments being effected in the national currencies of the countries of the region."[20] Not only did this obviate the necessity of using scarce hard currency, but, in calling for the establishment of relations on a businesslike basis, he emphasized the reciprocal, mutually beneficial character of his proposal—an arrangement holding great appeal for nations concerned with the appearance as well as the substance of independence and equality. Moscow was not offering a larger package than the United States, but it was trying to make the package more appealing.

However, initially the Soviet offers did not meet with an uncritical reception. Several South Asian delegates denigrated the Soviet stress on barter agreements, holding that "a bilateral approach would only tend to perpetuate a colonial economy; only multilateral trading could bring about the much desired development of the area."[21] This objection, reflecting as it did the fundamental assumption that bilateralism benefited the strong more than the weak, was raised at a time when Moscow had not yet embarked on its program of extending long-term loans to non-Communist countries. But it was overlooked when bilateralism and barter agreements became, politically and pragmatically, a precondition for Soviet aid and expanded trade with the Soviet bloc. Former objections were overridden by more pressing considerations: the need for development capital and for new markets for the accumulating surpluses of raw materials, which constitute the main way underdeveloped countries can earn foreign ex-

[20] E/CN.11/389, p. 55.
[21] E/CN.11/I & T/101, pp. 124, 128.

change. However distasteful was the prospect of being bound to a self-limiting bilateral framework of trade, the under-developed countries acceded on the assumption that this kind of trade was better than no trade at all. This line of thinking acquired importance among the underdeveloped countries after 1955, when the magnitude of Soviet-bloc offers of loans and trade convinced them that an alternative to dependence on the West was at hand.

But in 1954 and 1955 Soviet offers continued to encounter skeptical reactions. At the Sixth Session of the Committee on Industry and Trade, held in January-February 1954, the Indian delegate, alluding to the preliminary Soviet overtures to underdeveloped countries, commented on the Soviet failure to consider measures "to supply short- and medium-term credit facilities to allow countries of the region to purchase adequate quantities of capital goods during the transition period of their development plans." Letting one cat out of the bargaining bag, he concluded on a disappointed note: ". . . his country was quite ready to trade with the USSR and countries of Eastern Europe, but recent contacts had shown little hope of increasing the volume of trade with the countries of Eastern Europe, as the products of this region were not offered at the most favourable prices."[22] The Soviet delegate, Mr. Volkov, annoyed at this disclosure, retorted sharply that such matters "were normally to be discussed between the trading partners and not before the Committee." The Soviets had still to prove that the wine, as well as the bottles, was new. This they did, in international organizations, through technical assistance, and bilaterally, through their 1955 offers of loans to India, Afghanistan, and Egypt.

For the first time, the Soviet Government invited specific requests for the services of Soviet specialists and the training of Asians in the Soviet Union through ECAFE channels. Thus, at the Third Session of the Inland Transport Committee, the

[22] *Ibid.,* p. 140.

Soviet representative offered to assist the Railway Training Center for Operating and Signalling Officers with educational materials, railway equipment, and technical films; at the Sixth Session of the Committee on Industry and Trade, the Soviet Union expressed a readiness to accept experts interested in electric power station construction and operation methods; at the 1957 session of ECAFE, the Soviet Union supported the proposal to create in Southeast Asia an All-Asia Polytechnical Institute and indicated that it was prepared to participate in constructing and equipping such an institution; at the same session it suggested that a conference on economic planning be convened in Moscow. In all of these and similar proposals made with increasing frequency in recent years, the Soviets specifically requested that the financing be undertaken by funds available from its contribution to the UN Expanded Program of Technical Assistance.

Although the UN ordinarily has complete freedom to allocate the contributions of member states, the Soviet Government has, in fact, retained effective and visible control over its annual contribution. Pledged primarily in nonconvertible rubles, it cannot be spent outside the Soviet Union, and thus can procure only Soviet equipment, materials, and technicians. This has limited the usefulness of the Soviet contribution, already small when measured by that of other countries, and made it an essentially bilateral operation. The Soviet Government has never offered any justification for the restrictive character of its contribution. Challenges on this subject by Western members of ECAFE have been evaded or ignored; the neutralists prefer not to become involved in this issue, especially since many of them also contribute to the UN in blocked currencies. Several interpretations have already been offered, none entirely satisfactory: the Soviet insistence upon contributing in nonconvertible rubles may stem from a desire to ensure that EPTA utilizes Soviet experts and equipment, and in a manner acceptable to Moscow; perhaps the Soviet

Government is short of hard currency and therefore reluctant to contribute in convertible currency; finally, the self-limiting and limited contribution to EPTA has served Moscow well enough, and there is no compelling reason for any change at this time.

Soviet "Point Four" in ECAFE

The neutralists have been noticeably slow in accepting Soviet funds under UN auspices. They have negotiated far more extensive and varied technical assistance agreements with the Soviet Union on a bilateral basis than through international organizations. They have manifested little interest in acquiring Soviet technicians and equipment through EPTA. Isolated visits of Asian specialists have been sponsored by ECAFE, but most of those who have visited the Soviet Union have done so as a result of negotiations concluded directly with the Soviet Government. Bilateral arrangements are clearly preferred: Afghanistan negotiated economic and technical assistance agreements with the Soviet Union on January 27, 1954, in February 1955, and again in December 1955 during the Khrushchev-Bulganin visit; Indian-Soviet economic relations expanded after the February 1955 accord which called for the building and equipping of the steel plant at Bhilai; Burma, Cambodia, Ceylon, and Indonesia responded, but more slowly, to Soviet trade and aid overtures. By 1958 every neutralist country in ECAFE had signed bilateral agreements accepting long-term loans, using Soviet-bloc specialists and equipment, and expanding foreign trade.

During the 1953-1955 period, before the South Asian neutralists had overcome their reluctance to accept Soviet aid, Soviet delegates occasionally attempted to take premature credit for grants of technical assistance not yet negotiated. They also tried to clothe strict business deals in the mantle of Soviet benevolence to give the impression that Moscow was lending large sums to Asian countries. Member nations quickly debunked such Soviet claims. For example, at the Eleventh Session of ECAFE, in April 1955, the Soviet delegate stated that Rumania and East Germany had provided technical assistance to Indonesia for the construction of a cement factory, a sugar refinery, and the exploration of new oil fields. The Indonesian delegate promptly informed the session that negotiations were still in the preliminary stage and: ". . . as to the project for purchase of a sugar factory from East Germany, the purchase contract specified, as was usually the case for such transactions, that the establishment of the factory and the initial work would be done by engineers from East Germany. Indonesia does not consider such clauses as 'technical assistance.'"[23] The Afghan delegate was moved to make a similar comment: "In connection with what the USSR representative had said at the previous meeting . . . his country had obtained from Czechoslovakia an interest-bearing loan of 7.5 million dollars to construct several factories and start operating them. This could not be considered as technical assistance."[24] If Moscow had hoped, by premature and delusive claims, to induce a bandwagon effect, it must have been surprised by these sharp reprovals. But time and neutralist needs were running in its favor.

The post-1955 Soviet campaign to develop closer ties with the South Asian neutralists has been carried on in the diplomatic, political, economic, cultural, and scientific spheres; it has been comprehensive, sustained, and adapted to the desires of these countries, even when the aid requested was designed not to promote economic development but to enhance the internal prestige of the ruling group, e.g. the construction of a sports stadium in Djakarta. In this saturation public-relations drive, ECAFE has served as a convenient outlet for Soviet pronouncements. Though all efforts did not bear immediate results, the cumulative effect has been satisfactory.

[23] E/CN.11/SR. 150, p. 236.
[24] Ibid., p. 238.

To accelerate exchange programs, the Soviets offered at the Twelfth Session in February 1956 "to provide up to 200 scholarships, at the rate of 40 to 50 every year, for students from underdeveloped countries of the region, to begin from 1956/57."[25] The offer evoked interest and good will, but few applied. At the same time, Soviet delegates expressed surprise that heretofore neither TAA nor any of the Specialized Agencies had sent students to the Soviet Union or utilized Soviet experts. Their statements reflected disappointment and wounded pride that these organizations were indifferent to the help proffered by the Soviet Union with its wealth of technical and scientific experience; they also indicated Soviet concern that their newly initiated and highly publicized diplomatic overtures were being ignored. In an effort to broaden the appeal of its offers, the Soviet Government raised the ante. At the next ECAFE session, it offered to accept in 1957-1959 one thousand experts and students for postgraduate training, under TAA auspices and on the basis of bilateral agreements. Similar offers were repeated annually and were the antecedents for Khrushchev's February 1960 speech in Indonesia in which he announced the intention to establish in Moscow a Friendship University for the Peoples of the East for students from underdeveloped countries. The University opened in September 1960, with an entering class of 500 students from 25 countries. The Soviet Union also expressed a willingness to share its experience in the peaceful uses of nuclear energy with ECAFE countries, and bilateral agreements have since been negotiated with Burma, India, and Indonesia.

Acceptance by ECAFE countries of Soviet aid through UN channels has, however, remained negligible. Since 1956, Afghanistan, Burma, Ceylon, India, and Indonesia have used

[25] E/CN.11/431, p. 115. V. Borovskii, "ECAFE and the Problems of Economic Development of the Countries of Asia," *Mirovaia ekonomika i mezhdunarodnye otnosheniia* (February 1957), pp. 121-122, *passim.*

Soviet experts assigned under UN auspices and have sent their nationals to the Soviet Union under ECAFE sponsorship. But the numbers are small. The main emphasis continues to center on the bilateral alternative, and, were it not for India, much of the Soviet contribution to EPTA would remain unexpended.

The preference of ECAFE countries for bilateral aid has been discussed previously: the convenience, the prospects of a large package-deal, the willingness of the Soviets to assume full responsibility for completion of any project which they undertake, and the minimum expenditure of effort and money in preproject surveys and post-project evaluations. Several other considerations mentioned by South Asian officials deserve attention. First, since the amount of UN funds which any country can draw on is limited, each prefers to take its "share" from the hard currency countries, the traditional suppliers of South Asian industrial and technological needs, rather than from the nonconvertible, self-limiting contribution of the Soviet Union. Also, once adequate financing is assured, a wider variety of goods and services can be obtained from Western sources. Second, students and specialists from ECAFE countries (as well as from Africa, Latin America, and the Middle East) prefer to receive their education in Western institutions. This stems largely from their greater familiarity with Western languages, customs, and culture. The need to learn Russian is an obstacle few have the time or inclination to surmount. Despite the undoubted excellence of Soviet technological and scientific institutions in fields of interest to underdeveloped countries, Soviet education is unusually compartmentalized; it turns out graduates qualified in one narrow phase of engineering, medicine, or science. With the exception of India, underdeveloped countries are at a stage of development where they have little need for, and relatively few students ready to benefit from, highly specialized, technological training. Most countries need broadly educated personnel, capable of adapting their learning to local conditions and of training and supervising subordinates in a variety of interrelated functions and responsibilities. As long as these limiting features of Soviet education remain, the bulk of students from underdeveloped countries will continue to seek their training in the West. Third, the United States, the Colombo Plan Powers, and the Western European countries currently provide thousands of these students with educational opportunities. Therefore, there is no urgent need for underdeveloped countries to send large numbers of students to the Soviet Union. Most foreign students now studying in the Soviet Union do so without the approval or sponsorship of their governments. The answer to filling national needs for educated personnel lies not in exporting larger numbers of students to foreign lands but in building up the educational systems in these countries. Fourth, for internal political reasons, most neutralists enjoying friendly diplomatic relations with the Soviet Union are chary of exposing their best students to extended contact with Communist authorities under rigidly controlled and manipulated environments, from which could return trained, but indoctrinated, graduates. Finally, the recipient countries may feel less obligated to support Soviet proposals in ECAFE, or elsewhere in international organizations, since the bilateral aid is not a manifestation of largesse, but the result of hard, businesslike negotiations for which a price is paid and for which the donor expects to reap a political advantage. These explanations are suggestive and not mutually exclusive. As with so much of Soviet policy toward ECAFE countries, future developments must be watched for additional clues as to Soviet behavior and the reactions of the South Asian countries.

The Soviet Stand on Trade Policy

In ECAFE there is a growing realization that expanding, dependable markets are the key to stable earnings with which to finance economic development, and that, useful and vital though foreign aid and help from international organizations are, they cannot be expected to continue indefinitely nor to provide more than a small portion of the total capital investment required for the take-off to a self-sustaining rate of growth. The interest in expanding international trade has been heightened by fear of the effect of the European Economic Community (EEC) upon their economies and continued accessibility to European markets. ECAFE countries are studying the recent influence of the Common Market on their trade patterns and potentials, particularly with respect to the primary commodities which they must sell to survive, i.e. rubber, tin, copra, jute, etc. For these one- or two-crop countries, national planning is complicated by their inability to anticipate foreign exchange earnings because of price fluctuations in the world commodity markets. Always in the background, the spectre of a Western recession raises uncertainties concerning their necessarily modest growth targets. Fear of indisposable surpluses is omnipresent. Their burgeoning population consumes productivity gains, and the pace of economic development has yet to reach a self-sustaining level; domestic pressures mount, intensifying bitterness and frustration and spreading a sense of futility. Finding markets for commodity surpluses is crucial, linked as it is with the prospects of many neutralists for political survival.

Reassurances from European delegates at ECAFE meetings that the Common Market will not jeopardize ECAFE countries' access to traditional markets offer no comfort; they are belied by preliminary statistical evidence which shows that while Common Market members are expanding their imports from abroad and increasing their trade with one another, they are purchasing less from ECAFE countries. No steps have been taken to allay these fears.

This situation buttresses Moscow's ideological, political, and economic analyses of Western policies. Playing upon the legitimate fears of ECAFE members, the Soviet Union paints the Common Market in the darkest hues, denounces "capitalistic monopolists," and injects disruptive issues into the Asian-Western discussions of trade and economic development. Soviet delegates exaggerate Western economic problems, purporting to see impending disaster in periodic disturbances, and lauding, by way of contrast, the inexorable Soviet advances in industry, agriculture, and welfare, the stability of the Soviet economy, and the benefits inherent in expanding trade with the Soviet bloc. They commiserate with neutralist delegates because "foreign monopolies impose unjust prices on raw materials upon the developing Asian countries, while selling industrial goods and equipment to them at monopoly prices." At the Eighteenth Session of ECAFE in March 1962, the Soviet delegate, Mr. M. A. Lesechko, seconded the complaint of the Indonesian delegate that it was difficult to plan and execute development programs without assurance of the steady flow of foreign exchange from export earnings and noted that: "Within the period of 1953-1961 the world prices of finished goods exported by the leading capitalist countries rose by 10 per cent while the prices of raw materials and food products supplied by the primary producing countries fell by 8-9 per cent. Consequently, the gap in the levels of economic development between economically underdeveloped countries and highly developed countries, far from decreasing, is growing year by year."

Such criticisms find a receptive audience and cannot be dismissed simply as standard Soviet conference fare. As a result of sharply fluctuating commodity prices, a number of ECAFE countries in given periods have indeed lost more income than they have received by way of foreign aid. One ILO official said that the Organization's research staff had come to the conclusion that "the money which the South Asian countries lost as a consequence of the precipitous drop in world commodity prices during the 1956-1958 period was greater than the total amount of technical assistance and economic aid they had received from all sources since the end of the war." A Ceylonese delegate observed that, during the 1951-1959 period, Ceylon had average about $10 million a year in foreign aid, for a total of less than $100 million; during the 1955-1957 period, Ceylon's foreign trade slumped from a $150 million profit in 1955 to a deficit of more than $200 million by 1957 because of the decline in world prices for rubber and tea. This is not an isolated experience, and the attendant bitterness should not be discounted. Economic tremors in the West have caused political quakes in Southern Asia. According to one neutralist official, Indonesia's recent drift toward the Soviet bloc has been due more to the severe post-Korean drop in world commodity prices than to any increase in effectiveness of the Indonesian Communist Party.

Suggestions to devote greater attention to stabilizing world commodity prices have been made in several UN bodies. In 1954 ECOSOC established an eighteen-nation Commission on International Commodity Trade (CICT) to investigate possibilities of stabilizing prices of raw materials at levels regarded as satisfactory by the producing countries. The underdeveloped countries had long fought for such a Commission; and over the opposition of the Western Powers, and with Soviet support, they finally brought it into existence. But CICT has bogged down in debate and disagreement. The Soviets hammer at the continuing instability of world demand for primary commodities and the role of the West in perpetuating international economic disequilibriums. Yet, despite reiterations of general support for "a system of automatic compensatory financing," they have not put forth any specific proposals which might serve as a basis for serious discussions. A telling case against indiscriminate Soviet efforts to blame the Western countries for slumps in the prices of primary products was made by the American delegate at the October 11, 1962 meeting of the General Assembly's Social Committee. Mrs. Ronald Tree suggested that the problem of commodity prices could be resolved by increasing consumption of commodities such as coffee and tea, and not, as was done in the Soviet Union, by State trading corporations limiting demand and making exorbitant profits:

"There was thus an Alice-in-Wonderland quality to the statements made by the representatives of State-controlled economies who blamed the deterioration in commodity prices on those who bought the most. The difficulty was, in fact, the opposite. If the Soviet Union were to import as much coffee *per capita* as Czechoslovakia, the whole problem of the coffee surplus would immediately be solved. The USSR representative might argue that the Russians were a tea-drinking nation; yet Soviet imports of tea, despite that country's increased prosperity, had dropped from 5 per cent of the total tabulated world imports before 1939 to less than 3 per cent today. On the other hand the United States, a traditionally coffee-drinking country which imported almost half of the total world coffee exports, also imported 9 per cent of the total world exports of tea.

"The reason for the difference in relative imports was that in State-operated economies, the price charged to the consumer was often so out of proportion to the world market price that he had no choice but to reduce consumption. That was monopoly-pricing at its worst. According to official USSR trade statistics published in 1959, the cost of tea to the consumer was thirty times the import price paid by the USSR government, and, in Poland, according to the Polish Yearbook for 1959, sixty-two times the import price; whereas in the United States the consumer in 1958 had paid four times the import price and in the United Kingdom 1.7 times."[26]

The Western Powers, though aware of how fluctuating prices affect the internal political stability of underdeveloped

[26] A/C.3/SR. 1150, p. 4.

countries, have yet to give commodity stabilization priority attention. In a speech before the UN, Ambassador Adlai Stevenson recognized that "little things, like stabilization of commodity prices, can mean more than economic assistance. The change in the price of coffee by half a cent per pound can wipe out all of the economic assistance that we (USA) could hope to give . . . for a long time." Though recent experiences with tin and wheat stabilization agreements show that thus far commodity stabilization is not as effective in practice as it is in theory, in the long run it is the real promise for relief from ever-greater demands by underdeveloped countries for foreign aid. A major step was taken on September 28, 1962, to stabilize the world coffee market with the signing of the first International Coffee Agreement between the major producing and importing countries. The five-year agreement was particularly noteworthy since the participation of leading coffee producers made possible the enforcement of quotas on exports.[27]

In the meanwhile, a partial solution can be found in the expansion of international trade. The 1962 ECAFE Resolution on International Trade recognized that "foreign trade still remains the primary instrument for economic development and therefore the expansion of international trade is of basic importance for the progress and welfare of all peoples in this area." Moscow strongly supported this resolution, since it requested the Secretary-General to consult with governments on the advisability of holding an international trade conference—a theme pushed by the Soviet Union since 1955. On May 30, 1962, at a reception honoring President Modibo Keita of Mali, Premier Khrushchev coupled denunciation of the Common Market, which he said threatened the new African states, with another call for an international trade conference. Anxious to discourage the African states from associating themselves with the Common Market in order

[27] *New York Times,* November 23, 1962.

to forestall their developing close economic links with the West (links which could lead to improved political relations as well), Khrushchev warned that "subordination of the young sovereign states of Africa to the Common Market would signify their consent to reconciling themselves to the role of agrarian and metropolitan raw-material appendages of former metropolitan countries."[28] Soviet persistence, buttressed by growing dissatisfaction among the underdeveloped countries with the existing state of affairs, finally bore fruit. On Soviet initiative, the Seventeenth Session of the General Assembly approved a resolution to convene an international trade conference in early 1964, over the opposition of the United States, France, Britain, Italy, and other Western countries. The Conference will consider: the need for expanding the trade of developing countries in primary commodities so as to increase export earnings; measures for ensuring stable, equitable and remunerative prices and rising demand for the exports of underdeveloped countries; measures leading to the gradual reduction of tariff barriers; methods and machinery to implement measures relating to the expansion of international trade.

Through a fortuitous combination of timing and circumstances, bilateralism now appeals strongly to ECAFE neutralists who seek secure markets for their export-earning primary commodities. Regionalism is weak, lacking roots in South Asian history or economics. Regional sentiment is overshadowed by an egocentric nationalist approach and absorption in national problems. Hence bilateralism, in all its forms, has more immediate appeal for ECAFE countries than multilateralism. In ECAFE, the Soviet Union is the foremost exponent of expanding trade within a bilateral, rather than a regional, framework. The commitment of Soviet trade policy and assistance to bilateralism may be due more to pragmatic considerations of power and necessity than to theoretical preconceptions. Though Moscow cites the present advantages of

[28] *Ibid.*, May 31, 1962. Also see *Pravda*, August 26, 1962.

171

bilateralism to neutralist nations, it points to the development of regionalism in "the socialist camp," and implies that it is not opposed to regionalism qua regionalism. It has not, however, been notably sympathetic in the past toward regionalist efforts, either in Eastern Europe or in the non-Communist world.

Economically, regionalism presupposes voluntarily imposed restraints on the strong of the community not to dictate to the weak and a firm commitment to deal with all members on a plane of equality. Politically, in Eastern Europe it threatens to counterpoise Soviet hegemony with growing autonomy for the satellites; in the underdeveloped world, to the extent that regionalism can strengthen the economies of bourgeois-nationalist regimes, it constitutes a barrier to increased Soviet and local Communist influence. The authoritarian character of the Soviet state, the tradition of imperial diplomacy, and the insistence upon exclusiveness in matters of ideology are antithetical to the multifaceted prerequisites of a workable regional system, be it political, economic, or cultural in character. Witness Moscow's difficulty, even within the Soviet orbit, to accommodate to even a tenuous economic regionalism. In June 1962 the Council for Mutual Economic Assistance (Comecon) met in Moscow to discuss closer bloc integration and possible responses to the Common Market. The Soviet plan to coordinate more tightly the long-range economic plans for the bloc encountered opposition from Czechoslovakia and Poland who seek to preserve and expand their trade ties with the West. Comecon's attempt to encourage a "socialist division of labor," whereby individual countries would specialize in the production of particular goods for the entire bloc, would tie the Eastern European countries closer to Moscow and proscribe their contacts with the West, a privilege they largely regained after the de-Stalinization drive and the Polish and Hungarian Revolutions of 1956. Ironically, Comecon may develop into a viable economic organ-

THE USSR AND ECAFE

ization as a consequence of the vitality of the Common Market. If the Common Market makes it difficult for the Eastern European countries to trade with Western Europe, they will then have to turn increasingly to Moscow and work to strengthen Comecon. Elsewhere, one may find the Soviets subscribing in theory to Pan-Africanism and Pan-Arabism, but their day-to-day maneuverings in Africa and the Middle East refute their declarations.

Nowhere is Soviet hostility to regionalism more sustained than in its attitude toward European unity, particularly the Common Market. Moscow regards the Common Market as a last-ditch effort by European capitalism to postpone the onrush of the next, inevitable depression, with all its accompanying political unrest and revolution; but it is nonetheless worried about the stamina of the moribund capitalist patient. The current Soviet image of the Common Market and European moves toward unity is an adaptation of the Leninist theory of imperialism to the conditions of the 1960's. Drawing on Lenin's denunciation of the idea of a United Europe, one Soviet commentator wrote that the idea was only another scheme for the imperialist powers to divide up "peacefully" world markets: "The disintegration of the colonial system of imperialism, the rise of new countries which are taking the road to national independence, the futile attempts by some imperialist Powers to crush the national-liberation movement in the colonial and dependent countries—all generate imperialist tendencies toward unification of efforts and aims in order to retain the exploitation of their colonies. This tendency is plainly shown in the launching of the guarantees of the economic prosperity and political might of 'Europe,' of the 'third force' on the international scene."[29] Moscow believes that Europe will not be able to unify, to surmount class and national rivalries and, in the futile process of trying, will not

[29] V. Knyazhinsky, "'United Europe', a Weapon of Imperialist Policy," *International Affairs,* No. 6 (June 1957), p. 56.

hesitate to strengthen itself through exploitation of Africa and Asia. As the Soviets see it, the movement toward economic regionalism in Europe has still to prove its mettle, to demonstrate its capacity to weather centrifugal strains and transcend national jealousies: "Adenauer views it as a means of protecting German imperialism from German socialism, De Gaulle looks on it as a means of consolidating the reactionary regime in France and of solving her colonial problems, while Italy's Christian-Democratic Party considers it a safeguard against the left. All of them, jointly with the United States, seek to 'protect' imperialism from Communism through the Common Market."[30] Until experience and the test of time convince the Soviets that their evaluation is not only incorrect, but damaging to Soviet interests, Moscow will continue to believe and disseminate this conception of Western regionalism to a wary, disturbed Afro-Asia.

Past and present ECAFE efforts at regional economic and trade cooperation—the frequent meetings of the Committee on Trade, the ECAFE-sponsored Trade Promotion Conferences, and the Asian Planners Conference of 1961—have yielded meager results. At the March 1962 Annual Session of ECAFE, the Secretariat, sensing the growing anxiety over the possible consequences of the Common Market, circulated to member governments a confidential report which recommended the establishment of an Asian counterpart—an Organization for Asian Economic Cooperation (OAEC). Bold and visionary in conception, the proposal has already encountered considerable opposition: India and Japan contend that their strong economic links to non-Asian markets preclude, at this time, their support; many of the smaller ECAFE countries fear that any specifically Asian organization would be dominated by India and Japan; and some argue that their economies lack the complementarity necessary for organizing

[30] A. Arzumanyan, "Socio-Economic and Political Background to West European 'Integration,'" *World Marxist Review* (October 1959), p. 69.

174

a highly integrated trading and development network. The difficulties of promoting effective economic integration even on a sub-regional scale in the form of the proposed Association for Southeast Asia (ASA) indicate that the political climate is not yet conducive to the establishment of a complex, integrated economic framework. OAEC is an aspiration, but it is not a present possibility. ECAFE countries have stronger economic and cultural ties with Western Europe than with their neighbors. Their political leaders plead that national priorities preclude the cultivation of closer regional ties. Meanwhile, the region's competitive power grows weaker in relation to other regions. Low agricultural yields, inadequate regional cooperation, and unproductive investment ventures could condemn Asia to decades of instability and weakness.

The trading problems of the region may be further sharpened when Communist China's impact is fully felt in Asian markets. Preliminary evidence bodes ill, for political prices have already been used by Peking to undercut Asian products in traditional markets. One neutralist Ambassador, who has served in China, minced no words: "One thing that is not adequately appreciated by well-intentioned Asians who want to be friendly with China, nor emphasized forcefully or skillfully enough by American diplomats, is the fact that once the Chinese start to invade the markets of Asia near chaos will result because the Chinese, bent on dominance in Asia, will undersell at political prices all Asian countries in any market they choose to do so. For example, one Indian manufacturer, noting that bicycles could be produced in India for half the price that they were being sold in China, offered to sell bikes to the Chinese. The Chinese thought the proposal over for a few days and then quoted the Indians a price for Chinese bicycles less than that which the Indians charged for their own in India. Similarly, the flooding of the Hong Kong market with Chinese textiles is only in its infancy. ECAFE countries had best become more wary and move to counter this inevitable Chinese trade thrust. Their future is the issue."

Against this bleak general background, the appeal of Soviet bilateralism is clear: it offers an outlet at stable prices for Asian commodities and a source of needed equipment and machinery. The Soviet refrain is repeated at every ECAFE session: "Foreign trade organizations . . . were ready to offer credits for the purchase of machinery and equipment, and those organizations were studying the question of long-term agreements and contracts for the purchase of some major export products at fixed prices, payment being made in the currencies of the purchasing countries."[31] These statements no longer nurture illusions. ECAFE neutralists have learned from one another's experiences about the limitations and problems inherent in acceptance of Soviet aid and in expanding trade with the Soviet bloc. Though rarely alluded to in public, they are freely discussed in private: tons of cement delivered during the monsoon season and caking on the docks of Rangoon; rupees paid to the Soviets for industrial equipment and later sold by them at a premium in Western Europe; Indonesia's experience with faulty equipment, improperly assembled refineries, and delays in receiving spare parts. One Indonesian official involved in negotiating agreements with the Soviet Union presented the following picture: "Trade with the Soviet Union had its problems. Although the Soviets have given Indonesia a $100 million credit at 2 per cent, the lowest interest rate charged by any country or international lending institution, Indonesia has been slow in utilizing it because of the higher prices charged by the Soviets for their factories and equipment, a factor nullifying the visible benefit of the lower interest rate. Loans from the United States bear a higher rate of interest and, because they must be spent in the USA, often result in Indonesia not getting as much for its money as it might if it could spend the money freely elsewhere. However, Indonesia has greater flexibility in its choice of equip-

[31] E/CN.11/483, p. 110.

ment purchased in the United States than in its shopping in the USSR. Negotiating with the Soviets is complicated by the fact that the Soviets seldom speak English or Indonesian, and all agreements must be translated into Russian, Indonesian, and English—a laborious, lengthy process. The Indonesians, lacking expert interpreters of their own, must rely upon Soviet translators. Also, Soviet negotiators seldom have the latitude or flexibility of Western negotiators, and any change, however insignificant, must be referred back to Moscow for approval."

That Soviet trade is viewed by the Kremlin primarily as an instrument of foreign policy appears not to worry Asian leaders, although past statements by Soviet leaders themselves clearly indicate that the purpose of imports is to make future imports unnecessary. In 1955, for example, Khrushchev remarked to a visiting group of Congressmen that "we value trade least for economic reasons and most for political reasons." Whatever motivates Soviet policy-makers, it has not deterred neutralist interest in improving trade relations with the Soviet Union. Because of domestic and foreign policy considerations, because alternative sources of aid and trade are not available in significant amounts, because the attraction of a balanced position between the Soviet and Western blocs still has an ideological appeal for neutralist leaders, and because continued fears and suspicions of the West invariably strengthen favorable interpretations of Soviet policies, any difficulties and doubts remain muted.

The Soviet Impact on ECAFE

ECAFE has made an important contribution in the field of research. Through its surveys and studies of various aspects of Asian economic problems, it has provided many countries with planning and programming data which they could not have obtained on their own. ECAFE also convenes meetings of specialists to deal with specific problems. The technical committees handle topics ranging from hydrology to housing, transportation to trade. The most publicized meetings are the annual sessions. Resembling minor General Assemblies, they are the most political and, by their nature, the least productive. But even they serve an educational function in helping to break down Asians' ignorance of Asia. They enable officials from all ECAFE countries to meet one another, discuss common problems, and develop an awareness of the things that unite, not divide, them.

The present weaknesses of ECAFE are irremediable, given the nature of Asian politics. To begin with, there is the diversity of Asia, the absence of a tradition of regional cooperation, and the prevalent belief that development is primarily a national affair and that help from outside the region is of greater importance than any which might develop as a consequence of intra-regional cooperation. All members profess support for ECAFE goals, but their support is vocal not operational. Each interprets its commitment in national not regional terms, narrowly rather than generously. Since the hopes of 1947–1948 for an Asian Marshall Plan administered through ECAFE were shattered, the Secretariat has labored in search of a *raison d'être*. It has generally not attracted the quality of personnel needed, since as an international organization it has only recently begun to convince its patrons that it is deserving of greater support and responsibility. Not infrequently, the Secretariat has been used as a dumping ground for deposed politicians no longer wanted at home, but for whom a status-satisfying position must be found. The highly qualified can find a welcome market for their skills in their own countries, an exception perhaps being the Nationalist Chinese, and only infrequently do they elect to make a career out of service in the Secretariat.

According to Asian officials, national animosities have been a feature of Secretariat life. For example, from the start, to

the annoyance of other Asians, the Secretariat has been dominated by Indians, few of whom are regarded as outstanding.
Feelings of national superiority are also observable: the Chinese consider themselves the best trained and have disdain
for the Indians; other nationalities resent the Indians and the
Pakistanis because they flaunt their superior fluency in English; the Japanese send few people to ECAFE, and these
usually remain only long enough to improve their knowledge
of English; the smaller countries who rarely have qualified
nationals to send nevertheless insist that they should be given
more posts. One observer of Secretariat politics said that "the
Secretariat is splintered into separate groups, and jealousies
exist between Departments and within Departments; too often
this petty political infighting is based on racial, ethnic, and
cultural affiliation: the Indians cluster together, as do the
Chinese, and Japanese, etc., and within these groups cleavages
develop along doctrinal and ideological lines." He thought,
however, that recent years have seen an improvement. Despite
these shortcomings, the ECAFE Secretariat has nonetheless
managed to perform useful activities—a testament to the devotion and determination of the few and to the potential importance of ECAFE for the future of Asia, which is implicit in
their dedication.

Through participation in ECAFE, the Soviet Union very
likely seeks to pursue simultaneously a variety of policies,
some of which may occasionally conflict or appear inconsistent
with others, and which entail different degrees of support for
different facets of ECAFE activities. These include a desire
to strengthen Soviet-South Asian relationships (in the short
run as a complement to extensive bilateral efforts, and in the
long run as part of a comprehensive drive to improve Moscow's position in the budding rivalry with Peking for influence
in the region), to impress ECAFE countries with Soviet
achievements, and to stimulate interest in aspects of the Soviet
model useful for their development. Furthermore the Soviets

hope to wean these countries away from the West, to exploit Asian-Western frictions, and to place in continued question Western policies and objectives in Asia by adopting a strong anti-colonialist stand. The Soviets want to use ECAFE as a forum for disseminating Soviet views, for encouraging neutralist countries to turn to the USSR for technicians and equipment, either through bilateral or UN channels, and for promoting trade with the countries of the area.

The Soviets have had little influence in the ECAFE Secretariat. There have never been more than three Soviet citizens on the staff at any one time, and they were in minor positions. Because of the Secretariat's preference for hiring Asian nationals, there is no opportunity for Moscow to play an important role. During the Stalin era, Moscow opposed any strengthening of the Secretariat, which it attacked for its too broad and diversified studies of Asian economic developments. Now it supports proposals to increase ECAFE's powers by divesting UN Headquarters of much of its present authority. Not only has it aligned itself with sentiments shared by ECAFE neutralists, but, through decentralization, Moscow hopes to weaken the center where it is permanently outvoted, to decrease the power of TAB to allocate UN aid, and to weaken American influence, which is greater at the center than in the regions.

Since 1954, the Soviets have become active contributors to the work of the technical committees. Here, in the unpublicized meetings, where the most constructive activities of the Secretariat are conducted, Soviet experts are demonstrating that impressive performance makes the best propaganda. The teams of experts sent by Moscow are competent, hard working, well prepared; they give the impression of having been carefully selected and briefed. The same cannot always be said for Western delegations who too often appear to be a heterogeneous group hastily drawn together to attend the meeting because some representation is expected.

In its approach to Asian technocrats on the relevance of Soviet experience, Moscow is tooling for the long haul and not overlooking any opportunity to show to advantage. It stresses basic themes: the need for national planning, the role of public sector investment, the nationalization of basic industries, and the advantages of elaborate centralized economic controls. No longer does it blindly push Soviet methods as in the Stalin period. Rather, the Soviets argue that particular features of Soviet economic experience, especially in planning and investment, might be suitable for ECAFE emulation. At times they belabor their target audience with the obvious, a tedium the neutralists seem prepared to endure, believing that Soviet criticisms account for heightened Western interest. They are aided inadvertently by the occasionally overemotional criticisms and counter-arguments of Western delegates who feel compelled to defend a free-enterprise system which has little doctrinal appeal in Asia and which, more importantly, is more regulated in their own countries than one would gather from hearing their impassioned defense of a semi-mythical, unregulated free-enterprise system. The American delegates, in particular, are guilty of oversimplification and of gracing Soviet remarks with an attention that is substantively unwarranted; they spend so much time refuting Soviet allegations and searching for snares in Soviet proposals that neutralists sometimes profess haziness as to the positive aspects of American policy in ECAFE. The gap, however, between what is proposed and what is practicable is appreciated by responsible neutralist leaders who, though attached emotionally to the moral and social goals of "socialism," know the limits of their ability to adapt policies suited to an industrially advanced society to their own agrarian societies. There is no precipitate or uncritical acceptance of the Soviet model.

Present Soviet expectations from membership in ECAFE are limited and hence more realistic. If its approach since 1954 is any indication of future policy toward the nonaligned South

Asian countries, the Kremlin will concentrate on bilateral arrangements while continuing to utilize ECAFE to disseminate its views and test experimental innovations. Intended for all ECAFE neutralists, the Soviet offer of scholarships, for example, had greater impact when announced in the Commission than it would have had under any other circumstances. The Kremlin has discovered that with a minimum of outlay and commitment it can effectively reach segments of the neutralist elites usually inured to the more patent forms of political proselytizing. This observation is being applied, albeit still sparingly, in other international organizations where the membership consist largely of underdeveloped nations that are harassed by domestic difficulties, resentful of their dependence upon Western aid, and eager for change.

Soviet aid to ECAFE has been negligible, yet Soviet prestige continues to grow—a paradox that inheres in the nature of ECAFE politics. To fully understand it, one must remember that the neutralists are receiving substantial Soviet aid bilaterally and welcome Moscow's diplomatic support in their major foreign policy concerns, i.e. India on Goa, Kashmir, and the border dispute with China; Indonesia on West Irian; Afghanistan on its feud with Pakistan. These factors greatly condition neutralist attitudes; the minimal Soviet financial help to ECAFE projects is considered understandable, given Western opposition to Soviet proposals and Soviet coolness toward the projects being financed. From the Soviet standpoint, the net effect is encouraging, bolstering Moscow's contention that aid and technical assistance given through bilateral, not international channels, is more efficient and less likely to become involved in Cold War feuding.

The most dramatic illustration of nonparticipation and noncontribution failing to affect Soviet prestige with the neutralists is the Lower Mekong Basin project, which is one of the two major operational programs thus far undertaken as a result of an ECAFE proposal (the other being the Asian Highway). In 1951 ECAFE's Bureau of Flood Control initiated a series of studies to determine the potentialities of the 2,600 mile Mekong River, which is tenth among the rivers of the world on the basis of the volume of water it carries. The Bureau submitted a report in February 1957 detailing the rich potential of the Mekong delta. Encouraged by the report, the four main states concerned—Cambodia, Laos, South Vietnam, and Thailand—agreed to establish in October 1957, under ECAFE auspices, a Committee for Coordination of Investigations of the Lower Mekong Basin. If the Mekong project receives the considerable financial commitments (some estimates run as high as $3 billion over a twenty-year period) necessary to construct the major dams and power stations, though the precarious political situation in the area makes this improbable, ECAFE may justifiably claim a good measure of credit. By conceiving the whole idea and playing an active role in its implementation, ECAFE would appear to have strengthened its claim to leadership for regional economic development in Asia; mineral and inland water transport experts from the Secretariat have conducted and supervised field work, and ECAFE is the Special Fund's executive agent for the Mekong project.

But though ECAFE's prestige may have been enhanced, its authority has not. Caution must be exercised in evaluating the organization's likelihood of developing into the centralizing institution for regional cooperation. Not everyone affiliated with the Mekong project and ECAFE affairs is sanguine about the future. One UN official, for example, who has been closely associated with developments in the area described the situation as follows:

"More than any single development, the proposed Mekong River Valley project has injected some life and hope into ECAFE. But it is largely spurious. Once it became evident that the project could depend on the support of the rich countries, a Committee for Coordination of Investigations of the Lower Mekong Basin was established. Though it reports to ECAFE, the Committee functions largely independent of ECAFE control, and deals directly with individual governments who are prepared to contribute to the project. Thus, in a real sense, ECAFE has but a limited voice in the determination of actual policy, though it continues to play up the project at its sessions because the idea originated in ECAFE, and the organization has so little else to boast about.

"The project is the result of the Cold War. There would be no support for a Mekong River Valley project if it were not for the Cold War. Of all the deltas in Asia deserving of support, the Mekong is perhaps the least likely candidate. If carried through, with power stations and dams, etc., the cost will run into billions. The Mekong delta is almost devoid of people. Who will use the 35 billion kilowatt hours of electricity which the complete complex is supposed to produce? There is no industry, nor any visible prospect of large-scale industry developing in the area to utilize the power produced. Nor are there sufficiently trained workers there to attract investment capital to the area."

A British scholar, who has carefully researched ECAFE developments, takes sharp issue with this interpretation: "The project began despite, not because of, the Cold War. Any study of ECAFE water resources publications would show that after the Indus Basin, the Mekong (a much neglected river) was probably the next most suitable river for development through international action. The big political (Cold War) problem was to get the four riparian countries together in the first place. The United States tried and failed; ECAFE succeeded and hence the Coordinating Committee."[32]

These conflicting interpretations demonstrate the difficulty

[32] Letter of October 25, 1962, from Professor David Wightman, University of Birmingham.

in getting at the actual situation. ECAFE officials have perhaps shown unduly possessive feelings toward the project, but then it is their brain child—and attempts have been made to shunt them aside. It seems probable, however, that the independent Committee was set up, at least in part, to keep the Soviets out or, this failing, to minimize their role in the enterprise. Also, political factors led to the creation of this separate Committee. Of the four riparian states involved, only Cambodia will now permit Soviet nationals to survey or conduct hydrological or geological investigations on its territory; South Vietnam will not permit any Soviet nationals to enter; Thailand, though accustomed to granting visas to Soviets attending ECAFE sessions in Bangkok, is also opposed to the use of Soviet specialists; and Laos is a no-man's land, hanging limply in a tightening Communist noose.

In this case the Soviet record is flawless. At the Fourteenth Session of ECAFE (March 1958), the Soviet Government expressed its willingness to provide specialists for the planning and construction of hydroelectric units along the Mekong. Similar offers were made at the 1959 and 1960 sessions. Each time the Mekong Committee turned them down because it was not interested in technical assistance that was not also accompanied by machinery and equipment, as in the case of other bilateral contributions. Moscow could, if it believed that participation would serve a political purpose, pressure for acceptance of its offer by raising the ante, with the understanding that it would be used only in Cambodia. It has not done so most likely because it believes that nonparticipation in no way diminishes Soviet stature among the neutralist nations that it is courting, and that the project itself arouses little interest elsewhere in Southern Asia. In fact, rejection of the Soviet offers has reinforced the publicly unvoiced, but nonetheless widely shared, reservations of many neutralists that Cold War politics rather than economic considerations dictated the decision to develop the Mekong delta, instead of other areas where benefits would accrue to more people more quickly. Thus, there is danger that the project may become a white elephant and be abandoned should the political situation in any of the four countries change significantly in the near future, i.e. Communist takeovers would most likely result in the principal donor powers withholding further financial support.

Many decisions in ECAFE reveal the extensive corroding effect of Cold War considerations. For example, at the 1956 ECAFE session, the Soviet delegate commented on the rewarding experiences of the fifteen Indian Government officials and the ECAFE-study group of geologists who had visited the Soviet Union under UN auspices. The ECAFE group, he said, had called attention to the value of translating Soviet technical literature on geology and mining into English, so "the Soviet Union was prepared to make its technical literature relating to other branches of industry and economics, including hydro-electric construction, irrigation, planning and statistics, available to all countries interested."[33] He proposed that a translation bureau be established in Moscow, financed out of the Soviet contribution to EPTA, and he encouraged the Secretariat to take the initiative in making the necessary arrangements.

Since the proposal was made without any preliminary notice, the delegates could not act until they had consulted their respective governments. The Secretariat and several neutralists expressed interest. The Western Powers, on the other hand, questioned the value of the proposal and the motives behind it. Why not, they argued, translate German, French, and Spanish technical literature? Why just Russian? The Indonesian delegate who had helped to draft the recommendation which was the basis for the Soviet proposal summed up the case for adoption as follows: "During their six-week stay in the USSR, the study group was impressed by the large amount

[33] E/CN.11/431, p. 200.

of specialized literature published in the Soviet Union. Unfortunately, this literature was available only in Russian. The group felt that the area as a whole would greatly benefit if it was made accessible in a language widely understood in the region, i.e. English. It was a well-known fact that translation of scientific publications could not be entrusted solely to professional translators, however qualified, and that this work should be closely supervised by engineers and scientists fully acquainted with the subject, and the original language. Hence the proposal to establish the centre in Moscow. The study group was not struck by the necessity of translating the technical literature of the other countries visited, partly because such publications were already existing in English and partly because French and German were spoken in technical circles at home which was not true of Russian."[34] The Soviets pushed hard but an unexpected hesitancy developed among initially sympathetic delegates. Insistence that the translating be done in Moscow added substance to the contention of opponents that the USSR, by seeking to control the expenditure of its own UN contribution—a move contrary to UN procedures—sought acceptance for a project for which it, rather than the UN, would receive actual credit. In addition, by 1958 much of Soviet scientific literature was already being translated by private organizations in the United States, hence the diminished need for the UN to enter the field. ECAFE finally decided that the problem should be handled by UNESCO in conjunction with its broad plan to establish scientific documentation centers.

The frequency of Cold War quarreling, which invariably results in stalemate, led one high-ranking neutralist national on the Secretariat to remark:

"The United States tends to reject out of hand Soviet proposals, without seriously trying to determine whether a basis for compromise exists. Admittedly, Soviet proposals are often

[34] E/CN.11/I & T/133, p. 94.

overly generalized and implicitly political. But American delegates are always on guard, perhaps too much so, for some hidden Soviet trick, for some devious implication. If the Asians propose something and the Soviets support it, as they now almost ritually do for tactical reasons, then the Americans will respond by a call for further investigation, the net effect of which is to prevent the expeditious implementation of the Asian proposal. This hypersensitivity of the United States to proposals supported by the Soviets, but also favored by the neutralists, inevitably benefits the USSR.

"Asians resent the paternalistic, patronizing attitude adopted by Western delegates when questions involving Communist countries are raised; they resent the assumption that they are incapable of dealing with the Soviets, that they will fall victim to those shrewd, tough, untrustworthy Soviets unless the West is there to protect them. Americans should realize that Soviet statements are not blindly accepted as truth, and Soviet proposals are studied carefully before a position is taken. Asians feel fully competent to handle such matters as they arise."

These views were also expressed by other neutralists, usually with a chauvinistic twist.[35] Thus, the Indians thought the Indonesians and Cambodians too willing to accept Soviet claims uncritically, whereas they had a sense of perspective and a realistic grasp of the situation; the Indonesians and Cambodians, on the other hand, felt quite confident of their political acumen, but questioned the wisdom of the Afghans binding themselves so closely to the Soviet Union, whereas the Afghans felt that decades of diplomatic contact with Moscow had left them well prepared to handle the Soviets. Many neutralist officials volunteered the observation that a distinction had to be made between *Asian* and *African* evaluations of Soviet policy. A composite of their interpretations might

[35] Private discussions were held with South Asian officials during a visit to the area in 1962.

be described in the following way: the African delegates, with few exceptions, were dominated by emotional responses rather than reasoned positions; they lacked critical capability. Their tendency to accept Soviet statements at face value, especially where criticism of the West was involved, was no doubt conditioned by their bitterness toward colonialism, their suspicion and hatred of the Western Powers, and their lack of trained, experienced elites. The Asian states, on the other hand, were to a large extent free of these distorting propensities.

Neutralists are wary of Soviet methods and often weary of hearing of Soviet achievements, but generally they regard Moscow as well intentioned. Gaining a good press is easy for the Soviets in ECAFE: they concentrate on advertising their wares and supporting projects favored by the neutralists. The list is long but requires little, if any, financial outlay; for example, support for the proposed Asian Institute for Economic Development, an offer to organize a two-week seminar in Moscow on planning methods, and a plan to establish, equip, and staff several vocational schools in the region. The Soviets have not initiated any important proposals, but the net effect of their manifestations of interest has been good. Moscow is successfully convincing the neutralists of its deepening interest. It is sending higher-echelon officials to ECAFE meetings, and its technocrats show to advantage in the technical committees.

Occasionally, neutralists imply a sympathy for the view that the USSR may be more attuned to their aspirations than the West, because it, too, until recently, was an underdeveloped country that suffered considerably and achieved industrial eminence by dint of its own labor and sacrifice. More to the point, they believe that Moscow's commitment to public sector investment, nationalization of industry, and economic planning is in line with their approach. They note that the United States did not, until lately, show much sympathy for economic planning, which has gained universal acceptance among underdeveloped countries. Also, the West has generally taken a conservative, go-slow position on matters which the ECAFE Secretariat and the Executive-Secretary have urged, e.g. for a long time, the United States opposed holding intra-regional trade talks on the ground that they would prejudice the extension of multilateralism and the expansion of international trade; also, the Western Powers opposed the establishment of the Steel and Industrial Committees, saying such developments were premature given the level of economic development of ECAFE countries. Whatever the merit of Western arguments, they made poor politics. The Soviets, in supporting the Secretariat and the neutralists on these issues, appeared to be in the vanguard of future lines of approach. The neutralists do believe that the United States wants to help solve the problems of the area; but they say that, though the caloric content of the Soviet and American menus may be the same, the dishes served by the Soviets are more palatable to local tastes.

ECAFE meetings may seem far removed from the global struggle of the Great Powers. To member nations, however, ECAFE is important as a clearing house for information and exchanges designed to promote the region's economic development; furthermore, it serves to nurture a sense of regional consciousness. Members know that ECAFE is a battleground in the context of a broader struggle but hope that Asia may, in time, become strong enough to take its destiny into its own hands. The present weakness of ECAFE is to a great extent a reflection of the region which it serves.

V

The USSR and the IAEA

SINCE its establishment on October 23, 1956, the International Atomic Energy Agency (IAEA) has received concentrated Soviet attention. The Agency's purpose—the promotion of peaceful uses of atomic energy—endows it with singular political significance because of the ever-present possibility that recipient nations might divert the fissionable material to the manufacture of nuclear weapons. Because it encourages the ambitions of the underdeveloped countries, who see in the atom the Aladdin's lamp to rapid economic development and technological progress, the Agency has become another battleground in the pervasive Soviet-Western struggle for the allegiance of these politically strategic countries. Probably it has engendered more controversy and disillusionment than any other Specialized Agency; perhaps because the promise was so great, the dissatisfaction has been so intense. The potential of the atom is unlimited but the patience of the underdeveloped nations is not, and the Soviets play on this fact of international life. Moscow has been quick to exploit their desires for nuclear technology and the Agency's inability to rise above encumbering national policies which severely limit the application of nuclear knowledge through an international framework. Analysis of Soviet behavior in the International Atomic Energy Agency involves a study of the complexities of Great Power relations and the attitudes and aspirations of the underdeveloped countries. It is a tale to which the prologue may well be the epilogue.

Background to the IAEA

In view of its responsibility for promoting economic and social development, the United Nations has moved since 1955 to extend to underdeveloped countries the budding benefits of nuclear energy in the fields of industrialization, power development, medicine, agriculture, and related areas. Thus direct UN involvement began only recently. The original impetus came from President Eisenhower's speech of December 8, 1953, to the General Assembly, in which he proposed the establishment of an International Atomic Energy Agency devoted to the cause of peace and progress, which would "begin to diminish the potential destructive power of the world's atomic stockpiles" and open new channels for peaceful uses of atomic energy, and which would work especially "to provide abundant electrical energy in the power-starved areas of the world." The speech was hailed as the most imaginative proposal for meeting the revolution in expectations of underdeveloped countries since President Truman's Point Four proposal of 1949.

Only the Soviet Union was guarded in its response. The Soviet delegate, the late Andrei Y. Vyshinsky, reflecting the preliminary comments in *Pravda* on December 22 and 26, noted that the proposal did not affect the growing atomic arms race, nor did it cover more than a small part of existing atomic materials. But he expressed the readiness of the Soviet Government to participate in discussions concerning the establishment of the new agency, provided that concurrently progress was made on Soviet disarmament proposals. Thus, during the initial period of uncertainty, Moscow linked acceptance of the Eisenhower proposal with adoption of the Soviet-sponsored plan for disarmament and prohibition of nuclear weapons. This was felt by the West to be a not too subtle attempt to obstruct and eventually to undermine the project through indirect means. But, since politically the Soviet Government could not risk being labeled obstructionist on a proposal which had received such enthusiastic support from the underdeveloped countries it was then starting to court, and since the United States Government realized that without Soviet participation the proposal would lose its potential for decreasing international tension, both governments entered into private discussions from January 2 until March 19, 1954.[1]

As the American proposals assumed more concrete form, Soviet insistence upon the accompanying prohibition on atomic weapons as a precondition for its support cast a cloud over the negotiations. Throughout the spring, Soviet Foreign Minister Vyacheslav M. Molotov remained inflexible. An intimation by President Eisenhower that the United States was prepared to push ahead without the Soviet Union brought a sharp rejoinder from *Pravda,* which wrote that such a move would intensify the arms race. On September 23, 1954, the Secretary of State, the late John Foster Dulles, reemphasized American determination in a speech before the General Assembly: "The United States is determined that President Eisenhower's proposal shall not languish until it dies. We are determined that it shall be nurtured and developed. And we shall press on in close partnership with those nations which, inspired by the ideals of the United Nations, can make this great new force a tool of humanitarianism and of statesmanship and not merely a fearsome addition to the arsenal of war."

Confronted with a phalanx of delegates favoring the proposal, Moscow shifted its approach. No longer able to prevent the Agency's establishment, it sought instead to circumscribe the Agency's sphere of competence. The day after the Dulles speech, Vyshinsky announced Moscow's willingness to

[1] For an excellent account of the negotiations leading to the establishment of IAEA see John G. Stoessinger, "Atoms for Peace" in *Organizing Peace in the Nuclear Age,* edited by Arthur Holcombe and sponsored by the Commission to Study the Organization of Peace (New York, 1959); see also Professor Stoessinger's article, "The International Atomic Energy Agency: The First Phase," *International Organization,* XIII (1959), pp. 394-411; also Bernhard G. Bechhoefer, "Negotiating the Statute of International Atomic Energy Agency," *International Organization,* XIII (Winter 1959), pp. 38-59.

forgo its previous insistence on the prohibition of the use of nuclear weapons and to proceed to immediate discussion of the American proposals. By November 12, 1954, the Soviet delegation agreed to the establishment of IAEA provided that it was placed under the Security Council and not constituted as an autonomous Specialized Agency. This arrangement was adjudged necessary because the production of atomic materials for peaceful purposes would also increase the amount available for military weapons and thus affect issues of international peace and security.

Negotiation of the Agency Statute was handled outside the UN. The negotiating group originally consisted of the United States, Great Britain, Canada, France, Belgium, Australia, Portugal, and South Africa—nations which were either advanced in nuclear technology or were substantial producers of raw materials. A preliminary draft Statute was ready by August 1955. Encouraged by the success of the International Conference on the Peaceful Uses of Atomic Energy, held in Geneva that summer, and the unofficial approval given to the draft Statute, the negotiating countries took two important steps: first, they invited the Soviet Union, India, Brazil, and Czechoslovakia to join them in drawing up the final Statute; second, they announced their intention of inviting all prospective members to an international conference on the final text of the Statute. On December 3, 1955, the General Assembly unanimously approved these steps and again called for the early establishment of the Agency.

The twelve-nation negotiating group met in Washington on February 23, 1956, and held intensive discussions for almost two months. Provision by provision, the Statute emerged in final form from the crucible of conflicting concepts, objectives, and interpretations of the structure and scope of the proposed Agency. An 81-nation conference was convened in New York in September, and on October 26 the present Statute was approved.

The International Atomic Energy Agency is an inter-governmental organization, functioning under its own Statute as an autonomous international organization and having a close-working relationship with the UN. It submits reports to the UN, coordinates its research and technical assistance operations with those of the appropriate UN bodies, and functions along lines common to all UN bodies. The Specialized Agencies recognize the primacy of IAEA in international activities concerning the peaceful uses of atomic energy. IAEA, on its part, recognizes "that certain activities involving the peaceful uses of atomic energy are within the particular competence of the Specialized Agency concerned and [that it] should recognize the right of the Specialized Agency to continue to take action in fields within its particular competence in which the application of atomic energy plays an incidental and subsidiary role."[2]

The Statute is a compromise document. The Soviet Government wanted the Agency to be subject to the Great Power veto in the Security Council; the United States favored its establishment as a Specialized Agency, free from both the potentially paralyzing veto and the pressures from the General Assembly; the Indian delegation, which has emerged as the leader of the neutralist members of IAEA, sought supervision by the General Assembly. The Statute incorporates elements of each. Thus, the Agency is required to "submit reports on its activities annually to the General Assembly"; and to submit reports to the Security Council if questions arise "that are within the competence of the Security Council . . . as the organ bearing the main responsibility for the maintenance of international peace and security." Finally, reports are also submitted to the "Economic and Social Council and other organs of the United Nations on matters within the

[2] Recommendation by the Preparatory Commission Concerning the Guiding Principles for Relationship Agreements Between the Agency and the Specialized Agencies (1956).

competence of these organs." The Agency is made up of three major bodies: a General Conference, which meets annually and at which all member nations are represented; a Secretariat, responsible for handling the Agency's administrative and operational activities; and a Board of Governors, consisting of 25 members. (The number was increased from 23 in 1963 in order to give added representation to Africa.)

Organizational Problems

The first General Conference of the International Atomic Energy Agency was held in October 1957 in Vienna, its permanent headquarters. The opening speeches were eloquent expressions of hope in the future of the Agency and in its ability to mobilize the atom for peaceful purposes. But international political experiments can rarely avoid being affected by the enmities of their creators, and organizational controversies have beset the Agency from its start.

The initial parliamentary hassle concerned the admission of Communist China and centered on Supplementary Rule G of the Provisional Rules of Procedure, which had been originally proposed by the Preparatory Commission. This rule set forth the categories of representatives who could attend General Conference sessions. They were (a) "States which have signed the Statute of the Agency but which are not Members of the Agency"; and (b) members of the United Nations and the Specialized Agencies. Citing provision (a) to buttress their position, the Soviet bloc insisted that the General Conference should be guided by the principle of universality of membership and permit any nation desiring to participate to send nonvoting observers to the Agency's proceedings; to do otherwise would reduce the effectiveness of the Agency. The Soviet bloc position was clearly stated by the Czechoslovak delegate: "The wider the cooperation the Agency obtained at the international level, and the more extensive its field of action throughout the world, the greater would be its success. It should grant equal treatment to all States regardless of their political system or their economic and social structure. There was no compelling reason for it to follow the example of the United Nations and the Specialized Agencies. The attitude adopted in the past by members of those organizations in refusing to admit certain States had not procured them any advantage. The Agency must take care not to make the same mistake; it must give evidence of a new spirit and, by not excluding any State, create conditions which would enable it to attain all its objectives."[3]

The Western Powers maneuvered to keep Communist China out. Commanding a majority both in the Conference committees and in the General Conference, they revised Rule G and placed the Agency's policy in line with that of the UN and the Specialized Agencies. The amended provision stated that only representatives of nations which are members either of the UN or of a Specialized Agency may participate in Agency meetings.

In 1957 and 1961 the appointments of a Director-General were marred by factious discussions which ill served the Agency. During the late spring and early summer of 1957, it appeared to many observers that the post would go to the well-known Swedish scientist, Dr. Harry Brynielsson, in order to emphasize the nonpolitical, scientific objectives of IAEA. Indeed, the Soviets subsequently declared that there had been an "understanding" between the United States and the Soviet Union on the appointment of Brynielsson. However, no documentary evidence which substantiates the Soviet assertion has come to this writer's attention. Careful investigation indicates that both Dr. Brynielsson and the Swedish Government were reluctant, from the beginning, to have this matter pursued. That they did not immediately issue a public statement unequivocally removing Dr. Brynielsson from further consideration may have been interpreted by a number of delegations

[3] GC.1(S)/OR. 12, p. 8.

as a sign that there was still a possibility of Brynielsson's acceptance, an ambiguity which contributed to the uncertainty and subsequent controversy surrounding the appointment of Mr. Cole.

Shortly before the opening of the first General Conference in October, the United States formally put forth the candidature of Mr. Sterling Cole, an American Congressman who had been Chairman of the Joint Committee on Atomic Energy. But the fact of Mr. Cole's candidacy had been no secret whatever and was known for many weeks by members of the Board of Governors as well as most of the members of the Conference.[4] Concerning the Soviet claim that the United States had disregarded their "understanding" to support Dr. Brynielsson, Admiral Lewis L. Strauss, at that time the Chairman of the U. S. Atomic Energy Commission and ranking representative of the United States Government in atomic energy matters, informed this writer that at no time had he "ever agreed to cast the vote of the United States for any other individual than Mr. Cole for the post of Director-General."[5] Therefore, stated Admiral Strauss, "any assertion to the effect that the United States Government reversed its position with respect to the Director-General is incorrect." With the arrival in Vienna of Admiral Strauss the die was cast. The Soviet delegate, Professor Vasily Emelyanov, said that Admiral Strauss flatly told him that the United States wanted Cole, and that it had the votes to back up its choice. "Once the question had been placed on that basis," Emelyanov noted later, "the atmosphere was no longer one of cooperation but of dictatorship."[6]

Despite misgivings, the Soviets accepted this *fait accompli* and did not raise any formal objections to Cole's appointment. But four years later, because of Khrushchev's insistence upon

---

[4] Letter from James J. Wadsworth of March 13, 1963.
[5] Letter from Admiral Lewis L. Strauss of November 20, 1962.
[6] GOV/OR. 261, p. 8.

acceptance of a troika arrangement in the allocation of UN posts, they openly fought against giving the post for a second time to a Westerner. The circumstances surrounding the 1961 appointment are even more riddled with gaps in information and controversial interpretations.

From what can be reconstructed from documents and interviews, it appears that Indonesia put forth its own candidate, Mr. Sudjarwo, in November 1960. Early in 1961, after several Western members of the Board of Governors had tried again unsuccessfully to persuade Dr. Brynielsson to accept the post of Director-General, the United States Government communicated to Moscow its intention of recommending Dr. Sigvard Eklund, the eminent Swedish scientist. According to Canadian Ambassador Wershof, "at the beginning of 1961, before the Government of the United States or any other Government had approached Dr. Eklund, it had been known that the Soviet Union had decided to support Mr. Sudjarwo, without consulting other Governments."[7] The Soviet decision to support the Indonesian candidate without prior consultation with other Governments led to inconclusive discussions at the February and March 1961 meetings of the Board of Governors. At the June meeting of the Board several neutralist delegations tried, with Soviet support, to push the candidacy of Mr. Sudjarwo. However, only Dr. Eklund obtained a substantial vote of approval, and the Board, by 17 votes to 3, with 3 abstentions, recommended him formally to the General Conference, which convened in late September. During the June-September interregnum, there were no further neutralist or Soviet representations to the United States about the possibility of a compromise candidate. At no time did they offer any other specific candidates of their own (though some diplomats in Vienna detected a desire by one leading Indian official to have himself promoted as a compromise candidate), from which the Western Powers concluded that Moscow

[7] GC(v)/OR. 57, p. 5.

sought solely to prevent Eklund's appointment and was not concerned about finding a suitably qualified candidate. Not until the September meeting of the Board of Governors, held a few days before the opening of the General Conference, did the Soviets push for reconsideration of the June decision to recommend Dr. Eklund, a move designed to exploit existing neutralist sentiment for reconsideration of the Board's nominee.

At the General Conference Moscow reacted sharply, labeling Dr. Eklund a representative of NATO and protesting that "the Agency was not an estate in which the post of Director-General could be handed on by right of succession from one representative of the West to another."[8] Emelyanov castigated the West for arguing in 1961 that the Agency needed to be led by a scientist, although during the previous four years "no delegate had ever said in the general debate that the work of the Agency would have been more productive if the Director-General had been a scientist instead of an administrator." He argued that this thesis was now being put forward "in order to place the Afro-Asian countries in a difficult position and prevent them from aspiring to leadership." In this he echoed the sentiments of a number of neutralists, including Burma, Ghana, India, Indonesia, Iraq, and the U.A.R., who requested the Board to reconsider its decision and "place before the General Conference a nomination which is acceptable without opposition."[9] Had it been adopted, the effect of the neutralist resolution would have been to delay by at least another year the appointment of a new Director-General, a circumstance which the Soviets apparently were quite willing to accept in view of their support of the resolution and their equally strong opposition to Dr. Eklund.

However, the neutralists were poorly organized and the Western voting majority, overriding all objections, approved

[8] GC(v)/OR. 56, p. 6.
[9] GC(v) 176.

Dr. Eklund. Professor Emelyanov stalked out of the meeting, saying that he "did not want to be sent back to the Agency," but the rest of the Soviet delegation remained seated throughout the episode. For a few days there were fears that a Soviet withdrawal from the Agency might be imminent, but Emelyanov's "walkout" had apparently been only the personal response of a volatile individual.

One Indian scientist, who objected bitterly to what he termed "American steam-roller tactics," expressed regret at the unwillingness of the American delegation even to have permitted a reconsideration of the Eklund candidature, adding that if the Board of Governors had still, after further discussion, thought the Swedish scientist to be the best available candidate, then the Indian Government would have supported him. He resented the "obnoxious, high-powered public relations people sent in from Washington to collar votes in the corridors with the scarcely veiled threats of cuts in United States foreign aid—a mode of lobbying which breeds contempt and hostility, and serves to split friends needlessly." An Indonesian delegate cited the incident to bolster his contention that the Soviet Union is more sympathetic than the United States toward Indonesian views and sensibilities. To him, Soviet support for Mr. Sudjarwo was more significant than the aid which Indonesia received from the Agency as a result of American contributions.

The West has fought and won several minor and passing electoral battles in the IAEA, e.g. the issue of the presidency of the General Conference (an honorific post), the composition of the Board of Governors, and the blocking of accreditation for the WFTU. These pyrrhic victories have not advanced the cause of the Agency, nor helped the West gain acceptance for its policies among the neutralist nations. They have only confirmed the Soviet image of Western insistence on domination of the Agency and brought in their aftermath a high degree of politicization rare even for international organizations.

Programs and Policies

In its first report to the General Assembly the Agency distinguished between two types of activities: those which could be undertaken promptly and inexpensively and those which required extensive planning and financial support. The first category included plans to train specialists in nuclear technology, to establish programs for the interchange of scientific information, to convene scientific conferences and seminars, and to formulate international standards in the fields of health and safety. The second category called for the development of nuclear reactors for use in power-poor underdeveloped countries.

Current dissatisfaction with the Agency stems from the belief prevailing among many neutralist countries, and encouraged by the Soviet Union, that the Agency has failed to expedite the use of nuclear power and has, instead, become too engaged, as a result of Western pressure, in the marginal aspects of atomic applications to peaceful uses and in the question of safeguards and controls. In September 1958 the second General Conference recognized the urgency of the situation and passed a resolution which emphasized that "one of the Agency's primary functions under its Statute is to assist the less developed countries," and that "the main need of the less developed countries will be for medium and small power reactors to develop their economies." It commended the Board of Governors to give early and earnest consideration to:

(a) Initiating action for a survey of the needs of the less developed countries with their consent, in the matter of nuclear power generation plants suitable for their specific circumstances;

(b) Adopting measures so that a continuing study be made of the development of the technology and economics of small and medium scale nuclear power reactors which may be suited for the economic development of less developed countries;

(c) Disseminating [information pertaining to the above];
(d) Assisting the less developed countries in planning and implementing their training programmes at their request so that they may have, as soon as possible, adequate numbers of scientists, technicians, and engineers to take full advantage of the developments in the technology and utilization of small and medium scale power reactors.[10]

ATOMS FOR POWER: HOW SOON?

The most important long-term issue confronting the Agency centers on the extension of nuclear power reactors to underdeveloped countries. The United States and its allies note that, though nuclear power holds great promise for the future of the economies of power-poor countries, its present cost, which includes the larger initial capital investment needed for the power station, is so much higher than that of conventional power as to preclude its widespread application. They agree that every effort should be made to place nuclear power on a competitive economic basis with conventional fuels, i.e. coal, oil, hydroelectric power. But in the meantime, underdeveloped countries are advised to concentrate on training the necessary scientists and technicians, developing competence in the application of the atom in agriculture, medicine, and biology, and working to build a sound economic and technological foundation for the eventual utilization of nuclear power reactors.[11]

This Western partiality to the gradualist approach at a time of increasing disparity in wealth between the developed nations of the West and the underdeveloped nations of Afro-Asia and Latin America helps to account for the inability of the West to capture the sympathy of elites in most under-

[10] GC(II)/RES/27.
[11] The speech delivered by Dr. Glen Seaborg, the United States delegate at the sixth General Conference, is illustrative of the Western position. GC(VI)/OR. 66, pp. 7-16.

developed countries. Speeches by American delegates in IAEA are usually sound and sober; they are competent appraisals of the complex problems facing underdeveloped countries in their quest for nuclear power, but they lack a sense of urgency. Western prescriptions are devoid of political potency or emotional appeal. They call for hard work and constrained expectations; they offer no cure-all for economic backwardness. True, many countries accept Western advice, but they do so not necessarily because of conviction, but because the West is footing the bill.

One should not underestimate the political and psychological appeal of nuclear power reactors. A decade ago the underdeveloped countries wanted steel mills, even though they may have lacked coal, iron, and other prerequisites; a steel plant was the status symbol of industrial power and modernization. Today, nuclear power reactors exert an even greater attraction. They represent the latest technological advances and reinforce visions of rapid, uninterrupted economic development which would solve the economic and social ills of society in the shortest possible time. The reasoned arguments with which Western spokesmen appraise the feasibility of nuclear power for underdeveloped countries find no enthusiastic response. Western officials too often sound like those who, having themselves achieved a measure of prosperity and affluence, can afford to advocate progress at a snail's pace and to counsel patience and fortitude to others who thirst for change and are unconcerned with the niceties of orderly progress. Psychologically, they give, almost by default, the mantle of leadership in this field to the Soviet Union.

Moscow has taken an unequivocal stand by insisting that "the essential function of the Agency lay in the assistance it could give in the atomic field to the less developed countries, so that the present disparity between the industrial and the nonindustrial countries might be reduced."[12] The Agency,

[12] GC(II)/OR. 17, p. 10.

it held, should not become a center for fundamental research or a broker for technicians and seminars; rather, it must help underdeveloped countries build nuclear reactors. The vulnerability of the Agency to Soviet-bloc criticisms is immeasurably heightened by the fact that no nuclear power reactors have yet been built in Afro-Asian neutralist countries with Agency funds or assistance. On the other hand, it should be noted that the Soviets have not demonstrated any readiness to contribute funds to the Agency that would make possible an extensive program of reactor construction.

What the Soviets shrewdly do is capitalize on the unsatisfied aspirations of underdeveloped countries, including some which are allied with the West. At the second General Conference, the Pakistani delegate emphasized that "power generation was in fact essential for developing the resources of an underdeveloped country and for raising the standard of living of its people. Where the conventional sources of energy were inadequate, impractical, or uneconomic, it was necessary that they should be supplemented by nuclear power."[13] The Burmese, Egyptian, Ceylonese, and Moroccan delegates seconded these remarks. The Moroccan delegate noted that all power used in his country was expensive, the average cost of electricity in the arid areas being more than six times the cost in areas having access to some reasonably inexpensive fuel. Therefore, the high cost of nuclear power was not a deterrent and nuclear reactors could, he concluded, compete favorably with other fuels in such situations. Reinforcing these views, Professor Emelyanov has written that "United States monopolies are against developing atomic energy cheaply because they now have ample fuel resources" and want to keep nuclear development in its infancy to keep their profits on conventional fuels high.[14]

[13] GC(II)/OR. 19, p. 12.
[14] Vasily Emelyanov, "Marking Time," *New Times,* No. 47 (November 1960), p. 11.

The more Western spokesmen defended the Agency's approach—to develop programs for training the scientists and engineers needed to operate the reactors which will be built in underdeveloped countries when they become economically feasible—the more they carped on the economic and expensive character of small reactors, the sharper grew the criticisms of the underdeveloped countries and the attacks of the Soviet bloc, and the more pronounced became the divisions in IAEA along bloc lines. Soviet delegates assailed the Agency for its procrastination and for its failure to put "one gram of fissionable material at the disposal of countries needing it." Their contention that the West and the Western-dominated Board of Governors—the executive policy-making organ of IAEA—are intent upon transforming the Agency into an organization primarily occupied with overseeing safeguards and controls has gained widespread acceptance among the neutralists.

By adopting an impatient and radical stand, Moscow escapes criticism for its opposition to the constructive but less ambitious Western proposals. For example, in 1958 the United States proposed the establishment in Vienna of a permanent laboratory with the latest research facilities, to serve as the Center for the Agency's research and training. The Soviet Government refused to contribute, allegedly because it opposed the diverting of Agency resources from the paramount goal of building nuclear reactors, the goal toward which all else had to be subordinated. This withholding of financial support did not upset the underdeveloped countries who have yet to derive much benefit from the laboratory which began operations in 1961. Their appetite for reactors remains unchanged. Moscow talks continually of the pressing need for rapid economic development, for the application of the atom to the energy needs of power-poor countries, and for proportionately greater investment in the public sector. It derides the implication of the Western position, that underdeveloped countries are not competent to operate nuclear reactors, a view which they vehemently reject, maintaining that with proper supervision they can learn-while-doing. Such Soviet statements elicit appreciation, for they seemingly signify Moscow's greater sensitivity to the psycho-political objectives of underdeveloped nations. In this realm of conference behavior the Soviets often display a "feeling for the jugular" which makes for effective public relations.

The Soviet position has a double purpose—one, propaganda, the other, political and economic. First, by echoing the belief, popular among underdeveloped countries, that nuclear fuel is in many situations nearly competitive with conventional fuels, Moscow places itself squarely behind the neutralists and against the Western Powers who insist that this view is premature. Second, and perhaps of greater long-term significance, by aiding politically important neutralist countries to build experimental reactors now, thereby leading them to commit valuable portions of their scarce supply of available investment capital to nuclear projects, Moscow adds several more silken links to their ties with the Soviet bloc. Friendship with Moscow becomes that much more a political and economic imperative for these countries. A deterioration in relations could jeopardize their nuclear development because of their dependence upon the Soviet Union for fabricating components not manufactured in the recipient country. Spare parts loom large in the thinking of any country embarking on a program of industrialization which depends primarily upon foreign imports of machinery. The purchase of heavy machinery places the less developed country in a vulnerable position with respect to the supplying nation. This is especially true in the case of complex, intricate nuclear power reactors. In the event of political difficulties, the less developed country might find its supply of spare parts reduced seriously or cut off completely, thereby subjecting its economy to costly losses and dislocation. Hence the inducement to political friendship that inveigles a heavy borrower who cannot easily find alternate sources, or who knows he is dealing with a Government that has no compunctions about playing a squeeze game. Egypt encountered such a situation during 1959-1960 when, at a time of tension arising from Soviet criticism of President Nasser's handling of local Communists, Moscow held up the supply of spare parts needed for heavy machinery and for the ceramics plant being constructed by the Czechs.

Even before the Statute was adopted in October 1956, the Soviet Government, as part of its foreign aid program, embarked on a policy designed to make the Soviet Union the principal benefactor of neutralist countries seeking nuclear reactors. It quickly signed agreements to build small experimental reactors for Egypt and Yugoslavia, and thereafter for Ghana, Indonesia, and Iraq. General Agreements for the peaceful uses of atomic energy have been signed with India and other neutralist countries. Moscow has sought to retain the initiative, to demonstrate to the neutralists that it, not Washington, is prepared to undertake the construction of reactors in Afro-Asian states.

It would be an error to assume that most neutralists accept at face value all Soviet professions of disinterested concern and their sanguine estimates concerning the present applicability of nuclear reactors to the power needs of underdeveloped countries. Just as the helpful actions of the Western Powers often efface the impressions left by their delegates, so do the trifling financial offers of the Soviet Union in the Agency frequently vitiate the favorable impression made by Soviet speeches. The discrepancy between the optimistic views propounded by Soviet officials in public and their realistic evaluations given in private has been clearly evident, for example, on the question of whether nuclear fuels are competitive. Several members of the Secretariat stated that, in private talks, the Soviets show full awareness of the difficulties and expense presently limiting attempts to introduce nuclear reactors on a wide scale in underdeveloped countries.

Yet, sensing the eagerness of the underdeveloped countries, and the opportunity for depreciating the value of current Agency programs, they have staked out a position popular with the neutralists and have disputed Western and Secretariat analyses that nuclear power is "not yet generally economic." The Soviets have associated themselves completely with the views of the Indian delegation, the leading proponent of building reactors in underdeveloped countries and, by virtue of its own advanced atomic energy program, the generally acknowledged leader of the neutralist bloc in the Agency. Indeed, that Soviet delegates implicitly acceded to the leadership of the Indian Government on this issue can be seen from the frequency with which they quoted in their own speeches, examples and experiences previously cited by Indian officials.

Neutralist officials also realize that the Soviet Union either is not devoting much attention to the problem of reducing the capital costs of nuclear power stations (the major item of expense) or is not prepared to share its advances with other nations. For example, at the Agency's Conference on Small and Medium Power Reactors, convened in Vienna from September 5-9, 1960, to discuss what could be done to reduce their cost, the Soviet Government did not make any recommendations nor present any information regarding what was being done in the Soviet Union. Again, at the February 1961 session of the Board of Governors, the Soviet delegate, Professor Emelyanov, criticized the Agency for recommending that El Salvador abandon plans to construct a nuclear reactor because of the uneconomic character of that type of power for the country. "Studies had been made," he asserted, "of the economic feasibility of using 12, 20, and 50 MW nuclear stations in various regions of the Soviet Union, and it had been found that such power plants would be advantageous in several areas."[15] This statement elicited the immediate interest of the American delegate who observed that "the work that had

[15] GOV/OR. 231, p. 4.

been done, and was being done in the Soviet Union was obviously of great importance, and the Agency could benefit greatly from full knowledge of that work. Could more detailed information," he asked, "be given to the Agency, with a view toward helping the less developed countries?"[16] Emelyanov's reply marked a considerable retreat from his previous statement. Volunteering no information concerning the cost of the reactors, he modified his remarks by noting that "Soviet experience showed that small nuclear power plants competed favorably with small thermal plants *in certain circumstances, although certainly not always*" (italics added). In substance, therefore, his position differed little from that of the West.

The strongest case for providing nuclear power reactors now to underdeveloped countries has consistently been made by the Indian delegation, headed by Dr. Homi Bhabha, a noted physicist and Chief of the Government of India Department of Atomic Energy. Dr. Bhabha has often dismissed the high-cost argument as irrelevant and based on a superficial evaluation of the situations existing in underdeveloped countries. At the second General Conference, he observed that: "The problem facing the less industrialized areas was not that of the high cost of power but rather that of there being practically no power at all, unless atomic energy were utilized. For all those areas, at least in the immediate future, small 20 megawatt power stations would prove very useful even if the power produced by those stations was more expensive than that produced by large stations. Moreover, it had to be remembered that the areas in question were, in any case, used to high cost power."[17] Adding that nothing had been done despite periodic resolutions by the General Conference, he called upon the Agency to facilitate the reactor building program. At another session, Dr. Bhabha deplored the lack of interest shown by the Great Powers in making nuclear energy

[16] *Ibid.*, p. 6.
[17] GC(II)/OR. 21, p. 22.

commercially competitive, although "the expenditure on the development of military uses of atomic energy throughout the world is running at about the ratio of 100:1 with the expenditure on peaceful purposes."[18] Citing the experience of India to show that the cost of energy from nuclear fuel was already less than the cost of energy from conventional fuel in many situations, he urged the Agency to direct its resources toward developing nuclear reactor technology and helping underdeveloped countries to build reactors with which to train their scientists and technicians.

In June 1962 a State Department advisory committee, noting that "nuclear power is on the verge of becoming of practical importance in various parts of the world" and will be used increasingly around the world, recommended that the United States give greater support to the Agency in promoting the development and construction of nuclear power reactors.[19] Only time can tell whether this recommendation will be translated into an effective policy.

THE CASE OF THE UNUSED U-235

On October 1, 1957, at the first session of the General Conference, the American delegate announced that the United States Government had made available for acquisition by the Agency 5,000 kilograms of contained U-235 and that President Eisenhower would increase that amount by adding to it again as much as all other nations might place at the Agency's disposal by July 1960. Ten days later, the Soviet delegate announced his Government's offer of 50 kilograms. Other uranium-producing countries later followed with modest offers, so that the Agency had available 5,140 kilograms of U-235 during the 1958-1963 period. This amount is sufficient to operate between 500 and 600 medium-size nuclear power

[18] GC(v)/OR. 55, p. 7.
[19] Report of the Advisory Committee on U. S. Policy Toward the International Atomic Energy Agency (Washington, D. C.: Department of State, May 19, 1962), pp. 5-6.

211

reactors, a number many times more than the most optimistic estimates made for reactor construction by underdeveloped countries for the coming generation. Prior to 1962 no uranium for reactors had been allocated to any underdeveloped country (Pakistan became the first to sign in agreement in March 1962); and to date none has been used by any neutralist country of Africa, Asia, and the Middle East. The foremost obstacle has been the unwillingness of Afro-Asian neutralists to accept the accompanying safeguards and controls required by IAEA.

In a major article in the October 18, 1957 issue, *Izvestiia* denigrated the American offer because it was made "on a commercial basis," while lauding the Soviet offer for its willingness to sell the uranium at the lowest price prevailing in the international market. In ensuing sessions, Soviet delegates reiterated the theme that "the Agency should not be a commercial organization enabling those who provided materials and equipment for the Agency to make profits. Otherwise, the Agency would hardly be in a position to offer disinterested assistance to underdeveloped countries, which would then have to find other ways of satisfying their requirements."[20] They contrasted, on the one hand, "capitalist" United States offering to sell fissionable materials at exorbitant commercial prices which would bring profit at both ends of the business deal: profit for the seller and dependence of the buyer; and on the other hand, "socialist" Soviet Union eager to assist underdeveloped countries, scorning commercial gain by offering to sell at the lowest prices prevailing on the world market. Despite the fact that their offer of 50 kilograms was unimpressive quantitatively, the Soviets, by sounding less commercial, gained politically, particularly since they coupled their offer with a willingness to accept minimal Agency safeguards. On this latter point the Soviets made their biggest political gains.

[20] GC(II)/OR. 17, p. 11.

For a time, this theme made good Soviet propaganda. But there was never a real issue. During the Agency's early years, world prices, that is the prices charged by the United States Government, were high (relatively speaking, for they have since been lowered) because at the time nuclear materials were in short supply, expensive to process, and it was thought they would continue to be hard to obtain. The amounts which the United States Government "sold" to the Agency were charged against the quantity of fuel the U. S. had agreed to make available to IAEA,[21] and the prices were pegged at an artificial level, since they were fixed by government and not subject to competition. All prices for nuclear materials are controlled by government and are artificial, since it is almost impossible to calculate accurately what would be a fair price, i.e. cost plus a reasonable profit. Furthermore, the stated Soviet willingness to sell "at the lowest prices prevailing on the international market" was nonsense, since there was no commercial trading in U-235 and no price differential to be negotiated. The Soviets made the offer to sound generous and to make propaganda out of their charge that existing levels were set high in order to assure substantial profits for big business (which in the Soviet lexicon is synonymous with government). But the whole question was academic, because, according to Agency officials, the price of U-235 never constituted a serious barrier to purchases from the Agency.

Inexplicably, none have questioned Soviet motives publicly in IAEA on this issue. Why, for example, if the Soviet Government was so desirous of disinterestedly assisting underdeveloped countries, did it not offer to sell the modest quantity of uranium which it made available to the Agency at *cost*, rather than "at the lowest price on the international market?" It is, after all, not bound by "capitalist" price levels. Unless,

[21] There is no monetary relationship between the value of this material and the voluntary contributions *of money* to the Agency's General Fund.

of course, Soviet acceptance of these levels is a tacit admission that they are not glaringly out of line with the cost of production, processing, and distribution. As the matter stood, if international price quotations were, as they alleged, exorbitantly high, then the Soviets still expected to earn a considerable profit on their proposed sale to IAEA, because the differential between the lowest and the highest price was nonexistent. To this date, no nuclear fuel has been purchased through the Agency from the Soviets, who have never stated the specific price at which they are prepared to "sell." Nor have they ever made public the prices which they have charged the neutralists who purchased nuclear material and equipment from the USSR on a bilateral basis. When a country seeks nuclear fuel, it is for a specific type of reactor. No country working through Agency channels has yet requested a Soviet reactor, hence there has been no need for Soviet fuel elements. The reactors which the Soviets are building in neutralist countries are the result of bilateral negotiations, which also cover the purchase of fuel. Only one country—Finland—has requested Soviet assistance through the Agency. Commenting on this incident, one Agency official said that "Finland requested a critical assembly reactor from the Soviet Union at the same time that she requested one from the West. But she never heard anything further from the Soviets."

For several years, Western spokesmen interpreted the failure of underdeveloped countries to purchase fissionable material from the Agency as a consequence of the changed supply conditions in the world market—from one of scarcity to one of surplus. When President Eisenhower made his proposal, there was a severe shortage of reactor fuels, but as new deposits of uranium have been discovered and extraction techniques have improved, the facts of supply have altered. Against this new background in the world uranium market, the hope, often expressed by Western officials, that underdeveloped countries would still seek to satisfy their requirements through the Agency rather than through bilateral channels has had a hollow, politically unrealistic sound. The cost of U-235 is not the deterrent factor; the political price demanded by Agency safeguards and controls, *that* is the deterrent. Dr. Bhabha held that, given abundant supply conditions, the Agency could play "a useful and practical role only if it is prepared to offer terms no less advantageous than those of its competitors." But he warned that "if the Agency burdens itself with a cumbersome and expensive safeguards system, and one which raises difficulties for recipient countries, it can only blame itself if these countries turn to other suppliers or prefer to exploit, even at greater expense, domestic sources of supply."[22]

When one considers the 5,140 kilograms available to the Agency, not to mention the staggering amount in the possession of the major nuclear powers, then the little more than 300 kilos which have been used in international trade since the dawn of the atomic age suggests the magnitude of the problems still to be faced. On April 2, 1962, Mr. Sterling Cole, former Director-General of IAEA, speaking before the League of Republican Women in Washington, D. C., stressed this point: "Recently this government at Geneva offered to dedicate 55 tons (55,000 kilograms) of contained U-235 to peaceful purposes—a very impressive and generous offer but it is completely meaningless when we stop to consider that the only possible peacetime use for this material is as an enrichment for nuclear fuel in a power reactor. Therefore, in order to give some life and meaning to this offer we must take the next and necessary step by devising a method by which this material can actually be put to work for peace: otherwise our offer is empty and senseless." All nations agree that IAEA will never become a major supplier of nuclear fuel until the issue of safeguards and controls is settled. Unless it is resolved soon to the satisfaction of the neutralist countries, the Agency

[22] GC(III)/OR. 28, p. 16.

faces a future limited to educational and informational activities.

AGENCY SAFEGUARDS: PRINCIPLES AND POLITICS

No other issue has raised controversy comparable to that surrounding the application of safeguards and controls to fissionable materials provided by the Agency. Around it swirls the Cold War and the East-West competition for neutralist support. For IAEA, its future as an international organization hangs in the balance—to grow or to stagnate; for neutralists, inviolable issues are involved—repugnance to politically discriminatory conditions and possible infringements of national sovereignty, and a desire for *de facto* recognition of the equality of all members in regard to Agency policy; for the West, a bid for international acceptance of its views on inspections is implicated, not only for nuclear power factors but for disarmament as well.

Under a mandate from the General Conference, the Board of Governors drew up the principles which guide the Agency's application of safeguards, meant to ensure that no nuclear material supplied by the Agency would be diverted to military purposes. The Soviet bloc and many neutralists argued that the General Conference should discuss the principles *before* the Western-dominated Board submitted its recommendations for final approval, but they were outvoted by the Western majority. On April 17, 1960, after more than a year of consideration, the Board submitted its proposed Agency Safeguards to the General Conference, where final approval was forthcoming at the fall session—once again over the opposition of the Soviet and neutralist blocs.

The position of the United States is that the Agency Safeguards are necessary as reasonable assurance that Agency assistance would not be used to further any military purpose, and as an important first step which would lend encouragement and a tangible promise to Great Power disarmament negotiations: "Such a system would show the world that it was possible to conclude an international agreement providing for the application of safeguards and inspection by international inspectors; and that would represent a step towards an international disarmament agreement. It would be further evidence that States recognized and accepted international regulations and order. . . ."[23] The Soviet delegation held, to the contrary, that as long as the production of nuclear weapons continued, the establishment of safeguards would only create the illusion that the first step had been taken toward disarmament when, in fact, "not even the smallest step had been taken toward solving the problem."[24] It reaffirmed its support, in principle, for a system of safeguards and controls, but maintained that the system adopted for the Agency was out of all proportion to the amount of assistance it rendered.

The Soviet Government sided with the neutralists in insisting that controls be kept to a minimum, that they not be discriminatory, and that they, under no circumstances, infringe on national sovereignty. In effect, the Soviets argued for no controls. During early IAEA sessions, they derided the West for its concern over safeguards at a time when the Agency had yet to build or finance its first nuclear reactor, and they unalterably opposed any move which would have the effect of transforming IAEA into a supervisory body rather than one devoted to practical programs of assistance, alleging that this would divide member nations into two categories: "countries exercising supervision and countries subject to supervision." Though acknowledging that the failure of underdeveloped countries to apply to the Agency for nuclear fuel or for assistance in building reactors might, in part, be due to their lack of experience in nuclear matters, to shortages of trained personnel, and to the expense, the Soviets placed the main emphasis for the virtual boycott of the Agency on the strict

[23] GOV/OR. 197, p. 7.
[24] GC(iv)/OR. 44, p. 6.

control which it sought to exercise over the assistance it provided. They ridiculed Western fears of diversion of nuclear materials to military purposes, observing that no underdeveloped countries would be in a position to engage in such activities, whereas the countries imposing controls on others would themselves not be subject to them since they did not need the Agency's help: ". . . requests for assistance in the form of fissionable materials and facilities will mostly come from less developed countries which do not possess a developed industry and are unable to manufacture nuclear weapons. On the one hand, countries which do possess such facilities are not and will not be the recipients of Agency assistance, and will subsequently be outside the range of that control upon which some countries—be it noted, incidentally, countries which will in fact not be subject to control themselves—are insisting. Thus the Agency's safeguards system is of no possible use as a means of controlling countries which are intent on embarking upon a nuclear rearmament programme."[25]

The most comprehensive statement of the Soviet position was made by V. M. Molotov. The old Bolshevik, exiled as Ambassador to Outer Mongolia after having failed in his challenge to Khrushchev's control of the Party in June 1957, was assigned to Vienna less than two years later, where he remained as permanent representative to IAEA until October 1961, when he returned to Moscow to attend the Twenty-second Party Congress and thereafter faded into an unspecified obscurity. He presented the case against the Agency Safeguards proposal with the telling belligerence and skill that had won him the grudging respect of Western diplomats and had led John Foster Dulles to describe him as the ablest negotiator he had ever encountered.[26] Dismissing the Western view that the safeguards system would help prevent the pro-

[25] GC(III)/OR. 27, p. 8.

[26] John Foster Dulles, *War or Peace* (New York: The Macmillan Company, 1953), pp. 27-29.

liferation of countries manufacturing nuclear weapons, he said that "however ingenious the proposed system of control and supervision might be, it did not prohibit receiving countries from manufacturing nuclear weapons"; nor would it prevent countries which had no need to apply to the Agency for assistance from producing weapons. The Western-formulated document was nothing but a reflection of the unacceptable Western position on disarmament: "The policy adopted by those who advocated the Agency's safeguards system—supervision first, assistance afterwards—was the same policy as the Western Atomic Powers and their allies adopted to disarmament, that of raising obstacles to disarmament and obstructing any measure likely to hinder them from continuing the armaments race."[27] He associated himself with the Indian position that the voluntary acceptance by a recipient of the responsibility not to use Agency assistance for military purposes should be adequate at the present stage in the Agency's activities. It was clear, he held, that the United States was trying to transform the Agency into a control instrument to prevent the nuclear development of underdeveloped countries from threatening the profitable activities of Western monopolies.

[These arguments have been posed by the USSR in disarmament talks concerned with the problem of devising an "adequate" inspection system. Inherent in Moscow's rejection of the Western position is not only an irreconcilable suspicion of Western motives and trustworthiness, and an unwillingness to open the Soviet Union to international inspection (which is regarded as a front for American espionage), or to commit Soviet security to non-Communist institutions, but also the Soviet conviction that a Power intent on circumventing the controls could not be detected, or even deterred through fear of detection. Soviet leaders often paraphrase Stalin's cynical rejoinder to a Westerner's remark about the influence of the

---

[27] GC(iv)/COM.2/OR. 19, p. 7.

Pope in international affairs: "How many divisions does the Pope command?" Here they might ask, "Whom, after all, do international control commissions and inspectors command?"]

From IAEA debates, the Soviet Union emerges as the Great Power most sympathetic to the political apprehensions and aspirations of the underdeveloped nations; by opposing stringent Agency safeguards and incorporating negligible controls in its bilateral agreements with these countries, the USSR has demonstrated a willingness, in practice as well as in theory, to accept the pledge of recipients that they will not use for military purposes the fissionable material which they receive. Playing upon continuing fears of neo-colonialism and monopoly domination, it finds a receptive audience to its warning that "the nascent atomic industry in these countries could easily become dependent on various companies and corporations in the countries which are technologically most advanced. What purport to be safeguards against the possibility of producing atomic weapons would really become economic controls over the development of atomic industry and science in the less developed countries, and possibly over their economies as a whole."[28]

An added dividend accrues to the Soviet Union—support for its position on disarmament. By deemphasizing the control features, by stressing the need for mutual trust and good will, and by using its bilateral nuclear agreements with neutralist countries as examples, Moscow seeks to establish the workability of its disarmament proposals.

On occasion even allies of the United States cautioned against inflexible, excessive emphasis on safeguards and controls. A French delegate warned "that control had psychological and political as well as purely technical aspects. Flexibility and some measure of empiricism, taking into account in particular the stage of development reached by the receiving

[28] GC(III)/OR. 27, p. 11.

countries, were essential if it was desired that the Agency should be asked for substantial assistance."[29]

In its criticisms, the Soviet bloc, joined by most neutralists, has followed the lead of India, which does not need nuclear assistance from either the Agency, the Soviet Union, or the West. It is the Indian delegation which has had the greatest impact on the position of the neutralist countries. Their criticisms are as cogent and extensive as any made by the Soviet Union, and their effect upon the neutralist countries is greater. Dr. Bhabha expressed prevailing neutralist sentiment when he stated that "if the nuclear powers are unwilling to accept effective safeguards, whatever the reasons, how can they expect other countries to accept them? If the reasons for not accepting safeguards are good enough for the nuclear countries, the other countries will naturally tend to be suspicious, if they alone are asked to accept them. The history of colonialism is not such as to inspire confidence on this point among those who have suffered from its effect." On several occasions he observed that the system of safeguards "was intended, to use an analogy, to ensure that not the slightest leakage took place from the sides of the vessel while ignoring the fact that the vessel had no bottom. Even today, although, or perhaps because, attention continues to be focused on the sides of the vessel, it still has no bottom."[30]

Dr. Bhabha pointed out that even while the Statute was being negotiated there was deep-rooted opposition among many countries to the safeguards provisions, and acceptance of the Statute by the Government of India had been assured by inclusion of the Indian suggestion that the responsibility for applying safeguards be exercised only "to the extent relevant." The Indian Government interpreted this to mean, so far as nuclear material was concerned, simply a statement from the recipient country that the material would be used

[29] GC(III)/OR. 28, p. 9.
[30] GC(III)/OR. 30, p. 17.

solely for peaceful purposes. Meanwhile, the matter could be kept under continuing review and more elaborate procedures considered if circumstances warranted. Dr. Bhabha had urged the Board of Governors, in drawing up the principles on which the Agency's safeguards would rest, to refrain from attaching onerous conditions to material purchased from the Agency, lest prospective buyers deal elsewhere and the Agency atrophy. Safeguards should be devised in such a manner, he argued "that even those countries which do not require assistance from the Agency would be prepared to buy uranium through the Agency. It cannot be too strongly emphasized that the effectiveness of the safeguards system is a function not only of its intensity but of its coverage. Perfection is sterile when it applies to nothing."[31]

He also observed that, as the Indian delegation had indicated at the time of the Agency's establishment, the proposed safeguards imposed undue burdens upon those countries which were not in a position to manufacture nuclear weapons, while leaving unaffected those who were either already producing them or were capable of doing so. At a later session, he carried his argument one step further. Not only should the burden of safeguards not fall on the less developed countries who were not in a position to create a nuclear weapon threat, but the safeguards must not be used to justify a theoretical political proposition which had never before been shown to work: namely, if a viable inspection system could be devised, nations would be willing to disarm. Dr. Bhabha dismissed the "first-step" argument propounded by the American delegation, that safeguards should be instituted by the Agency with respect to nuclear reactors to demonstrate to the world their applicability in the field of disarmament: "He doubted very much whether that would serve any useful purpose, and thought that a false sense of security and com-

[31] *Ibid.*

placency would result from adopting a system which would bring under safeguards only those national programs which were a long way from the capacities required for the manufacture of nuclear weapons. His delegation therefore believed that the establishment of a safeguards system was inherently part of the problem of nuclear disarmament. If the nuclear powers were unwilling to accept effective safeguards, they could not expect other countries to accept them."[32] In a bit of philosophical rumination, he offered that "the problem before the world was not to put a puppy into a cage in order to ensure that when it grew up it would not bite someone; the problem was how to cage the tiger of nuclear armament which now roamed the world."[33]

America has been slow to allay the apprehensions of the neutralists. One American delegate cited situations in which similar procedures had already been carried out by the United States in conjunction with its bilateral nuclear aid programs without any objections thus far being raised by the recipients. He "advised those who still felt some concern on that score and who might want to know whether their concern was justified, to ask the advice of the countries where an inspection had been made by the U. S. Atomic Energy Commission."[34] But neutralists continue to view Agency Safeguards as skeptically as ever. In answer to my query, one Indian official wrote: "Even if a country accepts safeguards, what is the machinery which would be capable of enforcing them, should that country subsequently decide to renounce them and divert whatever assistance it may have received to military purposes? How would inspections obviate such an eventuality? In our estimation, there is no satisfactory reply to these questions. At most inspections may only be able to eliminate an element of surprise, if a country decides on the switch-over.

[32] GC(iv)/OR. 40, p. 16.
[33] *Ibid.*, p. 17.
[34] GC(iv)/COM.2/OR. 21, p. 12.

In the ultimate analysis, therefore, one cannot help concluding that the successful implementation of an effective system of safeguards would depend preponderantly on the bona fides of nations and on very little else. The basic essential of such a system should in our view be an inherent principle of uniform applicability of the system to all nations without any discrimination whatsoever. However, until a stage is reached when confidence and trust amongst nations can be established, we concede that a system of limited safeguards is necessary but we emphatically aver that such a system cannot be onerous, unrealistic or discriminatory."[35]

As long as neutralist countries can obtain nuclear material and equipment from the Soviet bloc or can develop their own sources, as India is doing, the present system of Agency Safeguards is not likely to gain widespread acceptance or be applied operationally on any sizeable scale.

[NOTE: Supporters of the Agency have found encouragement in two recent developments. First, at IAEA's General Conference in September 1963, the Soviet delegation voted to extend Agency Safeguards to large nuclear reactors, whereas previously, the inspection procedures applied only to small reactors of less than 100 thermal megawatts. This is the first time that the Soviet Union has come out unequivocally in support of applying Agency Safeguards to nuclear facilities which have been supplied through the Agency or placed under Agency jurisdiction. Proponents of a greater role for the Agency have optimistically interpreted this as more than a token gesture to improve East-West relations in the wake of the signing of the nuclear test-ban treaty; they are hopeful that it will be an important step along the tortuous path to the establishment of an international inspection system which could perhaps be applied to an arms control agreement. But until more is known of Soviet intentions, prudence and past

[35] Letter from the Department of Atomic Energy, Government of India, March 28, 1962.

experience caution against any expansive projection of the Soviet shift on this narrow issue to larger policy questions in the nuclear field.

Second, the Indian Government has agreed to permit Agency Safeguards to be applied "at a suitable time" to the 380 megawatt nuclear power station in Tarapur, north of Bombay, the financing and construction of which was negotiated in an agreement signed by India and the United States on August 8, 1963. Since the Government of India is not opposed to the application of safeguards to the supply of fissionable material, but only to equipment, and "since the Tarapur Station will be operated only on enriched uranium supplied by the United States or on plutonium produced therefrom," the bilateral agreement was so worded as to enable each Government to maintain its basic position regarding the attachment of safeguards to equipment.[36] The agreement does not directly strengthen the Agency, but it could serve a beneficial purpose.

---

[36] See the Joint Press Statement of the U. S. and Indian Governments issued on June 29, 1963, which was quoted in a letter of July 22, 1963, to this writer from the Department of Atomic Energy, Government of India. The Statement also noted that "the U.S.-Indian arrangement would include an agreement in principle that, at a suitable time, the Agency will be requested to enter into a trilateral agreement for the implementation of the safeguard provisions in the proposed bilateral agreement subject to the following conditions: After the Agency has adopted a system of safeguards for large reactors, and at a reasonable time to be mutually agreed, the U. S. and India will consult with each other to determine whether the system so adopted is generally consistent with the provisions in the bilateral agreement. If the system is generally consistent, the Parties will request the Agency to enter into a trilateral arrangement covering the implementation of safeguard responsibilities. The Agreement would permit deferring implementation of the arrangement with the Agency until after the Tarapur Nuclear Power Station has achieved reliable full power operation."

From the above it can be seen that there has not been any fundamental shift in Indian policy, although the proposed bilateral agreement has so been interpreted in some Western newspapers, and that it may be a number of years before discussions for Agency inspectors are even opened.

While India would feel free to continue its general critique of Agency Safeguards as applied to equipment, it would simultaneously be indicating a willingness to accept, subject to further negotiation, international inspection of an Indian reactor—an accommodation that might lead other neutralist critics to review their position on the safeguards' issue. On the other hand, U. S. insistence upon inclusion of the provisions calling for the assignment, albeit at some future time, of an operational role for the Agency represents a timely demonstration of American support for the Agency and gives rise to the hope that the Agency might someday become a major factor in international inspection of nuclear reactors to ensure their functioning for peaceful purposes.]

Another possible complication involves the unwillingness of the Brazilian Government to accept nuclear material from the Agency for fear that it would have to admit an inspector who is a Soviet citizen. Since important factions in that country are politically left-of-center, and would not want to embarrass the Soviet Government, the Brazilian Government is in a quandary for which it has yet to find a suitable answer. The result is the bypassing of the Agency as a source of nuclear assistance.

The Soviet Union's generally permissive attitude toward safeguards and its willingness to accept the pledge of neutralists not to divert to military uses the fissionable material which they receive distinguishes Moscow's policy from Washington's, which fears the consequences of a spread of nuclear weapons to small countries. Moscow's position is less overtly apprehensive and seemingly more realistic in terms of present-day conditions. It believes that none of the neutralist countries represents a military threat to it now or in the foreseeable future. Even if some of them should decide to make their own atom bombs, they could not afford the cost of building a large enough number, or of investing in the prohibitively expensive delivery systems, without which a major nuclear attack could not be undertaken. The high cost of modern military arms has priced the poorer, less developed countries out of the running. Thus, from a military point of view, Moscow is not worried about strengthening a potential enemy; its present nuclear capability and level of sustained technological development are sufficient for it to remain unconcerned over the possible diversion of small quantities of fissionable material. Moscow does not seem to share the West's forebodings concerning the potential consequences of a multiplicity of nuclear-armed powers. It does not appear alarmed at the prospect of, let us say, Egypt and Israel, or India and Pakistan, acquiring nuclear weapons, and at the inevitable increase in military tension which could upset the present precarious stability in these areas. Except for the United States, a nuclear-armed Germany, or an industrially powerful China (which is still a decade or two away from posing a major threat to Soviet security), the USSR remains confident of its own strength.

Another factor accounting for Moscow's stand is its concept of the integral relationship between military strength and political warfare. By adopting a flexible position on the issue of nuclear power for underdeveloped countries, it strengthens its political standing in these critical areas while aggravating the conditions under which the West must function in its dealings with the neutralists. For example, in promoting the nuclear programs and military buildup of Egypt and Iraq, Moscow simultaneously encourages their traditional feud and their opposition to Western policies, both in the IAEA and in the Middle East.

The United States' aim of keeping to a minimum the number of countries possessing a nuclear capability is based on the hope that Moscow may one day agree to an arms control agreement, which would be easier to negotiate if there were relatively few nuclear powers. Though well-intentioned, it seems rather quixotic in view of the history of twentieth-century efforts at restricting the incorporation of the latest military advances into the military establishments of nation-states. Yet, no agreement can anticipate every contingency; nor can it, however skillfully framed, fulfill the purposes for which it was intended if the parties bound by the agreement are not prepared to interpret it in a spirit of accommodation and fairness.

At the February 1962 meetings of the Board of Governors, a game of musical chairs was performed with the question of whether Agency Safeguards should be applied to Japan. The United States argued against the inflexible and inappropriate application of the safeguards which they themselves had been instrumental in establishing as Agency policy, while the Soviet Union, the arch opponent of these provisions, called for their strict application.

Before there was an official system of safeguards, the Japanese Government had purchased from the Agency three tons of natural uranium, which constituted half the supply of the initial fuel loading for one reactor. The Director-General recommended that Japan be exempted from current inspection requirements because the provisions under which Japan had agreed to initial inspection of its reactor were more stringent than the Agency Safeguards operative since October 1960 (earlier, safeguards were put into effect whenever the Agency provided assistance of any kind), and because the Agency's assistance was not "substantial" within the terms of the document. The Soviet delegate observed that the document on safeguards stipulated that the Agency would take into consideration *all* nuclear materials and nuclear facilities within the purchasing country in determining whether safeguards should be applied; and he insisted that Agency Safeguards should definitely apply to the Japanese reactor, because Japan possessed all the necessary facilities for producing nuclear materials, and with "its scientific and industrial infrastructure, Japan was amongst the States Members of the

Agency best equipped for the production of nuclear weapons."[37] To Professor Emelyanov, the American position was a bit of political legerdemain. He noted that: "It was not the Soviet Union which insisted on the introduction of safeguards. The representatives of the Western Powers were however now maintaining that an exception must be made in the case of Japan and that safeguards must not be applied. At the same time they were proposing to bring under the Agency's control and apply safeguards to the four reactors in the United States. Safeguards, it was said, were not appropriate in the case of Japan but they were appropriate in the case of the research reactors in the United States. That was simply ridiculous nonsense."[38]

Emelyanov met with an unsympathetic response. The Board, including India and the other neutralist nations, decided that safeguards should not be applied to Japan because the three tons of natural uranium supplied by the Agency did not constitute "substantial" assistance, the minimum amount necessary to warrant safeguards being ten tons. Only the Soviet bloc opposed the ruling.

Too much should not be read into the Soviet position in this case, because Japan, as a political and military ally of the United States, might be expected to incur the opposition of the USSR. An isolated incident, it did not foreshadow the seeming shift in mid-1963 in Soviet attitude toward the Agency safeguard provisions. What it did indicate was that, in certain circumstances, the Soviets would be willing to invoke Agency Safeguards, if by so doing they could embarrass the United States.

Emelyanov's allusion to the United States' offer to open four small nuclear power reactors to Agency inspection is another, as yet minor, episode in the continuing controversy over IAEA inspections and controls. In October 1960 the United States

[37] GOV/OR. 279, p. 19.
[38] GOV/OR. 280, p. 5.

made the offer to the Agency in order to demonstrate the reasonableness and workability of the Agency's system of safeguards and to give Agency inspectors experience in conducting inspections; Washington sought to convince the neutralists that the presence of Agency inspectors and the application of Agency Safeguards would not result in any violation of their national sovereignty. Final agreement between the Agency and the United States was announced in March 1962, on the eve of the eighteen-nation UN Disarmament Conference. The agreement, and its timing, opened the United States to the charge of trying to persuade the neutralist members at the Conference of the merit of the American position on inspections. The Soviets labelled the entire offer undisguised propaganda: "If the Agency had to test its system of safeguards, it could do so with one of the projects in which it was a participant" instead of commencing its inspection education on projects not financed by the Agency, nor legally subject to its safeguards.[39] Professor Emelyanov charged that the United States had made the offer for patently political reasons, and that the inspections would prove nothing since they did not attack the core of objections to the Agency's inspection system: "The very fact that such a matter had been raised in the General Conference and in the Board created the dangerous illusion that the United States was beginning to curtail military production and that it intended to place plutonium-producing reactors under Agency control. However, that was far from being the case. Inspectors visiting the United States would merely be able to verify that the reactors in question were of no military importance, all that was known in advance of the inspection. . . . [The Soviet delegation] could make other comments on the draft agreement, but the main consideration was not the details and individual provisions, but the viciousness, harmfulness and illegality of the very idea of

[39] *Ibid.*, p. 13.

applying Agency safeguards to four small United States reactors."[40]

It is a regrettable, but nonetheless established, feature of Soviet policy that Moscow is not now prepared to accept any system of international inspection which involves control posts in the Soviet Union or restraints upon Soviet actions in cases where it believes that its national interests are involved. Premier Khrushchev is on record as having made it clear that "even if all the countries of the world adopted a decision which did not accord with the interests of the Soviet Union and threatened its security, the Soviet Union would not recognize such a decision and would uphold its rights, relying on force."[41] If the Soviet Union will not sign an agreement calling for controls-with-inspections—be they designed to detect nuclear explosions, missile sites, or troop concentrations—on Soviet territory, then it cannot and will not, for political and propaganda reasons, advocate such controls for the under-developed countries, in the Agency or elsewhere, as long as these countries remain opposed to such procedures.

Soviet Performance: The Record

Though the Agency's proceedings have been dominated by discussions of nuclear reactors and Agency Safeguards, a modest record has been achieved in technical assistance, training programs, and the dissemination of scientific information. The USSR evinced greater interest in these activities than it has in those conducted by most international organizations, but its record is unimpressive. The fault, say the Soviets, lies with the Agency and with the Western Powers which control it. A look at the record during the 1958-1962 period may place this allegation in proper perspective.

MONEY AND POLITICS

Agency funds are derived from two sources. First, there

[40] *Ibid.*, pp. 13-14.
[41] Khrushchev speech, July 11, 1961.

is the Regular Budget, which usually makes up about 80 per cent of the total budget and is financed by annual assessments levied against member-states at approximately the same rate as that levied by the United Nations. Out of it the administrative expenses and regular activities of the Agency are financed. Second, there is the General Fund, which is supported by the UN through the Expanded Program of Technical Assistance, by voluntary financial contributions from members of IAEA, and by donations in kind, which include equipment, the services of experts, and fellowships at national institutions of members. It is used to finance technical assistance activities and training and exchange programs, including fellowships, seminars, and research contracts. The financing of nuclear reactors would presumably come from the General Fund, though this is an assumption that has never been publicly discussed or acted upon by the membership.

The Agency's utilization of only a small fraction of Soviet-bloc contributions precipitated Soviet charges of Western discrimination and jeopardized future support. In May 1959 the Soviet Union pledged an amount equivalent to $125,000 to the General Fund, with the condition that the contribution was to be spent for nuclear equipment made in the Soviet Union and destined for use in an underdeveloped country approved by them. As with Soviet contributions to other UN technical assistance programs, the funds were offered in rubles —in a nonconvertible currency. For several years the funds were not used. Accordingly, at subsequent sessions, Soviet delegates informed the Agency that no more funds would be pledged until the amount already placed at its disposal had been utilized, and they bitterly criticized the Secretariat for its discriminatory policies. The Soviets frequently repeated their charges in the Board of Governors and at the annual sessions of the General Conference. Their argument rests essentially on the allegedly discriminatory treatment encountered on several specific projects. What follows below is a review of Moscow's case against the Agency during the 1957-1961 period.

Professor Emelyanov, the principal Soviet spokesman, declared that the United States and the American Director-General refused to use the Soviet voluntary contribution because they feared "that the appearance of Soviet equipment on the scene would damage the reputation of United States firms, concerned only with making enormous profits." He accused the Secretariat of "pursuing a policy of discrimination," of deliberately ignoring Soviet requests that the Director-General use Soviet contributions to fill members' requests for equipment, materials, and experts. He noted that early in 1960 the Soviet Union had sent a qualified expert, with catalogues of equipment, to Vienna on a special mission to negotiate with the Agency. During these negotiations, the USSR had stated its willingness to supply a wide range of equipment but had been rebuffed by the Secretariat. "He himself had long been asking the Secretariat to communicate to him the prices of equipment on sale in the Western market. He would like to be able to draw comparisons, but had not been given the necessary data."[42] At another time, he complained that:

"The Soviet Union had twice stated that it was prepared to meet Afghanistan's request for complete equipment for the Nuclear Physics Faculty of Kabul University. It had also been ready to comply with the United Arab Republic's request for equipment for medical establishments. One example of the ill will shown by the senior officials of the Agency with regard to making use of the Soviet Union's voluntary contributions was to be found in the intolerable and inexplicable delays within the Secretariat in connection with obtaining a mass spectrometer for the Agency's laboratory. That apparatus had been supplied by the Soviet Union as a voluntary contribution, i.e. free of charge, yet the Secretariat was nevertheless spending an unconscionable time collecting funds to pay for something

[42] GOV/OR. 243, p. 18.

which was being given free! Had ever such nonsense been heard.

"For its part, the Soviet Union had done everything in its power to assist the Secretariat in using its voluntary contribution. From the time that it had offered the contribution, it had made proposals to the Secretariat regarding the supply of equipment and apparatus the total value of which had been more than double that of the contribution. If the Secretariat had really wanted to use the Soviet contribution and to supply Soviet equipment to developing countries, the amount of the contribution would have been used up long since."[43]

The Secretariat has not publicly challenged this interpretation, though the facts are available to contravene Emelyanov's presentation of pertinent developments. An information paper, known as the Webb Report, was prepared under the former Director-General Sterling Cole. It presented in detail the discussions and correspondence between Soviet and Secretariat officials concerning the proposed use of the Soviet voluntary contribution. In October 1961 Mr. Cole decided against issuance of this politically sensitive document (for which he was sorely criticized by the United States Government), believing that it would only worsen Agency relations with the Soviet Government and make cooperation even more difficult. When Dr. Eklund took office on December 1, 1961, he, too, decided against issuance of the Webb Report, for the same reasons.

Discussions with close observers of Agency developments have made possible the reconstruction of the sequence of events analyzed in the Webb Report and the record as seen by the Secretariat and contained in that Report. For clarity, the account of the Agency's negotiations with the Soviet Union is listed chronologically.

[John C. Webb of the Division of Technical Supplies, the division of the Agency responsible for utilizing the voluntary

[43] GC(v)/OR. 61, pp. 19-20.

contributions, ably conducted the negotiations until the first breakthrough was achieved in 1961. He was then reassigned by Director-General Cole and replaced by a Czech, Dr. Čestmir Šimáne, in April 1961. Mr. Cole believed that Šimáne would be a suitable person to fill the position and might be able, because of his nationality and technical competence, to heal the wounds which had been created and to expedite the use of the Soviet contribution.]

October 3. 1958: The Soviet Union announced at the General Conference that it was prepared to contribute to the General Fund an amount to be announced at a later date.

May 1959: The Soviet representative on the Board of Governors stated that the Soviet Union would contribute 500,000 (old) rubles or $125,000 for the purchase of equipment in the USSR.

May 8, 1959: The offer was acknowledged by the Director-General who asked for assurance that the amount would not be restricted as to use in any country.

June 19-25, 1959: The Soviet offer was accepted by the Board of Governors. The Secretariat requested the assistance of the Resident Representative of the Soviet Union in obtaining information concerning the availability of Soviet equipment, possible delivery dates, and prices.

November 11, 1959: The Director-General, not having heard anything further from the Soviet Government, informed the Soviet Permanent Mission in Vienna that the Agency was ready to purchase equipment and requested that an equipment catalogue and a Soviet consultant be sent to the Agency to expedite the matter. This was the diplomat's way of saying that the Agency was ready for business, what did the Soviet Union have to sell, and would they like to send someone to talk business.

December 11, 1959: There was no reply to the Director-General's letter. Another letter was sent with lists of equipment desired by the Agency. Still no information came from Moscow on the Soviet equipment available. The Director-General suggested that perhaps Moscow would like two men sent from the Agency to Moscow to discuss the problem.

January 12, 1960: The Soviet Mission in Vienna replied that it would not be necessary to send Agency personnel to Moscow; a consultant would be sent to Vienna (at Agency expense).

February 1960: Conversations were held between the Soviet consultant and Agency officials. It was apparent from the description of the equipment that Moscow was prepared to sell that there was only a limited choice available. The consultant explained that he was not authorized to give any information about prices or dates of delivery. Only the foreign trade agency, TECHNOPROMEXPORT, could give such information.

The Soviets were given full information on the equipment needed by the Agency and the prices contained in Agency catalogues.

The Soviet consultant indicated that Moscow was not interested in supplying individual items of equipment but in building and equipping a full laboratory, or a complete project. Particular interest was expressed in supplying laboratories to Afghanistan and Indonesia.

March 1960: The Secretariat inquired of the Soviet Union whether it would be willing to provide a sub-critical assembly requested by Indonesia under the Soviet voluntary contribution. Indonesia subsequently withdrew its request and the Soviet Government was so notified in early April.

April 19, 1960: Two representatives from TECHNOPROM-EXPORT visited the Agency to discuss the sale of equipment. They requested the prices of equipment purchased by the Agency. The Agency refused to give anything but its catalogue list prices, since all its purchases for items over $1,000 are arranged as a result of tenders (closed, competitive bids) and to give anything but the list prices would be a violation of trust; it indicated that the Soviets were expected to follow regular Agency procedure.

April 1960: The Director-General wrote the Soviet Resident Representative, enclosing a list of equipment needed for technical assistance projects in Austria, Iraq, the Philippines, Yugoslavia, and the U.A.R., which the Soviet consultant had indicated could be provided by the Soviet Union.

The Soviets did not reply to this letter.

The United States made an outright gift of $200,000 for the purchase of equipment in the United States; because of the U. S. appropriation schedule, the gift had to be acted on before June 30, 1960, to ensure its use.

The Agency sent the United States Government a list of technical specifications for *all* equipment needed for technical assistance projects, and asked for full particulars on which equipment it was prepared to provide. During the next month, in a series of individual letters, identical information was sent to the Soviet Government with a similar invitation.

June 1960: The United States was supposed to give information on what projects it was prepared to support at the June meeting of the Board of Governors. At that time, the USSR said that it would supply the needs of Afghanistan and the U.A.R. The United States offer, submitted a few days later, also listed the laboratory for Afghanistan. Since the Soviet communication did not contain any information on price or date of delivery, the United States offer, which did include this required information, was accepted for the Afghan project. The United States offer, made on June 26, was accepted by the Agency in order to use the gift within the prescribed period.

This issue has since been exploited by the Soviet Union which maintains that it was prepared to supply the laboratory for Afghanistan but was turned down because of the discriminatory policy of the Secretariat. From the Agency's standpoint, the Soviet bid was incomplete and therefore unsuited for acceptance. The Agency called Soviet attention to four other projects which still were to be acted on and left the way open for Moscow to supply Brazil, Turkey, Sudan, and Venezuela with equipment.

July 18, 1960: The Director-General invited the Soviet Union to supply equipment for a project in Ceylon.

August 11, 1960: For the first time, the Soviet Government submitted a list of prices for equipment which it could supply.

August 25, 1960: The Soviets agreed to provide $5,000 worth of equipment to Ceylon. The date of delivery, which had been stated as "early in 1961," later turned out to be early summer.

August 30, 1960: The Agency accepted the Soviet offer.

October 1960: The Director-General made two proposals designed to utilize the entire Soviet voluntary contribution: a) to utilize the 500,000 rubles by bulk purchases of equipment most commonly used by the Agency in supplying technical assistance, the equipment to be used as needed; b) to purchase Soviet equipment for use in the Agency's laboratory in Vienna.

December 1960: The Soviet Government rejected (a) outright, and accepted (b) on a limited basis. It agreed to supply a photospectrometer and a mass spectrometer, though extending the delivery date once the Agency had formally accepted. Also, the Agency asked for a reconsideration of the price quoted by Soviet officials, since it was above the international market price.

January 1961: The Director-General accepted the photospec-

238

trometer on the terms stipulated by the Soviet Resident Representative, but indicated that the price of the mass spectrometer was much higher than that quoted by other manufacturers and invited the Soviet Union to reconsider its price.

February 1961: The Soviet Government changed the delivery date of the photospectrometer to early 1962. Professor Emelyanov challenged the Agency's position that the price of the mass spectrometer was too high, noting that the Soviet instrument had a wide range of applications. Shortly thereafter, the Secretariat furnished the Governor from the Soviet Union with a list of "average prices" charged by commercial suppliers for items similar to the ones the USSR had offered to supply. The Soviet Union was furnished with detailed specifications of equipment required for projects in Argentina, Brazil, Iceland, Morocco, Pakistan, and Turkey, and invited to submit concrete bids.

March 1961: The Soviet Resident Representative offered to supply equipment for a research contract with the U.A.R.

May 1961: An order was placed with the USSR for part of the equipment required by the U.A.R.

The Director-General confirmed the order, placed in August 1960, for equipment for Ceylon.

June 1961: The Soviet Union submitted detailed specifications of the mass spectrometer which it offered in December 1960.

Summer 1961: The Soviets delivered their equipment to Ceylon. This was the first instance in which the Soviet voluntary contribution, made in 1958, was utilized.

The Webb Report shows the chronology of written communications between the Agency and the Soviets regarding the Secretariat's efforts to utilize the Soviet contribution, but it does not show the numerous personal conferences and discussions that Mr. Cole and others in the Secretariat had with the Soviets on this matter. The combination of the Webb chronology and the personal discussions negate the accusation that Mr. Cole had deliberately endeavored to avoid utilizing the Soviet gift; actually the facts are just the reverse. Among close observers of these developments, there was uniform agreement that the Agency was not practicing a policy of deliberate discrimination and that the Soviet charges were unfounded. After exonerating the Agency, they offered several interpretations of the Soviet behavior. Some ascribed the difficulties in utilizing the Soviet voluntary contribution primarily to the attitude of the first Director-General who, they contended, did not explore the possibilities with vigor or genuine interest; they thought that his successor would make greater efforts in this direction. Others thought the difficulties encountered in using Soviet funds during the Agency's first five years were understandable if one remembers that the Soviet Union does not operate commercially as the West does; it has no experience in providing nuclear equipment commercially for sale in world markets. The Soviets manufacture their equipment for specific projects in their own country and probably for other members of the bloc. They are not accustomed to thinking in terms of competitive costs and are reluctant to compete in closed bidding; price is merely an accounting device. Also, the date of delivery is a paramount problem, for in their own economy the Soviets produce equipment only as demanded by the current plan and thus have no available surpluses to meet unanticipated requests. Given these features of the Soviet approach, the difficulties between Moscow and the Agency had been inevitable but were not assumed to be of a permanent character. There was general agreement among these observers that the important contributing factors were the inexperience of the Soviets in competitive commercial situations, their hesitance about the entire process of submitting specific bids, and their resort to equivocation to conceal a combination of inefficiency, uncertainty, and inability to fill orders promptly.

One Indian official, however, cautioned against placing too much weight on these factors and suggested that Moscow was actually not as perturbed by the meager utilization of its voluntary contribution as it complained publicly: "The Soviets invariably respond favorably when informed that a neutralist is interested in availing itself of the Soviet contribution. But they surreptitiously make known their readiness to give much more on a bilateral basis than the small amount available through the Agency. The neutralist then concludes a bilateral agreement, and Moscow can continue to accuse the Secretariat of discrimination in utilization of the Soviet contribution." This stratagem enables the Soviet Union to improve its relations with neutralist recipients by providing a larger package, while retaining ample ammunition to discredit the Director-General and the Secretariat.

Consistently hostile to any increase in the Agency's Regular Budget, Moscow reacts sharply to Western charges of penuriousness. It maintains that IAEA could perform more constructively if greater attention were devoted to administrative efficiency, keeping the staff to a minimum, and fully utilizing national offers of cost-free experts, fellowships, and equipment. An activity which Moscow particularly inveighs against, regarding it as wasteful, is the Agency's placing contracts with various scientific organizations for investigation in what Moscow contends are peripheral areas of research that divert the Agency from its main task of promoting the peaceful utilization of atomic energy. One neutralist, for example, noted that of the first one hundred contracts assigned by IAEA only one dealt with a study of small and medium power reactors. The Soviets argue that the Agency should not supplement research on diversified topics, whatever may be their scientific merit, but should concentrate on subjects of immediate interest to underdeveloped countries.

A British proposal for establishing a single budget which would be financed solely by assessments of member states was rejected by the Soviets on the grounds that "its adoption would derogate from the established principle recognized by the United Nations, that contributions for technical assistance should be voluntary" and that "the transformation of voluntary into obligatory contributions would make it difficult for many states to participate in the Agency's work."[44] Professor Emelyanov pointedly insisted that voluntary contributions had become "a fixed rule" in UN financing of technical assistance, "a principle adopted once and for all in international practice."[45] He also noted the failure of previous efforts to induce members "to make voluntary contributions to the General Fund in amounts that were at least the same percentages of the target for each year as were their assessed contributions to the regular budget."[46] Not only did the Soviets argue against the British proposal as an unwarranted, unsound, discriminatory measure, but they emphasized that if it were adopted "they would refuse to ratify it and would not contribute to the additional expenses resulting from the change introduced in the financial provisions of the Statute."[47] For them, the move was an ill-concealed Western maneuver to control even more rigidly "both the scale of contributions and the allocation of budgetary resources."

Another accusation was that too many of the contracts went to Western countries. They called for a more frequent assigning of contracts to underdeveloped countries, i.e. India and Egypt, which the Agency was under an obligation to help in furthering the development of their nuclear programs.[48] Such a Soviet declamation led one British delegate to throw

[44] GC(vi)/OR. 66, p. 26.
[45] GC(vi)/COM.2/OR. 27, p. 17.
[46] *Ibid.*, pp. 17-18.
[47] GC(vi)/COM.2/OR. 29, p. 3.
[48] GC(v)/COM.1/OR. 35, p. 14.

into focus the readiness of the Soviets to propose ambitious activities but their reluctance to make them financially feasible. He pointed out that in the financing of research contracts a fundamental administrative distinction had to be made between topics of general interest to all members, which under the Statute had to be financed from the regular budget, and topics relating to a particular country, which had to be financed from the operational budget: "The general topics, being highly complex, could not normally be undertaken by laboratories in the less developed countries. The more specific projects were suitable for study in the less developed countries, but had to be financed out of funds provided by voluntary contributions. Therefore, if certain Governments wished more contracts to be placed with the less developed countries, they should be prepared to support their proposals with increased pledges."[49] [Since Moscow's voluntary contribution can be spent only in the USSR, it cannot help to finance any of the specific research studies contracted out by the Agency.] The Soviet delegate objected strenuously to the implication that "because the Soviet Union was opposed to any increase in the staff and budget, it was also opposed to an extensive program of assistance to underdeveloped countries."[50] Despite Moscow's protests, the impression, widely shared by Secretariat officials and neutralist delegates, is that the Soviet Union is not interested in making the Agency an important international institution. That this impression does not affect the national positions of the neutralists, is mute testimony to the marginal impact which the Agency has made upon its members.

Moscow's financial policy did cast the shadow of doubt over its intent. Yet, in this highly politicized world, few will be the adverse political reactions, because the Agency's programs are currently of only marginal importance to neutralist

[49] GC(IV)/COM.1/OR. 28, p. 3.
[50] GC(IV)/COM.1/OR. 26, p. 10.

countries. The Soviet Union will retain their friendship as long as it lends its political support on issues vital to them and continues its extensive bilateral aid program. The contrast between the degrees of Soviet and Western support for the Agency is vitiated by the fact that IAEA still remains neglected by the West and second in importance to Western bilateral operations. Thus, although the United States inspired the establishment of the Agency, and continues to laud its potential, provides fellowships, experts, and equipment, participates in scientific regulatory activities, and contributes to the operation of the laboratory, it has failed to sustain the initial enthusiastic support of the neutralists.

Western reluctance to give the Agency the decision-making power and financial wherewithal to undertake ambitious programs has dissipated much of the good will it received from the creation of the Agency; Western financial contributions are insignificant, inadequate to carry through any program of consequence. The entire budget of the Agency, in 1962, was less than $10 million, barely enough to build one small 20 megawatt nuclear power reactor. For several years, IAEA set a goal of $1.5 million to be raised through voluntary contributions to its General Fund, out of which technical assistance is supplied. This amount could scarcely be expected to arouse enthusiasm among underdeveloped countries who can often obtain a hundred-fold more aid through bilateral channels. Yet in no year was more than 75 to 80 per cent of the goal reached. The United States offered to contribute one-half of the total for each year: of this, $500,000 was paid unconditionally; the other $250,000, dollar for dollar, as the payments of all other members exceeded the half-million mark. That the full United States contribution was not made because of the failure of other countries to provide matching amounts is a commentary on the level of support for the Agency. During the 1958-1962 period, the total Soviet contribution was less than $200,000, the bulk of which remained unused.

This discouraging pattern of voluntary contributions places the Agency's future in jeopardy. Appeals for larger contributions to the General Fund go largely unanswered. The underdeveloped countries do not have the money, the Soviet bloc opposes strengthening the developmental functions of international organizations, and the Western Powers are not prepared to contribute on a scale which could raise the Agency to a level where its impact could be considerable. Whereas the parsimony of the Soviets may not be unexpected, that of the West is regrettable and shortsighted.

FELLOWSHIPS AND EXPERTS

Moscow's quarrel with the Agency also involves the administration of the fellowship program and the assignment and utilization of experts. Agency fellowships are of two types: type I, financed by funds received under EPTA programs and from voluntary contributions to the General Fund, afford IAEA maximum latitude in selection of the most suitable place and course of study; type II fellowships are granted by governments for use in their own national educational and scientific institutions. No type I fellowships have had to be used for study in the Soviet Union, because the number offered by the Soviet Government under the type II category has thus far been more than adequate to meet the number of candidates willing to study in the USSR. However, more than 20 per cent of the type I fellowships have been granted to Soviet-bloc citizens for study in Western institutions; their study is financed, therefore, by convertible Western contributions to the General Fund.

Difficulties in using Soviet type II fellowships have centered on the long-term (four to six years) awards. The fifty short-term (three to six months) fellowships offered in 1958-1959 were promptly utilized by the Agency. Shortly thereafter, the Soviet Government declared that it would not extend any more short-term fellowships until its offer of twenty-five long-term ones had first been used (as of late 1962, the initial offer, made in 1958, had still not been exhausted). By September 1961, however, Moscow reversed its attitude on the short-term fellowships, realizing the damage which it was doing to Soviet interests, and offered 40,000 new rubles (about $44,000) for twenty short-term fellowships to Soviet institutions. According to Moscow, the reason for the difficulties in using the long-term awards was clear: discrimination by the Agency. Soviet delegates rejected the Agency's explanation that the language barrier deterred applicants from choosing Soviet fellowship offers and insisted that "the truth was that the Agency did not want to send fellowship holders to the Soviet Union and was pursuing a discriminatory policy with regard to the use of opportunities offered by the Soviet Union."[51]

Agency officials deny the Soviet charge and insist that the language barrier is the principal factor deterring applicants from choosing to study in the Soviet Union. They note that fellowship requirements demand at least a first degree, and few applicants so far advanced are prepared to devote so much of their professional training to studying a new language. One Indian tartly remarked that "no scientist wants to go to Russia for so extended a period, which would be largely wasted because of the time needed to learn the language. The Soviet charge against the Agency is phony." In addition, the experience of several of the fellows in the USSR has not been favorable. For example, the first Indonesian long-term fellowship holder arrived in the USSR in January 1959; he was dropped from the program in early 1962 at his own request. He has since been joined by several others who found it difficult to acclimate to Soviet conditions for several years. The sources of their dissatisfaction were varied: an overwhelming sense of isolation because of the inability to communicate and because student contact with the faculty is ex-

[51] GOV/OR. 245, p. 5.

tremely difficult, since most of the instruction is given through lectures to large groups; an inadequate stipend, not sufficient to cover the purchase of books, equipment, and warm clothes (incidentally, Soviet fellowships pay only one-way travel); and an inability to adjust to the stringencies of Soviet society.

Moscow has also criticized the Agency for failing to use the services of the thirty Soviet experts, which it made available, cost free, and then for requesting additional appropriations to pay for other experts used by the Agency in technical assistance operations. It has expressed similar irritation at the Agency's reluctance to use more Soviet personnel on the various fact-finding missions which are sent to underdeveloped countries.[52] The Soviet delegation uses these situations as ammunition against budget increases: if the Agency does not avail itself of the free services of consultants offered by the Soviet Government, there is no basis for any increase in the budgetary allotment for payment of experts and consultants. On the other hand, the Agency insists upon a free hand in the hiring of consultants and upon retaining its own cadre of consultants, a few of whom are Soviet citizens. Its experience, say Secretariat officials, has proved the difficulty in obtaining the services of free consultants at exactly the time and in the specialty required by the requesting government. Nonetheless, the Agency has acted recently to use some of these experts.

IAEA's Future and Soviet Policy

When the Soviet Union first agreed to join IAEA, it did so uncertain of its role or objectives. As in chess where each move occasions a counter-move, always with the goal of checkmate in mind, so in the IAEA the Soviet Government became a member to keep a close and continuing watch on United States policies and to thwart them whenever possible. With participation came early appreciation of the Agency's useful-

[52] GC(vi)/OR. 65, p. 6.

ness as a clearinghouse through which passed the latest information on scientific developments in the nuclear field. Moscow had its citizens assigned to the staff in all the key divisions, where they keep abreast of the work being done in the West and send all available published data back to Moscow for evaluation. There is nothing insidious in this intelligence-gathering activity, since all the information is in the public realm, but the Agency does serve as a convenient collecting and assorting center for the Soviet Government. Moscow has also shown active interest in the Agency's training program, and tried to attract students and specialists to the USSR as part of its concerted effort to become the educational and scientific Mecca for underdeveloped countries. However, Moscow's most important objective has been to associate Soviet policies with those of neutralist countries, to demonstrate the scope of Soviet support for their aspirations, and to encourage them in situations whose effect is to embarrass the West, to estrange it further from the neutralists, and to minimize the worth of its efforts. To an extent unparalleled in any Specialized Agency or regional economic commission Moscow has succeeded in this objective. Its positions on every major issue that has come before the Agency have been deemed "correct" by the neutralists: e.g. nuclear power reactors, Agency Safeguards, and the need for studies of more direct benefit to underdeveloped countries. Moscow's stand on financial questions is a glaring exception. Yet even here it suffers minimally because of the considerable aid it does render bilaterally, and because of the unimpressive Western record of financial support for the Agency.

So great is the similarity between the Soviet and neutralist positions, that there is a tendency among many Westerners to link the two blocs together and to assume that the neutralists follow Soviet leadership, an impression Moscow is delighted to encourage. The coalescence of Soviet and Indian views, in particular, has encouraged the belief that India follows the Soviet lead in IAEA and does so largely for self-seeking reasons, e.g. Soviet support on Kashmir, economic aid, etc. These impressions are unfortunate and incorrect. When asked, "Why does the Soviet position in IAEA generally meet with greater support among the neutralist countries than that of the United States?," one Indian official answered that the question is based on an assumption that is not warranted by the facts:

"The experience of the underdeveloped countries in the Agency is, unfortunately, that in crucial matters their viewpoints receive more sympathy from the Socialist group of countries rather than from the Western countries, which at times are apt to give insufficient regard for the opinions of the developing countries. Two very good examples are the handling of the safeguards question and of the appointment of the second Director-General of the Agency. In both instances, the Western countries carried their viewpoints because they commanded a larger number of votes, despite the very strong opposition from the Socialist countries as well as the nonaligned Asian and African countries and despite persistent efforts by the latter group to find *via media.*

"In both instances it was not the Soviet Union but the nonaligned Asian and African countries which took up positions, and the Soviet Union extended its support to the developing countries because of a similarity of views. A perusal of the proceedings of the various meetings which dealt with the question of safeguards will show that it was India, which was mainly instrumental in formulating a position which was opposed to the Western position and in this India was supported by the Soviet Union, and not vice versa. Similarly, on the question of the appointment of the second Director-General, a candidate from a nonaligned Asian country was sponsored by the nonaligned Asian and African countries and supported by the socialist countries and not vice versa."[53]

[53] Letter from the Government of India, *op. cit.*

Seen in this light, the role of the Soviet Union in IAEA shows up in a new perspective, although, of course, it may legitimately be argued that this is so only because the present neutralist position accords with Soviet interests. But the statement is important because it expresses the views of a number of neutralists. It is doubly significant because it is an indication of official Indian thinking. Most neutralists followed India's lead on major international questions, certainly until 1961-1962. However, India's influence has waned in recent years, particularly among the African states. But with the most advanced nuclear development program of all the neutralist countries, India does have an unrivaled capacity to influence their attitudes toward the Agency. If the West and the Agency could reach a compromise with India on the application of a system of safeguards, the neutralists might be willing to turn more frequently to the Agency for assistance, thereby giving it a new lease on life. Though too much should not be expected, a promising step in this direction was recently taken when India agreed, in the Indo-American treaty of August 8, 1963, to accept in principle, and at some unspecified future time, Agency inspection procedures, "provided that they are consistent with the safeguards that would be exercised by the United States under a bilateral agreement."[54] This accommodation could serve as a precedent for other Afro-Asian neutralist countries to accept Agency safeguards.

Two conclusions may be drawn: first, neutralist opposition to the dominating policy of the United States in IAEA is the result of independent evaluation and not of any inherent predisposition toward Soviet views; second, Moscow's ability to improve its relations with the neutralists is facilitated by the current irreconcilability of Western and neutralist views.

The question may be asked whether the Agency was born prematurely or still-born? Should it continue to function as it does, even though its activities are different from the inten-

[54] *New York Times,* June 26, 1963.

tions of the Agency's founders? The Agency was created upon the assumptions that nuclear power would be promoted for widespread commercial use, that fissionable materials would remain in short supply, and that the Agency would become a major supplier of fissionable material and nuclear reactors. Nuclear technology has played loose with the assumptions of political leaders; it has either disappointed or outmoded them. Limited by meager financial resources and the unwillingness of the Great Powers to push the development of nuclear power reactors through the Agency, even though the production of electric power is the only application of nuclear energy that is specifically mentioned in the Statute, IAEA has shifted its emphasis to technical assistance, training, and minor research. The present Director-General is reputed to be a strong proponent of nuclear power reactors. It remains to be seen whether he will be able to convince the Great Powers to devote more attention to the task of making nuclear and conventional power competitive and to channel such efforts through the Agency.

Disillusionment is prevalent among the underdeveloped countries; no longer do they look to the Agency with great expectations. Such assistance as they obtain for their national nuclear programs comes predominantly from bilateral agreements. One neutralist cautioned against exaggerating the cooperation that does exist among nations in the Agency's modest programs; the major issues remain unresolved and are stifling the Agency: "It may be contended that such issues have not been many or frequent, but such a contention would be very misleading and may pave the way for a state of complacency which would prevent the Agency from developing in the manner in which it was visualized it should grow when it was established. The real feeling, albeit in a minority of countries, is that of frustration. The minority countries, however, represent most of the developing countries of Asia and Africa; they cover a vast area of the world and a population which is much more than that of the countries which have a majority vote in the Agency. The countries which are in a minority do not often press issues to a vote, as they are familiar with the pattern of voting and aware of the final outcome should an issue be so pressed. In the interests of harmony and of making a success of the objectives of the Agency, the minority countries have usually adopted a very conciliatory attitude, but such conciliation and acquiescence often tend to be deceptive and regarded by the majority countries as positive unstinted accord. Article III of the Statute of the Agency specifically enjoins on the Agency to give due consideration to the needs of the underdeveloped areas of the world. It is precisely such areas which are disappointed at the manner in which progress in the Agency is made." Neutralist officials frankly admit that the stand of their governments against Agency Safeguards, for example, is reinforced by the inability of the Agency to provide substantial assistance. Why should they then compromise on sensitive political issues? The resources of the Agency are so insignificant that there is no inducement for accommodation. But if the Agency had ample resources to finance the construction and equipping of nuclear reactors, neutralist countries might be willing to test the operation of a less objectionable system of safeguards.

The United States must bear a major responsibility for the apathy and antagonism which pervade the Agency. Just as it deserved acclaim for suggesting and promoting the establishment of the Agency, so, too, as its leading benefactor and dominating member, is it culpable for failing to nourish its creation. It has not offered nuclear material to the Agency at more attractive terms than those available through bilateral channels, nor helped the Agency to become a leader in the field of nuclear reactors, nor given the financial resources necessary to attract clients and make IAEA an important international organization.[55]

[55] In a statement before the Joint Congressional Committee on Atomic

The principal beneficiary has been the Soviet Union. It, alone, stands to benefit in the long run from the disenchantment with the Agency and from the strengthening of bilateral approaches to the development of nuclear energy. By supporting neutralist policies, it enhances its political stature among these strategic countries; by encouraging the neutralists to seek aid through bilateral rather than UN channels, it reinforces their belief that it is the Great Power struggle that gives them the greatest promise of extensive and extended assistance. Moscow's present purposes would appear to be served by an Agency of peripheral importance and dwarfed stature, an organization incapable of promoting meaningful cooperation between the developing and developed countries or of nurturing in the neutralist nations an appreciation of the potential that international organizations hold for them.

Energy on August 2, 1962, Dr. Henry DeWolf Smyth, the eminent atomic scientist and American Governor on the Board of Governors of IAEA, noted that the United States Government must now make a sharp decision on three questions: "1) Does the United States want to support the development of nuclear power around the world? 2) How important does the United States consider safeguards? 3) Is the United States really going to use the Agency or are we going to continue to work largely bilaterally or through regional groups?"

An indication of the marginal importance which IAEA holds in State Department thinking may be seen in the fact that no high-ranking official has, as a primary duty, responsibility for keeping abreast of Agency affairs.

VI ◈•——

Soviet Personnel in International Secretariats

CENTRAL to the Soviet prescription for political power is the importance of organization. Lenin, in his emergence from the crucible of exile and revolution, made a centralized and disciplined Party the cornerstone of the Bolshevik movement. He used it to overcome the unorganized, fragmented opposition groups and to establish Communist Party rule in Russia. For the exploitation of revolutionary situations in other countries, he counseled foreign Communists to adapt their tactics to each new situation, to infiltrate, divide, and dominate bourgeois organizations, while maintaining their own internal cohesiveness and discipline. In April 1920, in *"Left-Wing" Communism, An Infantile Disorder*, Lenin castigated the "Left" or "purist" Communists for disputing the need to participate in bourgeois parliaments, pointing out that participation "not only does not harm the revolutionary proletariat, but actually helps it to *prove* to the backward masses why such parliaments deserve to be dispersed; it *helps* their successful dispersal, and *helps* to make bourgeois parliamentarism 'politically obsolete.'"[1] He ridiculed those Communists who expressed their "revolutionariness" by hurling abuse at bourgeois parliaments and who, by repudiating participation in them, avoided "the difficult task of utilizing reactionary parliaments for revolutionary purposes. . . . The surest way of discrediting and damaging a new political (and not only political) idea is to reduce it to absurdity on the plea of defending it."[2] "The more powerful enemy can be vanquished only by exerting the

[1] V. I. Lenin, *"Left-Wing" Communism, An Infantile Disorder* (Moscow: Foreign Languages Publishing House, 1950), p. 74.

[2] *Ibid.*, pp. 81, 77.

254

utmost effort, and *without fail*, most thoroughly, carefully, attentively and skillfully using every, even the smallest, 'rift' among the enemies, every antagonism of interest among the bourgeoisie of the various countries and among the various groups or types of bourgeoisie within the various countries, and also by taking advantage of every, even the smallest, opportunity of gaining a mass ally, even though this ally be temporary, vacillating, unstable, unreliable and conditional."[3] Lenin argued that Communists must learn to make "all the necessary practical compromises, to maneuver, to make agreements, zigzags, retreats and so on," in order to weaken the stability of existing bourgeois institutions and pave the way for further Communist advances.

A few months later, in August 1920, the second Congress of the Communist International adopted a series of Lenin-inspired "theses," including one on "The New Epoch and the New Parliamentarianism." The Comintern instructed Communist Parties that to undermine bourgeois parliaments it was necessary to have "reconnaissance parties in the parliamentary institutions of the bourgeoisie." Communist participation was designed ultimately to destroy parliamentarianism: "It is only possible to speak of utilizing the bourgeois State organizations with the object of destroying them." This could be achieved by working with the parliaments while "making revolutionary propaganda from the parliamentary platform," denouncing class enemies, mobilizing the masses, "who especially in backward areas, still look up to parliaments and are captivated by democratic illusions." The degree of participation depends upon specific conditions. Communist deputies are always subject to the authority of the Central Committee of the Party and "each Communist member of parliament must remember that he is not a 'legislator' who is bound to seek agreements with the other legislators, but a party agitator sent into the enemy's camp in order to carry out Party decisions." Under

[3] *Ibid.*, p. 91.

255

certain circumstances a walk-out, boycott, or direct, violent challenge may be in order, though "chiefly when there is a possibility of an immediate transition to an armed fight for power."

Forty years later, Nikita Khrushchev moved "to apply to a world parliament tactics originally evolved for national parliaments."[4] On September 23, 1960, in the General Assembly, Khrushchev launched a frontal assault on the Office of the Secretary-General and on the entire concept of an impartial international civil service. Using the Soviet setback in the Congo as a springboard, he attacked the existing organizational arrangements in the UN, demanding a realignment of Secretariat posts and power commensurate with the new alignment of blocs and forces in the world:

"It is necessary that the executive agency of the United Nations should reflect the actual situation now existing in the world. The United Nations includes member-states of the military blocs of the Western Powers, Socialist states, and neutralist countries. This would be absolutely fair and we would be better protected against the negative phenomena which have been observed in the work of the United Nations; particularly during the recent developments in the Congo.

"We consider it wise and fair that the United Nations' executive agency should appear, not as one person—the Secretary-General—but should consist of three persons invested with high confidence of the United Nations—representatives of the States belonging to the three basic groupings already mentioned.

". . . Briefly speaking we think that it would be wise to replace the Secretary-General, who is now the sole interpreter and executor of the decisions of the Assembly and the Security Council, by a collective executive agency of the United Nations which would consist of three persons, each represent-

[4] C. L. Sulzberger, "The Lesson to UN of Mr. Khrushchev," *New York Times,* October 15, 1960.

ing a definite grouping of States. This would provide a definite guarantee against the activity of the United Nations' executive agency being detrimental to one of these groupings of States."

Khrushchev's demand for a reorganization of the UN Secretariat and a reapportionment of its personnel base has been extended to other international Secretariats. Though the focus of public attention is on developments in UN headquarters in New York, the principle and the demand have had their impact in other places where international organizations are located, in Geneva, in Vienna, in Rome, etc.

Khrushchev's troika proposal is lineally descended from Lenin's emphasis upon the importance of organization as an instrument for strengthening and extending Communist power, and from the Comintern's directives to foreign Communists on how to destroy bourgeois parliamentary institutions.[5] The

[5] Contemporary Soviet doctrine upholds the Leninist view of bourgeois parliaments. It has, however, evolved a more positive view on the possibility of transforming them into instruments susceptible to Communist control. Since the Twentieth Congress of the CPSU (February 1956), Soviet leaders have counseled a more systematic exploitation of bourgeois parliaments in order to make use of all available legal paths to the acquisition of political power. In *Fundamentals of Marxism-Leninism* (1959)—the latest compendium of official doctrine—Moscow specifically sanctions "the use of the machinery of parliamentary democracy to win power," but also emphasizes that the overthrow of bourgeois regimes in many countries will still have to be achieved through an armed struggle. This accommodation to present-day conditions is an indication of the growing self-assurance of Soviet leaders and of their belief that capitalist (non-Communist) countries are "ripe" for the peaceful and legal extension of Communist influence. The concept of "national democracies," enunciated by Khrushchev in his important January 6, 1961 speech, is intended as a theoretical justification for an evolutionary path for non-Communist underdeveloped countries to the status of "People's Democracies."

The House Committee on Un-American Activities (87th Congress, 1st Session) published in early 1962 a reprint of two chapters from a book written by Jan Kozak, a Czech Communist and Party historian, which cites the Czechoslovak experience as a guide to Communist Parties as-

application of these principles to international Secretariats has been late in coming because of the earlier Soviet underestimation of the value of these institutions in promoting Soviet interests. It may be recalled that Stalin was concerned only with the security function of the UN and with keeping it politically incapable of interfering with Soviet objectives. For these purposes the veto in the Security Council was adequate. Lacking interest, he refused to participate in most of the Specialized Agencies, and the meager number of Soviet nationals serving on their Secretariats was therefore consistent with his general depreciation of their value in promoting Soviet interests. (Out of the more than one thousand professional staff members at UN headquarters, other than linguists, Moscow never had more than 15 serving in any particular year during the Stalin period. By 1956, only 25 out of 1,163 were Soviet nationals.)

Despite the post-1954 attention to the activities of international organizations and to the use of their plenary and technical sessions for setting forth Soviet views and for courting neutralists, Soviet leaders, until 1960, virtually ignored the Secretariats. They never made sustained or systematic efforts to place their people in key positions where they could influence the operation and orientation of an organization. Strange that these men, trained with an eye to infiltrating and capturing the key positions in mass-supported organizations, made so few and such indecisive attempts to penetrate international Secretariats. At the plenary meetings of the UN and Specialized Agencies, Soviet delegates called for an end to "swollen" budgets, administrative inefficiency, and increasing staffs, and

---

suming power in Western-style parliamentary systems. The two chapters—"How Parliament Can Play a Revolutionary Part in the Transition to Socialism," and "The Role of the Popular Masses"—provide detailed information on how "it was possible to transform parliament from an organ of the bourgeoisie into an instrument . . . leading to the change of the social structure and into a direct instrument for the victory of the socialist (Communist) revolution."

also for a more equitable geographical distribution of professional posts. However, this latter interest was mainly vocal, aimed apparently for propaganda value, and did not result in a noticeable increase in the number of Soviet nationals in international Secretariats. Moscow made no serious effort to make available more of its citizens to Secretariats despite repeated encouragement to do so by UN officials.

Not until Khrushchev's troika proposal at the Fifteenth Session of the General Assembly did Moscow begin to act as if it really meant to avail itself of its unofficial quota of Secretarial posts. The troika speech and the consequent Soviet attitude toward the UN indicate that the residue of Soviet isolationism in, and underestimation of, international organizations is being discarded. Khrushchev's insistence upon greater representation for Soviet personnel in the Secretariat, particularly in the policy-making posts, may have far-reaching consequences for the future of international Secretariats and should be appraised against the Leninist image of the role which bourgeois institutions can play in furthering revolutionary objectives.

The recommended replacement of the Secretary-General by a three-man directorate, representing the three political blocs —Western, Communist, and neutralist—was justified on the ground that it was time the UN reflected the changed alignments of political forces in the world. Moscow's interpretation of the functions of the Secretariat is diametrically opposed to that of the West; it does not see the Secretariat as the administrative arm of the General Assembly and the Security Council, operating to fulfill the mandates of these political organs, independent of control by any particular government. Rather, it conceives of the Secretariat as a body openly constituted on an ideological and political basis, devoid of impartiality and independence. In effect, the troika is designed to give the Soviet bloc a veto in the running of the Secretariat and enable Moscow to thwart the will of the General Assembly. The Soviet Government has, in the light of the Congo experience, come to appreciate the political importance of the Secretariat and wishes to be in the position where it can exercise a veto in that organ, or at least exercise greater influence over the decisions that are made. Inherent in the troika proposal is also the Soviet quest for greater equality with the Western bloc in UN organs, as well as on the Secretariats.[6]

Khrushchev's reference to the application of the principle of equitable geographical distribution of professional posts, particularly at policy-making levels, in international Secretariats is not new; it has been raised many times by Soviet and neutralist delegations. Moscow is now stressing the issue because it has attracted widespread interest and support among the underdeveloped countries, both neutralist and com-

[6] Premier Khrushchev's troika proposal dramatically focused attention on Moscow's demand for formal, as well as actual, equality with the West in international Secretariats. For several years before, Soviet delegates in international organizations had been calling for a more equitable apportionment of honorific and committee posts at the plenary meetings of various organizations. For example, in IAEA the question arose in connection with the election of the president of the General Conference: at the 1957 conference a Westerner had been elected and at the 1958 conference an Indonesian had been elected to this honorific post. Moscow argued that it was time (at the 1959 Conference) to give the post to a member of the Socialist camp and proposed Mr. Nadjakov of Bulgaria. According to the Soviet delegate: "Until a week before [the 1959 Conference convened] no objections had been raised and no other candidates had been mentioned. Just before the conference had opened, however, the United States mission to the Agency had begun to exert pressure in order to have the representative of Japan elected president of the conference. No objection to the candidature of Mr. Nadjakov had been expressed, and all attempts to negotiate with the United States delegation had been fruitless. The introduction of the Japanese candidature, which placed before Member States a fait accompli, was a sign that the United States delegation was still pursuing the old bankrupt policy of negotiating from a 'position of strength'; it was a denial of the principle of cooperation about which the United States delegation liked to speak." GC(III)/OR. 25, p. 5. *Note:* The Japanese candidate was elected by a vote of 39 to 15. The following year Mr. Nadjakov was accorded the honor.

mitted. With the exception of ECAFE and ECA, international Secretariats are staffed primarily with Westerners, and thus quite naturally the Afro-Asians want more posts for their nationals. Moscow hopes to translate their common sentiment on this issue, as well as the existing dissatisfactions with the Secretariat's handling of the Congo affair, into support for its troika proposal.

The Issue of Equitable Geographical Distribution

The UN Charter does not call for fixed quotas from member-states for the allocation of professional posts. It mandates a Secretariat staffed by qualified personnel of high standards of integrity and recommends that recruitment be based on a broad geographical basis. Thus, Article 101(3) states:

"The paramount consideration in the employment of the staff and in the determination of the conditions of service shall be the necessity of securing the highest standards of efficiency, competence, and integrity. Due regard shall be paid to the importance of recruiting the staff on as wide a geographical basis as possible."

Further, in recognition of the fact that a truly international Secretariat is ensured not by a multiplicity of nationalities but by the attitudes and actions of its staff, Article 100 enjoins members of the Secretariat from seeking or receiving "instructions from any government or from any other authority external to the Organization" and from acting in any way "which might reflect on their position as international officials responsible to the Organization."

In 1945 most available competent and experienced personnel were Westerners, who composed more than 85 per cent of the UN staff. A similar situation existed in the Specialized Agencies. Over the years this imbalance has been slowly, but only partially, rectified. In 1948, for example, when the Secretariat had reached a relatively stable level, and when the General Assembly initially adopted the present system of "desirable ranges" as a guide to the geographical composition of the staff, approximately 75 per cent of the staff were Westerners; by 1962, this percentage had been lowered to 62 per cent.[7] Now with the membership more than doubled, international Secretariats come under persistent pressure to appoint greater numbers of nationals from both the Soviet bloc and the Afro-Asian countries.

On a number of occasions between 1955 and 1960, the Soviet Government protested against "the violation of the principle of equitable geographical distribution" in regard to the composition of the UN Secretariat and the Specialized Agencies.[8] It noted that there were ten times as many American as Soviet nationals on the UN Secretariat and that most of the key executive posts were held by nationals from the NATO countries. Though calling for changes, it did little—because of the leadership's inability then to perceive the advantages which the assignment of additional personnel might bring—to fill vacancies available for Soviet nationals, and attempts by the United Nations to recruit more Soviets met with no cooperation. From 1954 to 1961, the Soviet Union increased the number of professional posts which it held on the UN

[7] UN Document A/5270, p. 3.

[8] Economic and Social Council, *Official Records* (28th Session), July 1959, p. 83.

The principle of equitable geographical distribution has also been applied to the policy-making and technical organs of international organizations. Thus, Soviet delegates frequently condemn the ILO for its failure to accord adequate representation to the socialist countries on the Governing Body, the Industrial Committees, and various advisory committees. ILO, *Proceedings* (42nd Session), June 1958, p. 171. For a comprehensive account of Soviet policy in ILO, and of Soviet criticisms of the West, see Harold K. Jacobson, "The USSR and the ILO," *International Organization*, Vol. xiv, No. 3 (1960), pp. 402-428; and Alfred Fernbach, *Soviet Coexistence Strategy: A Case Study of Experience in the International Labor Organization* (Washington, D. C.: Public Affairs Press, 1960, 63pp.).

Secretariat from a little over 2 to a little more than 3 per cent—still far short of its "desirable range."

In the Specialized Agencies the imbalance was even more pronounced, giving rise to situations like the one at UNESCO's annual conference, in November 1958, when the Soviet delegate threatened a withdrawal of Soviet financial support unless more posts were made available to the Soviet bloc. In the ILO, where the Soviet Union had little more than 1 per cent of the professional posts, their delegates moved beyond denunciations of alleged discriminatory practices by the Secretariat to broader attacks on the composition of the executive organ and committee structure of the Organization, a precursor of Khrushchev's troika proposal and of the even more extensive demands for structural changes that have been made by Soviet writers: "In this century of extraordinary rapid changes the ILO is still creeping along at a snail's pace. Indeed, how can one speak of the existence of normal conditions—absolutely normal conditions—in the ILO if countries that represent 12 per cent of all States Members of the ILO have less than 4 per cent representation in the Governing Body of the ILO; if countries which contribute more than 15 per cent to the budget of the ILO are represented by less than 2 per cent?"[9] They contended that this imbalance in the Governing Body, as well as in the staffing of the Secretariat, was deliberately perpetuated by the West and that the lists of Soviet candidates submitted for consideration as staff appointments had still not brought any noticeable changes.

In the highly technical and patently nonpolitical Specialized Agencies, such as the International Telecommunication Union (ITU), the Universal Postal Union (UPU), or the World Meteorological Organization (WMO), Moscow has rarely demanded more posts. It is seemingly unconcerned over the composition of Secretariats of organizations in which politics

[9] ILO, *Proceedings* (44th Session), June 1960, p. 400.

has no publicity value, in which the Secretariat does not have the authority or opportunity to influence or interpret political decisions, in which attention does not pivot on the under-developed countries, and in which highly technical functions are carried on in a manner satisfactory to the Great Powers.

The situation in the International Telecommunication Union may be noted by way of illustration. ITU has three main purposes: "to maintain and extend international cooperation for the improvement and rational use of telecommunication, to promote the development of technical facilities and their most efficient operation, and lastly, to harmonize the actions of nations in the attainment of these common ends." (The ITU was originally established in 1865, thus making it the oldest intergovernmental organization; its present relationship to the United Nations was established in 1947.) The USSR was an active participant at conferences during the Stalin period (one of the few Specialized Agencies in which this was true). However, its views and desired allotment of radio circuits led to frequent and bitter clashes and to its withdrawal from a number of conferences, e.g. the meeting of the Provisional Frequency Board in October 1949 and the High-Frequency Broadcasting Conference in April 1950.[10] One Western specialist attributed the Soviet refusal to provide sufficient information on its use of various radio frequencies, or to cooperate in the assignment of such frequencies until 1956, to a number of reasons: a) Moscow was not prepared to reduce its requirements "to the point where a workable plan could be drafted"; b) its desire to retain all possible advantages accruing to it under the old list; c) the unwillingness to supply technical data; d) "the existence of two radically and apparently incompatible approaches" to the problem; e) the deterioration of

[10] George A. Codding, Jr., *Broadcasting Without Barriers* (Paris: UNESCO, 1959), pp. 104-105. See also Professor Codding's *The International Telecommunication Union* (Leiden: E. J. Brill, 1952), pp. 351-363.

East-West relations.[11] However, a number of other factors must be kept in mind: first, it was another aspect, no doubt, of the self-quarantining and isolationist character of Stalin's foreign policy; second, Moscow, with its xenophobic concern over security and intelligence information, was reluctant to give any data which might shed light on the state of Soviet telecommunications; finally, Moscow was not then advanced in many areas of telecommunications and preferred not to expose its weaknesses to Western appraisal.

By 1954, however, Soviet experts started to attend the meetings of ITU's International Telegraph and Telephone Consultative Committee (CCITT), and the International Radio Consultative Committee (CCIR). Developments in Soviet technology, an easing of the Stalinist proscriptions on contacts with the West, a realization that scientific exchanges could benefit the USSR, and an increased usage of radio frequencies, with attendant interest in their regularization, all served to induce Soviet participation.

Though the number of Soviet nationals working for the ITU has remained small—less than 3 per cent—Moscow has not insisted upon increased representation, as it has in other Specialized Agencies. The highly technical nature of the organization, the infrequent plenary meetings of the major bodies, and the relatively minor role played by underdeveloped countries in the ITU are partial explanations. Also, the United States and the Soviet Union, as the most dynamic members in terms of technological development and demands, frequently find themselves on the same side in voting situations; for example, in the International Frequency Registration Board (IFRB), a key body in the ITU, they share similar ideas concerning procedures for solving problems arising out of the exploration of space. Both Powers also share the belief that the problem of radio frequency jamming lies beyond the scope of ITU

[11] *Ibid.*

responsibility. The jamming of registered frequencies is a regular feature of the Cold War, with considerable importance in the cultural and propaganda competition in underdeveloped countries. Since each Power resorts to this technological weapon in the struggle for audiences abroad, and each is reluctant to publicize or subject its activities to systematic scrutiny, they refrain from raising this sensitive issue in ITU meetings. Both regard jamming as a *political* problem, and hence not the concern of the ITU.

Moscow fulfills its responsibilities within the Organization. On the important issue of registering frequencies with the ITU four months prior to operating on those frequencies, its abides by ITU regulations. Moscow pays 10 per cent of the regular ITU budget, the same amount as that paid by the United States. Assessment is by category of membership; both the United States and the USSR are in category 30—the highest category. Each pays, in addition, for the subordinate categories of, in the case of the USSR, the Ukrainian and Belorussian SSR's, and in the case of the United States, its overseas territories. Their parity of financial contribution is rare in international organization, existing also in the UPU; and it may be noted that the budgets of both organizations are small, approximately $1.3 million a year for the ITU, and less than a million dollars a year for the UPU. The Soviet Union participates in the study groups organized under the CCITT and CCIR. It is also very much interested in the space study group. In 1957 the USSR invited the study group on color TV to meet in Moscow, where for the first time it showed many of its latest advances to an outside organization.

Most ITU personnel are career civil servants. By contrast, the few Soviet personnel in ITU rarely remain for periods longer than two years. Moscow has shown no interest in changing this situation. The 1960 ITU annual report noted "that there was again little response to circular-letters advertising vacant posts which are not represented or are under-represented among the staff of the Union (ITU)." This may be accounted for by the relative political unimportance of the ITU. Since the ITU is a technical organization, Moscow may prefer to accept the existing situation as long as it believes its interests are being adequately safeguarded.

One notable exception to the general Soviet lack of interest, prior to 1960, in placing its nationals on international Secretariats was in the International Atomic Energy Agency, where the USSR took an active part from the beginning. There it did more than merely call attention to the need to staff the Secretariat with personnel from representative parts of the geographic spectrum; it came up with suitable candidates for every Department and at every level, with the result that it is represented by the second largest group (the United States is the largest) on the IAEA Secretariat. This departure from Moscow's usual indifference toward international Secretariats was, simultaneously, an indication of the special importance which it attributed to the IAEA—its desire to be kept fully informed of all phases of IAEA's activities, and to be provided with the most comprehensive account possible of the latest scientific developments in all nuclear fields—and a verification of its real absence of interest in the other Agencies. Moscow maintains an unflagging interest in the IAEA Secretariat's operations and takes concrete steps to ensure maximum representation—in obvious contrast to its relations with the Specialized Agencies.

Regardless of the political motivations behind Khrushchev's troika proposal, the intensification of Soviet demands for increased representation for the Soviet bloc and the neutralist countries on international Secretariats does rest upon a sound statistical base. In the thirteen Specialized Agencies (except FAO, which is now headed by an Indian) and IAEA, all Directors-General are Westerners, and most of the top posts are held by Westerners; very few come from the Soviet bloc or the underdeveloped countries. Less than 5 per cent of

UNESCO's personnel comes from the Soviet bloc, and few of them are in responsible positions. In the ILO, 80 per cent of the Division Chiefs are Westerners; none are Soviet citizens, and only 3 per cent of the professional posts are held by Soviet-bloc personnel. In IAEA, Professor Emelyanov, the chief Soviet delegate, lashed out against the Western stronghold. Calling for adoption of the troika proposal, he noted that more than 60 per cent of the 207 professional positions, and 70 per cent of the directorial posts, were concentrated in the hands of NATO nationals, with the result that the staff, heavily recruited from one bloc, particularly at the higher levels, was used to channel "the Agency's work in important spheres in a way that suited the interests primarily of the United States and its Allies."[12]

On November 16, 1960, the Soviet delegate, A. A. Roshchin, in the Administrative and Budgetary Committee of the General Assembly derided the one-sided composition of the Secretariat: "In its present form the United Nations Secretariat is actually not an international apparatus. It is an apparatus of the United States and the countries that are tied to the United States by military alliances. As regards its composition and the trend of its activity it is basically pro-American and pro-Western. It does not express the interests of other states, above all the socialist countries, and at the same time it does not pursue a policy in keeping with the interests of the United Nations as a whole." He further declared: "Even according to the figures contained in the report of the Secretary-General, which gives a far from accurate picture of the real situation, 779 persons out of a total of 1,168 employees subject to geographical distribution, are citizens of the United States and other countries that are members of Western military alliances. This accounts for 66.6 per cent of the total. The neutral states have 305 employees in this category, or 26.1 per cent, while the socialist states have only 84 persons, or 7.2 per cent."

[12] GC(v)/OR, p. 8.

The Secretary-General, Mr. Dag Hammarskjold, rebutted the Soviet charges of deliberate discrimination in recruitment of professional staff at UN headquarters. He indicated that while the Soviet Government complained about inadequate representation, it failed to suggest workable solutions or to supply recruits: "I get lists of candidates. We pick out those who seem to fit the vacancies and, then, it happens, too often in some cases, that after a short time of employment, without any pre-warning, those recruited go home again or, maybe, are withdrawn. In fact, it is in some cases difficult to keep such a pace of recruitment as to balance the pace of withdrawal."[13] One Western observer has called attention to the seldom publicized paradox "that the Secretary-General is occasionally under pressure *not* to apply the principle of geographical distribution to particular operations, but to give preference to persons from countries which, for geographical or ideological reasons, have a special interest in the operation, e.g. the fact that the UN Information Center in Moscow is staffed solely by Soviet citizens."[14]

Explaining the poor Soviet representation in the ILO, Mr. David L. Morse, its Director-General, noted that "the Communist countries" refuse to accept the competitive examination system used by ILO to recruit for professional posts. Instead, they present their own candidates for each available post, and even then the Soviet officials appointed on the recommendation of their Government do not stay very long with the ILO. After a few years, they return to national service: "We have had a large turnover of Soviet officials. Now an official who knows he is to return to national service is psychologically in a very different position from a career international civil servant. He has naturally less incentive than the career official to acquire the uniquely international view-

---

[13] *New York Times,* October 19, 1960.

[14] Sydney D. Bailey, *The Secretariat of the United Nations* (New York: Carnegie Endowment for International Peace, 1962), p. 101.

point."[15] Mr. Morse observed that the underdeveloped countries accept ILO recruitment procedures. The main obstacle to employing more of their nationals is the shortage of competent people from these countries seeking ILO employment.

The Soviet delegate, Mr. Goroshkin, disputed Mr. Morse's explanation of the "abnormal situation which exists within the ILO," and declared that he was trying "to shift the blame when he spoke of the difficulties of recruiting citizens of socialist countries, which he, apparently forgetting both the official terminology and his official position, preferred to call Communist countries. The Director-General maintained, for instance, that the Soviet Union does not agree to the usual procedure for recruiting staff by means of competitions and that even his conversations 'at the highest levels' brought no results. I most emphatically refute such an assertion. First of all, we are not aware of any conversations 'at the highest levels' on this question. Secondly, the Director-General himself knows perfectly well that, in the correspondence which took place some time ago between him and the Permanent Representative of the USSR in Geneva, we expressed full agreement with the procedure of recruiting Soviet citizens for the ILO proposed by the Director-General himself. Then why did the Director-General need to make such an assertion?"[16] Such acrimonious exchanges are not uncommon, and these conflicting interpretations have not been cleared up by any published review of correspondence between the ILO Secretariat and the Soviet Government.

The situation, as described by Mr. Morse, remains broadly true today. The Soviets do not accept the regular procedure for selection of ILO staff and they do not submit to the competitions. However, a modus vivendi appears to have been worked out by which the ILO informs the Soviet Government of the competition which is being organized for the recruit-

[15] ILO, *Provisional Records* (45th Session), June 1961, p. 505.
[16] *Ibid.*, p. 630.

ment of specific personnel. The Soviets then furnish the ILO with a list of names from which the official is finally chosen.[17] The main problems still in dispute are the length of time Soviet citizens serve in the organization before being reassigned and the continued failure of the Soviet Government to appoint to the organization significantly greater numbers than has heretofore been its practice.

The Soviet campaign for a more equitable distribution of Secretariat posts has found a receptive following among the Afro-Asian countries, especially the latecomers to national independence. These countries view their "quota" of posts as a means of satisfying their quest for prestige and equality with other nations and want to use international Secretariats as training grounds for their nationals who remain a few years and then return to serve in the government or Foreign Service. For the few underdeveloped countries with surpluses of college-trained personnel, e.g. India, Egypt, and Pakistan, greater representation would provide an outlet for people not needed or, for political and professional reasons, not wanted at home. In Specialized Agencies, where the apportionment of professional posts is so evidently disproportionate to the membership's composition, and where this issue is a political concern of the underdeveloped countries, Moscow's attacks on Western domination and discrimination have had an effect.

---

[17] To promote a more equitable distribution of professional posts, the Director-General of ILO issued instructions to the effect that vacancies should be filled in accordance with three principles: "first, that external competitions should normally be opened initially only in countries from which there were no nationals or too few nationals on the staff; second, that recruitment from countries in an intermediate group should be initiated only if all reasonable efforts to recruit nationals of countries in the first group prove unsuccessful; and third, that appointments should not be offered to nationals of countries from which there already were, for historical reasons, too large a number, unless justified by very special circumstances, such as special linguistic requirements, and unless specifically authorized in each case by the Director-General personally." ILO, *Provisional Records* (46th Session), June 1962, Appendix No. 38, p. VII.

The Ghanaian delegate to the ILO annual conference called for a radical change in the structure of the Organization to reflect the growing importance of the neutralist countries: "We know that the International Labor Organization was started by certain countries, and at that time there were few Asian and African countries, but that was over 40 years ago. . . . We cannot go on forever to be members of an Organization where we are discriminated against. We cannot continue forever to belong to the International Labor Organization when decisions about Africa are taken in Geneva."[18] In IAEA, the Indian delegation called for a revamping of the top levels of the Secretariat, a suggestion seconded by other delegations. The Philippine delegate noted that "it might be argued that the less developed countries could not spare any experts to fill technical posts, but that argument did not apply to the administrative posts."[19]

The Soviet Government hopes that this dissatisfaction among the Afro-Asians can be transformed into support for its troika proposal. It links the inequitable distribution of posts to vestiges of colonialism and an ingrained Western sense of superiority over non-Western peoples and encourages the view that a nation is slighted if it does not receive its due share of Secretariat positions. Moscow concludes that only a troika arrangement in which the Soviet, neutralist, and Western blocs are accorded equal representation can ensure the desired equitable geographical distribution of posts for all countries.

Moscow and the International Civil Service

Khrushchev's proposal has created an uneasiness among UN personnel. The pressure to hire more Soviets, East Europeans, and Afro-Asians is making UN officials self-conscious

[18] ILO, *op. cit.* (45th Session), p. 68.
[19] GC(v)/OR. 52, p. 26.

about seeking candidates in Western countries and is bringing about changes in recruitment practices. But most UN officials have permanent contracts, making expansion the only possible way (apart from normal retirement) to meet the demand for a change in the type of personnel. This, however, involves increased budgets, and the UN is already in dire financial straits.

A major effort to find a workable solution, satisfactory to all UN members, had been undertaken at the direction of the General Assembly by Dag Hammarskjold several months before Khrushchev made the subject a contentious political issue. In June 1961 a committee of eight experts, representing different national viewpoints, made a number of proposals for reorganizing the Secretariat, intending them also to guide subsequent policies for all international Secretariats. The committee proceeded "on the assumption that its recommendations must be in harmony with the provisions of the Charter which envisage a Secretariat organized and employed in such a way as to achieve independence, efficiency, and wide geographical distribution." The report[20] provided a series of recommendations designed to correct "the existing imbalance and inequality in geographical distribution of staff," including a plan to offer "not less than 100 posts" to the Soviet bloc. To obtain a unanimous vote, the committee went to some lengths to meet the Soviet position, but the Soviet member maintained all his original positions by reservations in the report and in his separate statement. The committee expressed its conviction "that the bulk of the staff should consist of persons who intend to make service in the Secretariat a career and that the efficiency of the Secretariat is dependent on the existence of a substantial core of career officials," and supported the view that a suitable proportion (25 per cent) of the UN personnel might be hired on a short-term basis to ensure a continuous flow of "new blood and new ideas." Mr. Roshchin would have

[20] UN Document A/4776.

none of this; he said the whole concept of a permanent civil service was "only a cover for the unsatisfactory practice of recruiting the personnel of the Secretariat on a clearly improper, one-sided basis."[21] Most committee members would not support the Soviet suggestion that an immediate end be made to the granting of permanent contracts. They said that this would mean the end of an independent, impartial international civil service, for personnel detached only temporarily from national administrations and dependent upon them for their professional future cannot possibly be expected to subordinate the special interests of their countries to the international interest. That the danger of national pressure on an international official is directly related to the terms of his appointment was emphasized by Mr. Hammarskjold in a major address at Oxford University in May 1961 when he noted that a short-term appointee is psychologically and politically in a different position from the permanent civil servant who does not plan a subsequent career with his national government.[22] In November 1962 the Fifth Committee (Administrative and Budgetary Affairs), and subsequently the General Assembly itself, upheld the Committee of Eight and the Secretary-General in their determination to maintain the percentage of permanent appointments at roughly the 75 per cent level. A Czechoslovak resolution, which sought to gain support for the expansion of the percentage of short-term contracts, met with such opposition, both from the Western and the Afro-Asian countries, that it was not even offered for a vote.[23]

Mr. Roshchin, in a separate opinion, said the report (of the Committee of Eight) failed to provide "for vigorous corrective measures" to improve the current unsatisfactory situation.

[21] *Ibid.*, p. 20.
[22] UN Press Release N. PM/85, May 29, 1961 (Geneva).
[23] A/C.5/L.749 (November 21, 1962).

He quoted the statistics that out of a total of 1,309 posts in the Secretariat, the Soviet Union had only 42, and the total of all the Socialist countries was only 84. (By late 1962 the situation had improved considerably: out of 1,389 staff members, 81 were Soviet citizens and 144 came from the Socialist countries.) [24] Mr. Roshchin noted that: "Such an incorrect and one-sided composition of the Secretariat has far-reaching consequences. Among these consequences, the fundamental one is that the Secretariat has, in effect, been transformed into an executive mechanism, not for the United Nations, but for the Western military allies. . . ."[25] Accusing the Western Powers of barring Soviet nationals from participation in most of the Secretariat's important executive functions, in political missions to crisis areas, and in most technical-assistance missions to underdeveloped areas, he sharply attacked Hammarskjold's handling of the Congo problem and called for complete reorganization of the Secretariat along lines set forth in Khrushchev's troika proposal.

Notwithstanding Soviet acceptance of U Thant as Secretary-General for a full term, to expire in 1966, it seems clear that Moscow has no intention of abandoning its fundamental demand for reconstitution of the Secretariat. What Moscow wants is an arbitrary and mechanical apportionment of *all* positions according to ideology, political alignments, and military alliances. On the eve of the seventeenth General Assembly, for example, an article appeared in the authoritative Soviet journal, *International Affairs*, which went far beyond the original Khrushchev troika proposal of September 1960. It insisted that the troika principle should apply not only in the Secretariat but in the distribution of seats in the Security Council, the Economic and Social Council, the International

---

[24] UN Document A/C.5/933, p. 3.

[25] A/4776, Appendix, p. 2. See also the Soviet analysis in the article, "To Resolve the Problem of Reorganization of the U.N.O.," *Kommunist*, No. 4 (March 1961), pp. 13-14.

Court of Justice, and the election of "the post of President of the General Assembly and Chairmen of its main Committees."[26] How Moscow expects, if indeed it does, to effect such sweeping reorganizations without formal revisions of the Charter is not yet apparent. It remains opposed to any revision of the Charter or the convening of a conference to consider changes in the Charter.

Developments during the early months of the Congo crisis awakened Moscow to the political importance that the office of Secretary-General and the Secretariat had acquired and to the realization that the veto it possessed in the Security Council might be circumvented by the action of the Secretariat itself. Consequently, it undertook a twofold course designed to resolve the situation to its advantage. Moscow produced the troika proposal to bring the office of the Secretary-General under effective control, and it stressed the need of wider geographical distribution in the Secretariat, including the placing of Soviet nationals in key political posts in order to increase their influence there. The failure, thus far, to attract widespread support among the Afro-Asians for recasting the composition and character of the Secretariat has been a bitter disappointment, but it has not led the Soviets to abandon this objective.

From everything that Soviet spokesmen have said, it is clear that they seek to discredit, weaken, and destroy the concept and structure of the International Civil Service. They do not accept the assumption that men may act independently, impartially, and responsibly in the interest of the international community. Soviet leaders do not believe that individuals will make decisions which contravene their class or political interest. The concept is anathema to their value system and their approach to social and political analysis. Premier Khru-

[26] M. Volodin, "U.N. in a Changed World," *International Affairs*, No. 9 (September 1962), p. 7.

shchev told Mr. Walter Lippmann that he "would never accept a single neutral administrator. Why? Because while there are neutral countries, there are no neutral men. You would not accept a Communist administrator, and I cannot accept a non-Communist administrator."[27] During a press conference in New York on September 24, 1960, he dismissed as impossible the ability of the Secretary-General to act with equal regard for "the interests of the countries of monopoly capital, the interests of the socialist countries, and the interests of the neutralist countries . . . . Now one man is the interpreter and executor of all the decisions of the Assembly and the Security Council, but an old saying goes: There are no saints on earth and there never have been. Let those who believe that there are saints keep their belief; we have no faith in such fables."

In his last annual report to the General Assembly, Mr. Hammarskjold defended the principle of a Secretariat which is international in its composition and international in its responsibilities. He dismissed the Soviet view of the UN "as a static conference machinery for resolving conflicts of interest and ideologies. . . served by a Secretariat which is to be regarded not as fully internationalized but as representing within its ranks those very interests and ideologies."[28] Directing attention to the provisions in the Charter calling upon member-states to respect "the exclusively international char-

---

[27] *New York Herald Tribune,* April 17, 1961. This Soviet dogma had its Western counterpart thirty years ago in the League of Nations. In a report reviewing the administration of the League Secretariat, two experts noted in a minority opinion that "so long as there is no Super-State, and therefore no *international man,* an international spirit can only be assured through the cooperation of men of different nationalities who represent the public opinion of their respective countries." However, this view was rejected, and the League was not thought of "as merely a piece of conference machinery," but as an institution having "an existence independent of its constituent elements; it possessed international personality and legal capacity." Sydney D. Bailey, "The Troika and the Future of the UN," *International Conciliation,* No. 538 (1962), p. 21.

[28] UN Press Release No. GA/xvi/1, August 25, 1961.

acter of the responsibilities of the Secretary-General and the staff and not to seek to influence them in the discharge of their responsibilities," he defended the institution of the international Secretariat, seeing no contradiction between a demand for a truly international Secretariat and a demand for a wide geographical distribution of posts: "It is, indeed, necessary precisely in order to maintain the exclusively international character of the Secretariat, that it be so composed as to achieve a balanced distribution of posts on all levels among all regions. This, however, is clearly something different from a balanced representation of trends and ideologies." In direct disagreement with Khrushchev's views on the international civil servant, Mr. Hammarskjold said that "while it may be said that no man is neutral in the sense that he is without opinions or ideals, it is just as true that, in spite of this, a neutral Secretariat is possible. Anyone of integrity, not subjected to undue pressures, can, regardless of his own views, readily act in an 'exclusively international' spirit and can be guided in his actions on behalf of the Organizations solely by its interests and principles and by the instructions of its organs."

Even among many of the nations (e.g. India and Nigeria) critical of the present heavily Western-dominated Secretariats, there is wide acceptance of the view that an international civil servant can act in an efficient, independent, impartial manner, irrespective of national origin or personal philosophy. A Burmese official cited U Thant as example of an individual who, on becoming an international civil servant, had completely detached himself from all contact with former colleagues and was making decisions without regard for the policy of the Government of Burma. He expressed the opinion that Soviet nationals, too, working on international Secretariats need not be necessarily influenced in their judgments and decisions by the policy of their Government. As to the specific issue of the troika proposal, he paused for a moment and then remarked

278

ruefully: "Mr. Khrushchev said that there are no neutral men. If he really believes that, then what else is there for us to say."

Soviet Citizens as International Civil Servants: The Record

How have Soviet citizens performed as international civil servants? In their official capacities on international Secretariats have they attempted to promote the policies of the Soviet Union? How have they behaved when situations arose in which their responsibilities to the UN conflicted with the policy of the Soviet Government? How has the employment of Soviet citizens affected the operation of international Secretariats? Would any changes result from the recruitment of large numbers of additional Soviet nationals? Information derived from interviews with officials of international Secretariats offers some tentative answers to these questions.[29]

In general, Soviet nationals have had little impact upon international Secretariats. In no Secretariat have they become a power in the decision-making hierarchy. Only in the Department of Training and Technical Information of the International Atomic Energy Agency have Soviet and Soviet-bloc personnel begun to establish their "presence," and then in a manner which has been largely beneficial to the Organization. Several reasons were suggested for this marginal influence: their short stay, the run-of-the-mill quality of most of the Soviets assigned, the language barrier, and the self-imposed isolation of the great majority of the men. Of these, the most significant, and one which reveals how little Soviet leaders attach to international Secretariats, is the brevity of their appointments. Soviet nationals are assigned by the Ministry of Foreign Affairs to work in international organizations,

[29] Interviews were conducted during the 1961-62 period with officials and former officials of the United Nations, ECE, ECAFE, ILO, WHO, IAEA, and ITU.

usually for two, and rarely for more than three, years, after which they return to the Soviet Union. They are not interested in becoming permanent international civil servants. By this policy of rapid turnover, Moscow has precluded its citizens from becoming influential in the day-to-day affairs of the Secretariat. In any organization power inheres not merely in the position of the incumbent, but in his ability to maximize its potential—and this is a function of time, attitude, and experience. Seniority appropriately used is a source of authority in any organization. But Soviet officials are denied its benefits and the influence which it can bring, by their own government. Soviet nationals have barely familiarized themselves with their positions when they are reassigned.

Various explanations have been given for Moscow's policy of short-term appointments. All non-Soviet officials interpreted it as a fundamental lack of interest by the Soviet Government in international Secretariats and, inferentially, in international organizations. One East European Communist diplomat agreed with this, but added that "the unwillingness to assign its citizens for long terms is a sign that Moscow has not fully learned that international organizations can be used to promote Soviet objectives more effectively than they are at present. Moscow understands well the value and power of control over organizations in other areas, but does not yet appreciate the importance of having Soviet nationals made an integral and continuing part of international Secretariats. Only after it learns this can the USSR hope to play a major role in these bodies. Also, the Soviet nationals themselves are reluctant to serve longer than two or three years in international organizations because of their fear that it will jeopardize prospects for promotion at home. They understand the marginal importance of their service and see that, with few exceptions, the men assigned are not of the best quality. They are often the misfits and the miscellaneous who haven't lived up to their promise at home, and the boss is trying to get rid of them." He knew of several instances where high ranking Soviet officials in the Secretariat in New York strongly requested that they be replaced after two years.[30]

One Soviet official, who has been associated with the UN section of the Ministry of Foreign Affairs since 1945, attributed the short tours of Soviet nationals in international Secretariats to the personal reluctance of Soviet citizens to work abroad indefinitely or for extended periods of time. "Would you," he asked me, "like to spend the rest of your life, or even five years, in Bangkok, Rome, or Geneva?" Moreover, he disputed the argument that the international civil service apparatus suffered as a result of the fluidity of its personnel. Noting that foreign-service employees of most countries have tours of duty at home alternating with changing foreign posts, he stated that Soviet personnel worked for international Secretariats on assignment, just as they served in foreign countries, and were

[30] Only one of the Soviet nationals who served as Under Secretary-General in charge of Political and Security Council Affairs—the highest post thus far held by a Soviet citizen in the UN—has remained longer than two years. Under a "gentleman's agreement," concluded in 1945 between the United States and the USSR, and approved by the five permanent members of the Security Council the following year, the post of Under Secretary-General of Political and Security Council Affairs has usually been assigned to a Soviet national. With one exception, none served longer than two years: Arkady Sobolev (1946-1948); Constantin E. Zinchenko (1948-1952); Ilya S. Tschernyshev (1953); Anatoly F. Dobrynin (1958-1960); Georgi F. Arkadev (1960-1962); E. D. Kiselev (died April 17, 1963); Vladimir P. Suslov (1963—).

Regarding Dobrynin, who was appointed Ambassador to the United States in March 1962, one correspondent gave the following assessment: "More than any other Russian before or since, Dobrynin took seriously his duties as an international civil servant. He ran an efficient, disciplined Office of Political and Security Council Affairs. He took a kindly interest in subordinates who came before the promotion boards. He spoke in policy matters not only for the Soviet point of view; frequently, colleagues recall, he represented Hammarskjold's viewpoints to the Soviet delegation in a brokerage operation often marked by success." Max Frankel, "Moscow's Man Intrigues Washington," *The New York Times Magazine* (July 29, 1962).

not interested in making a career out of their work in international organizations.

Several Asian officials thought that the Soviet Union shifted people in international Secretariats in order to keep national loyalties firm. Moscow was concerned that exposure to the West and periods of activity relatively free from close Party supervision might result in more critical attitudes toward the official ideology and policy, or even in outright defections. Westerners tended to discount this explanation. This difference in attitude, which will not be stressed here because of the limited sampling, may in part stem from the disparity of the experience of these two groups in dealing with Soviets and in their understanding of the cohesiveness of Soviet society. Also, the greater alienation of Asians from their own societies as a consequence of prolonged work and living in a Western environment, to the extent that they are sometimes dissatisfied with the thought of returning for permanent residence in their native countries, may lead them to attribute their own attitudes to Soviet citizens in similar situations.[31]

Secretariat officials observed that, in addition to making appointments on a short-term basis, Moscow rarely assigned outstanding personnel to work on international Secretariats. They admitted that this might be a hypercritical assessment, but insisted that Soviet staff members, particularly at the lower levels, "sit at their desks or wander around the corridors on long coffee breaks," and are either not industrious or lack in-

[31] We do know that there are thousands of individuals from underdeveloped countries who, once having acquired an education in the West and having spent a number of years abroad, choose not to return, but to "exile" themselves. Though they usually retain their citizenship, they remain abroad, working for international organizations, or for enterprises in Western countries, where they can earn many times their prospective salary at home and can experience relief and liberation from the confining, traditionalist pressures which await them at home.

As they adapt to Western society, they come to value not only the greater professional opportunities but the ability to lead their personal lives more independently than they can in their native country.

terest, perhaps because they know that their position is temporary. One official in IAEA observed that "most Soviet officials do nothing but fill a billet. They have no interest in the Agency. A Soviet official in the legal division has been there for two years and has done nothing but read newspapers. A few, however, have done good jobs." A colleague of his countered that the Soviet heads of IAEA's Department of Training and Technical Information, which is responsible for arranging conferences, fellowships, and training courses, "have performed diligently and well. But they have brought so many Soviet bloc citizens into the Department that it is beginning to acquire the reputation of a source of Soviet strength in the Agency's Secretariat."

A formerly high-ranking Indian on the ECAFE Secretariat offered the following evaluation: "There have never been more than three or four Soviet nationals on the [ECAFE] Secretariat at any one time, and they have not been very effective. Soviet personnel do not show any independent judgment, critical capability, or flexibility in approaching economic and political problems. They rarely stay longer than two years. Appointments are made by Moscow, and the Executive-Secretary has no choice but to accept the few that are sent. Moscow requests more posts for its nationals but refuses to send people who are linguistically proficient or professionally able to do work other than in their narrow specialty. This limits Soviet effectiveness. They are not and cannot be a decisive factor in Secretariat affairs." Several ECAFE officials commented that rarely can a Soviet official on an international Secretariat communicate effectively in English or French, a necessity for staff members. However, recent appointees, particularly among the young diplomats, are better prepared, and this difficulty is expected to be remedied in the next five years.

As a consequence the decision-makers among the permanent staff, who are invariably Westerners, are usually unwilling to give Soviet nationals much responsibility or substantive work

—an attitude reinforced by the residual mutual distrust. As relative transients the Soviets are at a severe disadvantage; they are not accepted as colleagues or international civil servants by the permanent professional staff. Thus, the Soviets are not taken into the inner circle of administrators, into "the power elite" which really runs the Secretariat's day-to-day affairs. By maintaining this distance, the permanent staff, in its turn, reinforces the Soviet staff's belief that they are in a hostile environment where they are not really wanted and are discriminated against, and this widens the gulf. One ILO official candidly admitted that the Soviets are not trusted: "We assume," he said, "that they pass along all information to Moscow on any issue. That is not to say that anything secret is involved, since the member governments must eventually approve of anything the Secretariat does, but during the negotiating phase, Soviet personnel can place the Secretariat at a disadvantage by premature and improper disclosures." It is no secret that Soviet nationals assigned to international organizations report regularly to Soviet Missions; Moscow does little to disguise the subordination to its discipline of all Soviet citizens working in international Secretariats. Although 10 per cent of ECE Secretariat posts are held by Soviet citizens, they have been used sparingly in research on the Soviet Union or Eastern Europe. ECE officials state that although a few of the Soviets are very good, in general it is difficult to use them on bloc developments because they "don't have the same questioning, probing, critical approach toward Soviet bloc problems that Westerners have toward both the Western European and the Soviet blocs. They will never criticize their government's policy."

From the foregoing, it is evident that Soviet authorities have numerous instances of antipathy toward the USSR on the part of many officials on international Secretariats with which to castigate UN officials in plenary sessions of these organizations. One Soviet official in Geneva, though justifying the present pattern of short-term appointments, acknowledged that it might create problems for the Secretariats and said that the Soviet Government was now preparing competent people for careers in international organizations and was anticipating extension of the period of assignment. If this proves correct, it could mark the first step in a concerted drive by Moscow to play a major role in the operations of international Secretariats.

To all these overlapping explanations must be added the ever-present human factor. Official Soviet policy may fluctuate from bellicose threats of nuclear annihilation to ingenuous appeals for cooperation and coexistence; but whatever the political climate in Moscow, Soviet personnel on international Secretariats, like most Soviet diplomats, continue to follow their self-isolating mode of everyday living, to create the cocoon-like existence which makes close contact with non-Communists impossible. There are exceptions but they are made rarely, selectively, and with deliberation. In all the essentials of routine living—choice of friends, housing, education for children, and enjoyment of leisure time—Soviet citizens restrict, or are restricted in, their range of experiences with foreigners. These inhibitions are pervasive and officially sanctioned. The situation in education and housing of Soviet nationals in Geneva may be cited by way of illustration. No Soviet child goes to a Western school or has any contact with foreign children. Before 1959 they were sent home for pre-university education. Now they go to a Soviet-operated school. Officials explain this by the parents' desire to prepare their children adequately for entrance to Soviet institutions of higher education, noting that the education provided in Western schools does not meet the entrance requirements of Soviet universities. In Geneva, where housing is short and rents are high, the Soviet Mission to the UN is building behind the Soviet headquarters an apartment dwelling which will house all Soviet personnel stationed in Geneva, including those attached to the Mission and those working for international organizations, i.e. ILO, WHO, ECE, ITU, UPU, etc. One Soviet attaché cited this housing project as an example of his Government's concern for the welfare of its citizens. The effect, however, as with the education of Soviet children, will be to keep Soviet nationals isolated from intimate and continuous contact with other groups and to intensify already deep-rooted feelings of exclusiveness and suspicion. In both situations the consideration of the Soviet Government for the welfare of its Foreign Service personnel perpetuates minimal and superficial relationships with foreigners. Group exclusiveness is further promoted by the social patterns of Soviet nationals: participation in biweekly cultural programs at Soviet headquarters, infrequent dining with non-Communists, and a pronounced reluctance to establish close friendships with them.

Among those who have worked with Soviet nationals in international organizations, the impression was generally shared that there was no appreciable change in the political and ideological outlook of Soviets who served several years on international Secretariats. The Soviets consider themselves employees of the Soviet Ministry of Foreign Affairs on temporary assignment, and not international civil servants. One Western European summed up the matter in this way: "The Soviets may become more socially poised, dress more tastefully, and chat more frequently with non-Communists about unimportant issues, but their basic political attitudes show no signs of change. Their conviction of the inherent superiority and durability of the Soviet system remains as strong as before. Nor does exposure to a non-Communist milieu dispel their suspicion of the West or lead them to question the correctness of Kremlin policies." A Japanese diplomat, recently returned from a tour of duty in Moscow, said that "the younger generation of Soviet diplomats is able, hard-working, extremely self-confident, and committed to the essentials of the Communist *Weltanschauung;* they are attracted by Western culture and

286

standards of living, but nothing else. Their outlook remains Marxist-Leninist."

It was generally agreed that at present we have no way to measure the effect of exposure to the West on Soviet officials, particularly as it may find expression in the decision-making process. Influence, if there is any, might not take effect for years; certainly no startling changes should be expected in the foreseeable future.

Conditions are not yet ready for a definitive study of Soviet performance on international Secretariats. Too few Soviets have served, and largely in nonsensitive posts. The test of whether Soviet nationals can meet the requirements of independence, integrity, and impartiality demanded of international civil servants is still in the future. So far, Soviet appointees have played negligible roles on the Secretariats. Khrushchev's pressure for more posts has alerted UN authorities to their responsibility and to the need to hire more Soviet-bloc personnel. But there is no convincing evidence that in taking this stand Moscow is genuinely interested in substantially increasing the number of its nationals working for the UN or is prepared to assign them for longer periods.[32] Only by appointing top quality people for long periods can Moscow expect to increase its influence. And only then could we begin to evaluate the extent to which Soviet personnel

---

[32] Professor Leland M. Goodrich has written that the Soviet "demand that more Soviet nationals be employed is a reasonable one; the difficulty arises when it comes to implementation. By denying the whole conception of an international career service, by seeking to place its nationals in what it regards as key policy positions, by denying the possibility of free recruitment, by insisting that all appointments be made from persons proposed and approved by the government for short terms, and by taking the position that its nationals refuse fixed-term career appointments, the Soviet Union makes the task of the Secretary-General in meeting its request for increased participation of its nationals extremely difficult, if not impossible." "Geographical Distribution of the Staff of the UN Secretariat," *International Organization,* Vol. XVI, No. 3 (Summer 1962), p. 481.

are capable of acting independently of Moscow's national position. At the present time it suits Moscow to have this grievance of inequitable representation. Khrushchev seeks to neutralize, not improve, the Secretariat, to prevent it from being used to thwart Soviet aims. He is deriving maximum benefit from using the charge of Western domination in the Secretariats, is gaining favor with the neutralists, and is making the Secretariats cautious of undertaking any activity which might expose them to combined Soviet and neutralist attack.

VII ❧—

The Soviet Image of the United Nations

Moscow's CHALLENGE to the prevailing structure of the United Nations has stimulated increased Western interest in the Kremlin's attitude toward international organizations. Soviet policy statements made on the floor of the UN are subjected to constant scrutiny, but little is known of how Moscow presents to its own people the activities and achievements of international organizations,[1] other than the general knowledge that all information and interpretations are channeled through Party-controlled media of communication and bear the imprint of government approval.

Knowledge of the image of the United Nations that Soviet leaders hold and present to their people is important for an understanding of the Soviet attitude toward international organizations and of the role which they play in over-all Soviet foreign policy. There are two aspects of the problem: first, to review the information that the Soviet Government presents to its own people and the channels that it uses. This reveals not only the limitations placed on what the people can learn, but also the information that it is expressly desired that they do know; second, to analyze the serious and scholarly writings. Since these may be presumed to mirror the political views held at the highest level, any change in their scope or quality or in the image they present can be considered a reflection of modification in the leadership's thinking on foreign policy problems. Soviet scholars tread with caution a carefully hewn path, in which guideposts are clearly marked and never far from view. Their writings offer no insights into

---

[1] One notable exception is Chapter VII of Alexander Dallin's pioneering study of *The Soviet Union at the United Nations* (New York: Frederick A. Praeger, 1962). I am indebted to Professor Dallin for many of the insights in this chapter.

the policy-making process itself, but they do express the existing official attitudes and thus serve as useful guides to current Soviet thinking.

Informing the Soviet Public

Several important, though little-known, organizations are primarily responsible for molding the people's views of the United Nations and other international organizations. Together with the controlled press and radio, they have succeeded in keeping the Soviet people ignorant of the potentialities and achievements of the UN and its affiliates. The perpetuation of this ignorance enables Soviet leaders to minimize the constructive role of international organizations. The Soviet populace have never developed any strong feelings about the United Nations such as may be found in many influential groups among various Western countries. Soviet leaders, who are always prating about their "internationalism," restrict its application to Communist-controlled organizations and automatically rule out the United Nations and the Specialized Agencies which they regard, after all, as "capitalist" organizations.

A gulf has always existed between the statements of support made by Soviet officials in international organizations and the carefully pruned information which is doled out to the people of the USSR. This was vividly demonstrated during the August 1962 visit to the Soviet Union of Secretary-General U Thant, who issued a statement with the understanding that it would be broadcast to the Soviet people. Noting that Soviet policy was motivated in part by fear and suspicion, he stated that the Soviet people do not apparently fully understand the true character of the Congo problem. In the statement broadcast to the Soviet people by Radio Moscow, all references critical of the Soviet Union were omitted.[2] The

[2] *New York Times*, August 31, 1962. According to Seymour Topping, the *Times*'s Moscow correspondent, the Soviet Government had appar-

Soviet people are told little of the contributions of the United Nations except when they accord with Soviet policies, for example, resolutions condemning colonialism. On several occasions, such as UN Day and Human Rights Day, newspaper articles observe that the UN could be a useful instrument for peace, but that it is now ineffective and has failed to live up to expectations largely because the American imperialists and their lackeys seek to subordinate it to their domination. They further report that only through the efforts of the Soviet Union, the People's Democracies, and some of the more "progressive-minded" neutralist nations has the UN been able to function as well as it has. This picture fluctuates according to whether a "hard" or "soft" line is being disseminated: from bitter hostility toward the UN during the Korean War period, to support during the 1956 Suez crisis, and back to denunciation at the time of the Congo affair. But the over-all image is invariably the same: that of a peace-loving Soviet Union working for general and complete disarmament, a lessening of international tensions, and freedom for all colonial areas— and everywhere opposed by the reactionary Western Powers who dominate the Security Council and the Secretariat. The Specialized Agencies and regional economic commissions are seldom mentioned, though, of late, scholars are beginning to write of their activities.

Nominally, the principal responsibility for "educating" the Soviet people about UN activities rests with the Soviet Association for Cooperation with the United Nations; actually, it is carried out by the All Union Society for the Dissemination of Political and Scientific Knowledge, operating in conjunction with the Association. The Soviet Association for Coopera-

---

ently decided to withhold publication of views critical of its policies as a result of the upsetting repercussions among its educated groups of the text of the interview with President Kennedy in November, 1961, which was published in its entirety and contained strong criticism of Soviet policies. *New York Times,* September 1, 1962.

tion with the United Nations was established on March 28, 1956, at a time when the Kremlin was initiating its courtship of underdeveloped countries, in part, by joining a variety of international nongovernmental organizations, as well as Specialized Agencies in which it had not previously been a member. In August 1957 the Association joined WFUNA, the World Federation of Associations for the United Nations, and has since attended all the annual meetings. According to one WFUNA officer, the Soviets manifested only perfunctory interest until the August 1960 session: "They attended the annual meetings and submitted their reports. Their delegates were generally friendly, but not very interested or active in the proceedings. However, with the setback to Soviet ambitions in the Congo, came a decided change. At recent sessions, Soviet delegates have used WFUNA to propound Moscow's position, especially on disarmament and the proposed reorganization of the Secretariat, and have tried to influence members of other delegations to report Soviet proposals favorably to their peers and public at home."

According to its constitution, the Association's objectives are similar to those of its American counterpart: "to popularize the aims and principles of the United Nations with a view to safeguarding and strengthening international peace; to give its support to the efforts of all peace-loving nations desirous of promoting international understanding and cooperation; to strengthen the friendship and solidarity with other nations." There are, however, several important differences between the two organizations. First, the Soviet Association, unlike the American, is government controlled; it expresses and disseminates only views and information approved by Soviet leaders. Second, membership is collective, not individual; organizations join as organizations. Since they are all government controlled, the Association's policies are formulated to advance national, not international, goals. Membership is composed of ten leading mass organizations of Soviet society: 1) the USSR Academy of Sciences; 2) Committee of Soviet Youth Organizations; 3) All Union Council of Trade Unions; 4) Union of Soviet Societies of Friendship and Cultural Relations with Foreign Countries; 5) Committee of Soviet Women; 6) Soviet Committee for the Defense of Peace; 7) the Union of Soviet Writers; 8) Moscow University; 9) Academy of Construction and Architecture; 10) and most important from an operational and propaganda point of view, the All Union Society for the Dissemination of Political and Scientific Knowledge.

Third, the Soviet Association for Cooperation with the United Nations has no vitality of its own; it is a political ornament designed to impress visiting delegations and to publicize Soviet policies abroad. It claims a membership of more than 18 million, a figure no doubt envied by other Associations of WFUNA. But these members have no independent political function; they are incapable of exerting any influence at variance with official policy. The appalling lack of balanced information available to the Soviet public supplies a truer index of the state of the public's political literacy than the meaningless membership statistics that totalitarian societies can always produce. The Association's budget of about $30,000 a year, which is supposed to cover its activities throughout the USSR, is financed by contributions from each of the ten member-organizations. The nine-member Governing Board is composed of prominent academicians and officials, who, according to one Soviet official of the Association, meet every four to six weeks to discuss the Association's plans and the topics to be stressed by lecturers in the field, but have very little to do with actual operations. Day-to-day matters are handled by a three-man permanent staff, which has three main functions: first, to attend the annual WFUNA sessions and send representatives on good-will visits to national UN associations in various countries; second, to provide visiting delegations with information, discussion sessions, and guided tours; third, to coordinate information programs about UN activities with the

All Union Society for the Dissemination of Political and Scientific Knowledge.

To the permanent Secretariat of the Association falls the responsibility for entertaining visitors. In 1958 the Association exchanged visits with its American counterpart, the American Association for the United Nations (AAUN). The fourteen-member group, headed by such eminent figures as Eleanor Roosevelt, Clark M. Eichelberger, Paul Hoffmann, and Arthur Holcombe met with Soviet officials and scholars, visited various cities, and discussed areas of common interest in which cooperation might be promoted irrespective of ideological or political differences, e.g. educating the public about the work of the UN and expanding cultural and scientific exchanges. To be a member of an officially invited delegation to the USSR is to be assured of red-carpet treatment, but although the American delegates met with Soviet officials and scholars, they were not taken to any of the regularly scheduled public lectures conducted under the auspices of the Association. The Soviets are reluctant to grant this experience to visiting foreigners, since the lectures are standard presentations of official policy or polemics against the West.

Educational and informational programs are handled for the Association by the All Union Society for the Dissemination of Political and Scientific Knowledge, an organization, established in 1947, to transmit official views on contemporary developments from the leaders to the average citizen. The Society numbers over one million and reaches into every area and level of Soviet life. It is a key medium for informing the people of the latest orthodoxies in foreign and domestic policies. Members of the Society are drawn from academic, cultural, and scientific circles; they function as voluntary, part-time organizers and represent an important mechanism for adult indoctrination. Approximately 18,000 members are assigned by the Society to work through the ten organizations composing the Association. They arrange meetings, distribute literature, and lead discussions of whatever UN activities are currently being emphasized by *Pravda* and *Izvestiia*. In addition, the Society's Section on International Life provides volunteer lecturers with varying degrees of competence, depending upon the audience. No one formally or systematically briefs the lecturers, nor are any UN booklets used in their preparation. Their "educational" endeavors consist principally of recitations parroted from the latest piece in *Pravda*, or of topical pamphlets especially prepared for the Society by Soviet writers. According to the Association's annual reports to WFUNA, the principal subjects dealt with since 1960 have been disarmament, developments in the Congo, the completion of the liquidation of colonialism, and the need to reorganize the Secretariat and the structure of the UN. One report noted that Soviet lecturers have "actively criticized the UN" for failing to justify "the live hopes that the people of the whole world have nourished in regard to it"; they have also made clear that the structure of the UN, and that of its "ruling and executive organs had become antiquated and did not reflect the new forces which have been created in the world."[3] Current emphasis is on the disarmament problem. It is clear from the lectures delivered and the resolutions passed that the All Union Society plays a vital part in the Government's campaigns to mobilize public support for its policies.

In contradistinction, the Association, which noted that it "responded regularly to important events which took place in the world," consists, according to one observer, "of a desk and a secretary." In fulfilling its domestic function, it works through the All Union Society, upon which it is dependent for lecturers, organizers, and an audience. The Association has no literature, no pamphlets, no written materials of its own for distribution. It relies upon newspaper accounts, books,

[3] *Rapport Annual*—Avril 1960/Mars 1961 of the Association for the United Nations in the USSR to the Sixth Plenary Assembly of WFUNA, Geneva, August 30-September 2, 1961.

pamphlets published by the All Union Society, and the small amount of free material provided by the UN Information Center. One of the Association's annual reports to WFUNA noted that it "maintained direct contact with the UN Information Center in Moscow, which has put at the disposition of the Association different materials and publications of the United Nations, as well as literature necessary for the active education of the Soviet Association on the subject of the UN." Unfortunately, this impressive sounding relationship is misleading, as are many exaggerated accounts found in the reports of insignificant organizations seeking to justify their existence.

The UN Information Center in Moscow—the only one in the Soviet Union—is a study in futility. Ill-equipped and located in a three-room apartment at Khokhlovski Pereulok 15, in a modest, out-of-the-way section of Moscow, its existence is unknown to most Moscovites, and certainly to Soviet people in general. Founded in 1948, it is staffed by Soviet citizens who are paid by the UN. The Center consists of a Director's office, nicely furnished and lined with bookcases containing UN publications and books on the UN, a bare and poorly lit research and reading room for students and specialists who want to use the reports of international organizations, and a small closed storage room holding most of the Center's materials. The pamphlets supplied by the UN are several-page throwaways. They are purely descriptive and do not discuss policies or issues. Occasional mimeographs are run off to publicize the visit to the Soviet Union of a UN mission, the convening of UN meetings, or the statements of Soviet officials at the meetings of international organizations. They have limited distribution and are, no doubt, a formality that is gone through for the sake of visitors. According to one of the officials—(who have fluctuated in number from four to seven) about ten to twenty people come in daily asking for pamphlets or literature. Certainly no journalist or official would be interested in such innocuous information handouts. There is no card catalogue or filing system, and the UN documents piled in the storage room give no indication of organization or use. The Center entertains requests from schools for lectures, several of which are delivered by its personnel but most of which are handled by the All Union Society for the Dissemination of Political and Scientific Knowledge. This Center represents the limited extent of what the UN can do at present to get its message across to the Soviet people.

All available information strengthens the impression that the Soviet leadership places little importance on educating its people about the UN, either at the adult or school-age level. One Western analyst who has thoroughly investigated the question has written that "the official syllabus on Soviet foreign policy and international affairs [in Soviet schools] makes no reference to the United Nations as a separate topic. Likewise, the Party's model outline of the lectures on recent Soviet foreign policy and world affairs does not list the U.N."[4] But despite the skimpy treatment of UN affairs internally, Soviet leaders in their statements abroad give an impression of purposeful, extensive efforts. For example, in response to a questionnaire sent by the Secretary-General to all member-states regarding the "Teaching of the Purposes and Principles, the Structure and Activities of the United Nations and the Specialized Agencies in Schools and Other Educational Institutions of Member States," the Soviet reply presented a glowing account which stated in part: "Every young man and woman who has completed a secondary education in the USSR is familiar with the activities of the United Nations and the specialized agencies through two courses given to all graduating classes. . . . Information about the United Nations is widely disseminated. . . . United Nations Day and Human Rights Day are observed in the schools. . . . The State history courses and textbooks for higher educational institutions also

[4] Dallin, *op. cit.*, p. 93.

include basic information on the background and activities of the United Nations and the specialized agencies. . . ."[5] This rosy picture is in evident contrast to the material we have on Soviet course syllabuses, content analyses of Soviet textbooks, and reports of academic visitors to the Soviet Union.

International Organizations in the Mirror of Soviet Scholarship[6]

In a confined and compartmentalized society, criticism is carefully regulated, and scholarly writing in the social sciences leans toward the descriptive rather than the analytical, the hagiographic rather than the critical. Since 1954, and particularly since the 1956 Party Congress, Soviet leaders have emphasized the need to improve the quality and quantity of studies devoted to international relations and Soviet foreign policy, especially current problems and events, and developments in the underdeveloped world. Their desire for systematic coverage of these areas reflects the increasingly diversified and extensive range of Soviet foreign policy interests and their realization that effective policy requires accurate information.

The initiative to raise the standards of scholarship in politically sensitive areas could come only from the top. Grappling with controversial subjects in the fields of foreign policy and international relations was alien to the docile generation of

[5] A summary of the Soviet reply to the questionnaire was published in UN Document E/3322 which covered the January 1956-December 1959 period. See Economic and Social Council, *Official Records,* 29th Session (1960). Annex, p. 21.

[6] I would like to express my appreciation to the editors of *Survey* (London) and the Institut Universitaires de Hautes Etudes Internationales (Geneva) for their permission to use sections from my paper on "Soviet Historiography and Soviet Foreign Policy" which was presented at the Conference on Contemporary History in the Soviet Mirror which they co-sponsored in Geneva in July 1961.

scholars reared under Stalin and conditioned to produce stereotyped ideological tracts, devoid of substance and bearing a dreary resemblance one to another. Soviet scholarship emerged slowly from the chrysalis of the Stalin period to meet the manifold demands of the present; entrenched patterns were not easily overcome. But taking heart from the public denigration of Stalin, the thaw in Soviet society which spread after the Twentieth Party Congress, and the urgings of Party leaders, a number of scholars wrote letters later to the editors of *Mezhdunarodnaia zhizn'*, the leading monthly journal on world affairs which was revived in 1954. These letters castigated the State Publishing House for Political Literature (Gospolitizdat) for its failure to publish "new and original scholarly works of research" on contemporary international problems and for its preoccupation with low caliber works of little value; they also noted that "so far there has not been a single work of any importance . . . generalizing and offering a scientific evaluation of the activities of the UN and its agencies."[7]

Quick to perceive the drift of impending change, S. Mayorov, one of the editors of Gospolitizdat, agreed with his critics about the lamentable state of Soviet scholarship on international affairs, but placed the blame on the research institutes for their continued failure to analyze "the present-day relations among capitalist states," the growing significance of the underdeveloped countries, and the diverse activities of international organizations. He observed that scholars were preoccupied with the past, wedded to the trivial and the noncontroversial, and apparently unwilling to help overcome "the absolutely unsatisfactory state of the study of Soviet foreign policy."[8]

[7] *International Affairs*, No. 12 (December 1956), pp. 98-99. The letter was signed by Academicians E. Korovin and A. Guber, and Professors N. Lyubinov and A. Manfred.

[8] "Literature on World Affairs," *International Affairs*, No. 1 (January 1957), pp. 159-161.

A number of new journals were started, each with a particular purpose, but all designed to broaden the coverage of contemporary international developments and to provide outlets for the results of research in neglected areas.[9] Despite the newly available opportunities for publication, and the hortatory statements of Party officials for fresh interpretations of present-day events, the academic community responded cautiously, unwilling to analyze the economic, social, and political developments in the non-Communist world and in international organizations in any but the most general of terms. Articles too often consisted of a series of lengthy quotes from

[9] The monthly journal, *Mirovaia ekonomika i mezhdunarodnye otnosheniia* (World Economics and International Relations), commenced publication in the summer of 1957 and was given the principal responsibility for analyzing developments in the capitalist world; to encourage historians to deal with affairs of this generation, *Novaia i noveishaia istoriia* (Modern and Current History), was established at about the same time; Orientalists were provided in 1957 with their own journal for the first time since the 1930's—*Sovetskoe vostokovedenie,* which was superseded in early 1959 by *Problemy vostokovendenie* (Problems of Orientalist Studies), and *Sovremennyi vostok* (Contemporary East), a semi-popular, obviously propagandistic monthly which was superseded in 1961 by *Asiia i Afrika segodnia* (Asia and Africa Today); finally, in September 1958, as a result of the November 1957 Moscow Conference of Communist and Workers' Parties, a new monthly, *World Marxist Review,* commenced publication in sixteen languages.

In addition, other measures have been taken to make available more current material. An annual yearbook on international affairs, *Mezhdunarodnyi politiko-ekonomicheskii ezhegodnik,* and one on international law, *Sovetskii ezhegodnik mezhdunarodnogo prava,* have been published since 1958 and 1959, respectively. The three volumes of *Istoriia diplomatii* (History of Diplomacy) are being revised, and two additional volumes added; second edition of *Diplomaticheskii slovar'* (Diplomatic Dictionary) has been published in three volumes, rather than the previous two. In 1959, the State Publishing House for Social and Economic Literature revived publication of the discontinued Foreign Policy Library series, consisting of the memoirs of prominent Russian, Soviet, and foreign statesmen, and studies in diplomacy and international relations. Other extensive additions have been made for the study of Soviet Foreign Policy and International Relations.

Lenin and Khrushchev (since 1956 Stalin is rarely cited) linked by innocuous reaffirmations of principles.

Their inadequacies elicited self-examination. Widely publicized "dialogues," part self-criticism and part exhortation, were carried on in various journals. Some critics noted the non-availability of documentary and reference materials necessary for scholarly research, particularly on Soviet foreign policy and UN affairs: "Collections of the United Nations documents need to be published. The specialists in world affairs cannot be satisfied with newspaper reports on the work of the various United Nations bodies, since reports are perforce, much too brief."[10] Some condemned the persistence of meaningless rehashings of old quotes in articles on contemporary affairs; others lamented the neglect of current history in secondary schools and universities; still others emphasized the absence, more than forty years after the October Revolution, of any adequate study of Soviet foreign policy.

Every year the number of published works increases. Since 1956, a profusion of studies on Soviet foreign policy (there were none prior to 1955), international relations, and under-developed countries has been published. The great bulk of these deal with international relations and the underdeveloped world, few with international organizations. For example, the 1960-61-62 research plans of the Institute of World Economics and International Relations of the USSR Academy of Science, which was established in 1957 in response to pressure for more information about the capitalist world, contained only three works on the UN and other international organizations. Though the growing political literature still does not provide any new information about the formulation of Soviet foreign policy, or the points of view disputed in decision-making circles, several changes in quality have led one close Western observer of Soviet scholarship to write: "Recent Soviet output

[10] *International Affairs*, No. 2 (February 1957), p. 136.

is distinguished by its relatively high level of scholarship, sophisticated approach to ideological questions and its varied use of foreign publications, albeit, selected from among those Western works which either present the Soviet position in sympathetic light or represent extremely hostile positions which seem to confirm Soviet preconceptions and expectations of 'bourgeois' behavior. Tendentious and stereotyped propaganda tracts, shorn of the more vulgar and crude trappings of the Stalinist era, continue to appear but with diminishing frequency, and they must now compete with the output of genuine Soviet scholars for attention."[11]

But the study of international organizations remains the stepchild of Soviet scholarship. UN affairs, in all their varied and far-reaching ramifications, continue to attract the least attention from Soviet scholars, students, and publishing houses. There has been some increase in coverage as a by-product of the revival of the study of contemporary international developments, but nothing remotely comparable to the mushrooming attention given to international relations, Soviet foreign policy, and underdeveloped areas.[12]

The subordinate status of the UN and international organizations is evident in the attitudes of the Soviet leaders. For example, on January 6, 1961, Nikita Khrushchev delivered a major foreign policy speech to leading Party officials. In discussing prospects for an end to the Cold War, he made no mention of the peace-promoting functions or potential useful-

[11] Vernon V. Aspaturian, "Diplomacy in the Mirror of Soviet Scholarship" (MS), p. 10. Professor Aspaturian's paper was presented at the Conference on Contemporary History in the Soviet Mirror (1961).

[12] For a review of Soviet writings on various aspects of Soviet policy in international organizations, see the author's "Selected Bibliography of Soviet Works on the United Nations, 1946-1959," *The American Political Science Review*, Vol. LIV (December 1960), pp. 985-991. For a comprehensive Soviet bibliography on international relations, international law, and related areas see *Sovetskaia literatura po mezhdunarodnomu pravu:* bibliografiia 1917-1957 (Moscow, 1959), edited by V. N. Durdenevsky.

ness of the United Nations as an instrument for helping to ensure the orderly transition of political power in underdeveloped countries and for settling international disputes. Khrushchev's only allusion to the UN was in conjunction with his praise of the Soviet proposal, submitted to the Fifteenth Session of the General Assembly (December 1960), for granting independence to all colonial countries and peoples. Again, at the Twenty-second Congress of the CPSU in October 1961, Premier Khrushchev presented a new Draft Program blueprinting the building of a Communist society. In discussing the possibility of peaceful coexistence between the "socialist camp" and the "imperialist camp," he noted that "the issue of war and peace is the principal issue of today." Hailing the efforts of the socialist camp on behalf of peace, he also stressed the important role in championing the cause of peace played by the neutralist countries, the international working class, and "the anti-war movement of the masses" (in non-Communist countries). Nowhere in his listing of the forces working for peace is there any mention of the United Nations.

Nor is there anything in the literature to indicate that Soviet leaders have discarded, or visibly altered, the essentials of the Stalinist image of the UN. A volume, published by the all-important Higher Party School of the Central Committee of the CPSU, on contemporary history designed "for teachers of contemporary history, propagandists and party activists, and also for wide circles of Soviet readers" does not have a chapter or a section dealing with the UN or the activities of international organizations.[13] To the extent that references to the UN—especially quotations from Khrushchev's 1959 and 1960 speeches before the General Assembly—are to be found in recent studies on Soviet foreign policy, they are invariably bitterly critical of the UN and those who oppose the Soviet

[13] L. M. Shestova (editor), *Noveishaia istoriia*, Vol. II (1939-1959) (Moscow: Publishing House of the Higher Party School of the Central Committee of the CPSU, 1959).

position on the Congo, the proposed reorganization of the Secretariat, and the Soviet plan for general and complete disarmament.

The inference seems clear that for the Soviet leadership and intelligentsia the UN is still of marginal importance, despite a noticeable change in the style of Moscow's behavior there and in its greater willingness to use the organization to further Soviet objectives. Discarding the indiscriminate hostility and pervasive obstructionism of the 1945-1953 period, particularly where underdeveloped countries are involved, the Soviets are adeptly aligning themselves with the neutralists on all the issues of fundamental importance to these countries —anticolonialism, greater representation on international Secretariats, etc. In this way, they are enhancing the effectiveness of their opposition to Western policies and their reputation as a friend of underdeveloped countries. Soviet contributions to EPTA, participation in the countless discussions of international organizations, and support wherever possible for neutralist positions have developed mainly as a consequence of the expanding UN membership and the accompanying Soviet policy of courting the new members of Africa and Asia. Though they appreciate the value of the UN in serving to publicize Soviet policies and, perhaps more important, to intensify strains within the Western camp, there is no evidence that more extensive and active participation in UN affairs is accompanied by any fundamental change in attitude. The Soviets have not altered their view that neither the UN nor its Charter affects, in any basic fashion, the character of the contemporary international situation or the relations between states. Soviet leaders are still, as they were in Stalin's day, opposed to any expansion of UN economic, financial, and political functions. Paradoxically, since 1955, as a concomitant of the new focus on contemporary international developments, Soviet scholars have increased their attention to those international organizations concerned with underdeveloped countries, though quantitatively the number of articles is extremely small. Their writings continue to emphasize the importance of Soviet bilateral aid, the relevance of Soviet industrialization experience for the Afro-Asian, Latin American countries, and the need for rapid economic development and expansion of international trade.

On questions affecting the functioning of the UN, Soviet scholars make amply clear Moscow's opposition to any revision of the Charter, maintaining "that under present circumstances all attempts to revise it would not only be futile, but even harmful. . . . The Soviet Union was, and still is, opposed to abolishing the unanimity principle, which is indispensable for the effective operation of the United Nations."[14] Indeed, according to one Soviet scholar, the preservation of the veto power in the Security Council is essential to the continued existence of the United Nations: "Only the Security Council, establishing the presence of a threat to peace, of any violation of peace or act of aggression, should determine what measures, up to the use of armed force, must be taken. The attainment of agreement among the powers, who are permanent members of the Security Council, is supposed to be a *sine qua non* for action. This is to preclude the possibility of armed forces being utilized in the interests of any particular group of governments."[15] Soviet writers regard Western, and particularly the United States', efforts to revise the unanimity provision as an attempt "to bring about a paralysis of international bodies," undermine the Charter, and perpetuate Western domination in the UN at a time of rapidly changing power relationships. They defend the Soviet use of the veto on the ground that

[14] V. Shvetsov, "Another Attempt to Revise the U.N. Charter," *International Affairs*, No. 7 (July 1957), p. 109.

[15] G. I. Morozov, *Organizatsiia ob'edinennykh natsii: k 15-letiiu ustava OON* (Moscow: Institute of International Relations Publishing House, 1960), p. 137.

the West, with the aid of a "mechanistic majority" in the General Assembly, has in the past disrupted the legitimate functions of the Security Council and illegally expanded the scope of the General Assembly. However, warned one Soviet scholar, "the expectation of such a 'majority' is becoming less sound with each session of the General Assembly," due to the growing "anticolonial majority in the General Assembly."[16] Khrushchev himself emphatically stated in his 1959 speech to the General Assembly that "if there is no veto there will be no international organization, it will fall to pieces."

Not only do Soviet writers inveigh against any revision of the Charter, but they also vehemently denounce all proposals designed to transform the UN into a "World Parliament," holding that such arrangements are "extremely unpopular and unrealistic" and constitute a major challenge to the traditional concept of national sovereignty. Premier Khrushchev, speaking at the UN Journalists' Association in New York on October 7, 1960, unmistakably spelled out what he thought the UN was, and what it was not: ". . . it [the United Nations] is not a parliament, but an international forum established to settle issues in a way that will not harm any country represented at the forum." In this same speech he stated:

"If you like, I will put the matter more bluntly. Suppose the delegates of U.N. member countries suddenly hit on the 'grand' idea of resolving to abolish the socialist system in the Soviet Union. What would happen if everybody voted for it except ourselves, the representatives of the socialist countries? What would we say to that? We would say what we Russians usually say in such cases: 'Get out!' You took the decision, so live with it; as for us, we will live under our socialist system as we have lived so far. And whoever pokes in his nose— excuse me for the coarse but rather lucid expression—will get a punch in the face!'

[16] *Ibid.*, p. 143.

"Gentlemen, a very serious question has been raised here. That is why I want to say more about it, and beg you to ponder on it thoroughly. It is the countries of the imperialist, colonial bloc that so far control the biggest number of votes in the United Nations, which consist of imperialist, socialist and neutralist countries. We, the socialist countries, are today a minority in the United Nations. But that is a changing situation. Today we are in the minority, and tomorrow—we predict this to you—you will be in the minority. Consequently, you must not abuse your temporary majority in the United Nations in order to impose your decisions on the minority because, I repeat, it is not a parliament. What we discuss there are not the internal problems of a particular country, but international problems, with due respect for sovereignty and without interference in the affairs of other countries. This should be borne in mind and serve as the point of departure."[17]

By investing the principle of national sovereignty with an inviolable status, the Soviet Union assures itself, on this issue, of the full-fledged support of underdeveloped countries who are now undergoing a militantly nationalistic phase of their development. Having recently acquired independence, they are hostile to any proposals which would entail a diminution of their national prerogatives.

The rostrums of international organizations, particularly that of the UN, are used by Soviet leaders to proclaim their commitment to peaceful coexistence of different social and

[17] N. S. Khrushchev, *On Peaceful Coexistence* (Moscow: Foreign Languages Publishing House, 1961), pp. 286-287.

In an interview, on July 13, 1962, Premier Khrushchev told a group of visiting American journalists that "the United Nations, in point of fact, is a branch of the U. S. State Department. The United Nations does not as yet constitute united nations in the full sense of the term. In the future the United Nations will really become united nations, but so far it falls far short of such functions; it is dominated by certain groups of western states, with the U.S.A. at their head. But that period is already running out for the United Nations, and it will soon end."

political systems, and to impress neutralists with their desire for peace and disarmament. Thus, during his speech before the General Assembly on September 18, 1959, Premier Khrushchev lauded the UN, noting that it "is itself an embodiment of the idea of peaceful cooperation between states with different social and political systems," and stressed the UN's importance in promoting the independence of colonial peoples and the development of their economies. But when talking outside the UN about the need for peaceful coexistence, for example, on his tour of the United States, Khrushchev rarely alluded to the UN. In his article "On Peaceful Coexistence," written especially for American consumption and published in the October 1959 issue of *Foreign Affairs,* the UN did not appear once in his exposition on the need for peaceful coexistence.

During the Stalin period, the Soviet public was seldom informed of the activities of international organizations. Very few articles dealing with UN efforts to improve economic conditions in underdeveloped areas appeared in Soviet journals, in contrast to the frequent statements made in the UN by Soviet delegates. Occasionally, commentaries would appear attacking Western policies and praising Soviet proposals, but they were few and published sporadically. From them it would have been impossible for a Soviet scholar to reconstruct a picture of what was going on in international organizations, unless he had access to data which was not available in the regular journals. Such articles as did appear, purporting to review the record of UN endeavors, usually consisted of attacks on the West.[18] Other than a few studies on the International Court of Justice and international law, and one on the trusteeship system, only one book on the UN was published prior to 1954, an innocuous collection of UN documents.

Since 1954, the writings have been relatively devoid of the

[18] For example, see G. Slavianov, "Economic Problems at the Thirteenth Session of the United Nations Economic and Social Council," *Planovoye khoziaistvo* (November-December 1951).

polemics characteristic of the Stalin years. Soviet scholars mention the economic development and technical assistance programs of international organizations, but the articles are generally brief accounts of the Soviet position in the plenary sessions and the technical committees in which the Soviet Government has a special interest, e.g. the most frequently reported discussions are those relating to international trade. Soviet scholars emphasize the bilateral approach to economic development and either ignore or belittle the potentialities of aid channeled through international organizations. They stress the desire of the Soviet Union to aid underdeveloped countries, the inadequacy of UN efforts, and the significant role that the Soviet bloc is playing in stimulating the growth of the public sector of the economies in underdeveloped countries. Western aid is presented as given for "mercenary political and military objectives" and as doing little to promote the development of the national economy since it does not concentrate on heavy industry. The point stressed is that Western economic aid is negligible compared to its military aid, and that, relatively speaking, little is given through the UN: "If the Western countries give underdeveloped countries, through the UN, economic and technical assistance of approximately 34 million dollars, then the military expenditures, which are carried out on a bilateral basis, exceed this amount by almost 100 times."[19]

Soviet commentaries on UN economic assistance programs dwell increasingly upon their futility and their inability to make a major contribution to underdeveloped countries. Though extolling the value of Soviet aid,[20] its importance to

---

[19] "The XXI Congress and the Further Strengthening of the World Socialist System," *Voprosy istorii*, No. 5 (May 1959), p. 20.

[20] Whereas serious studies do not dwell long on Soviet contributions to UN efforts to help underveloped countries, the pamphlets disseminated among mass audiences in the Soviet Union invariably inflate the extent of Soviet aid: ". . . significant aid is rendered to backward countries by the USSR through the United Nations by means of the annual

the economies of recipient countries, and its stimulative effect on Western giving, some Soviet studies have argued that foreign aid, whether given through bilateral or international channels, can only be of peripheral importance in encouraging economic growth. One writer, A. Kodachenko, quoted Paul Hoffman, the Director of the UN Special Fund, as saying that underdeveloped countries need $70 billion in the next decade for them to attain a moderate, steady, self-sustaining rate of growth, and that half of this sum has already been found and will be allotted, but for the remaining $35 billion other sources must be found. From this, Kodachenko concluded that "the unrealistic imperialist plans of expanding aid, which are advertised by bourgeois propagandists as 'the chief means of stimulating progress in the underdeveloped countries,' do not evidently correspond with the needs of these countries for foreign exchange for financing economic development."[21] Observing that the *plans* are a long way from realization, he returned to a fundamental of Soviet development doctrine, namely, that for the economic transformation of society, the underdeveloped countries must rely upon their own efforts and resources, and not upon foreign aid. Kodachenko added that United States aid is designed not to promote economic independence of these countries, but to perpetuate their dependence on the United States. This, in turn, enables the United States to enmesh weak countries in military alliances against "the mythical danger of Communism." He maintained that the "aid" of the Western Powers was directed toward strengthening "the position of foreign capital and the pro-

---

payments given to the program of Expanded Technical Assistance, and the despatch of experts and machinery to these economically backward countries." P. N. Tret'iakov, *Ekonomicheskaia i tekhnicheskaia pomosh' SSSR slaborazvitym v promyshlennom otnoshenii stranam* (Moscow: Znanie Publishing House, 1960), p. 12.

[21] A. S. Kodachenko, *Sorevanie dvukh sistem i slaborazvitye strany* (Moscow: State Publishing House for Social-Economic Literature, 1960), p. 90.

imperialist stratum of the bourgeois and feudal elements who impede the carrying out of the policy of progressive social-economic transformation." Kodachenko is one of a growing number of Soviet writers who seek to impress the under-developed countries with the need to support the Soviet position on disarmament and nonalignment in order to end the heavy drain on their economic development that military expenditures entail.[22] In elaborating this theme, he observed that not only are those countries that are drawn into the Western military alliance system forced to spend a disproportionate amount of their available capital on armaments, thus precluding their investing in economically useful projects, but the neutralist countries, too, are compelled to assume a heavy arms burden which retards their economic development. Only the Soviet plan for general and complete disarmament could end this enervating cycle of economic futility and backwardness.

Soviet participation in the Specialized Agencies is sketchily treated in Soviet scholarly literature. One source is the 1960-1961 second edition of the Diplomatic Dictionary (there was no mention of these organizations in the 1948 edition, since the USSR was not then a member of most of them). Another is the encyclopedic Yearbook on international affairs, published since 1958. The 1959 Yearbook contained, in addition, the first extensive survey of UN materials. Both of these references are legalistic and fragmentary presentations of the work done by these Agencies. A recent textbook, widely used in Soviet law courses, cautioned against too expansive an assessment of the importance of the Specialized Agencies and other intergovernmental organizations, asserting that they "have been the subject of considerable study in the bourgeois doctrine of International Law, which greatly exaggerates the importance of international associations of this kind. . . . [The

[22] A. S. Kodachenko, "Disarmament and the Underdeveloped Countries," *International Affairs*, No. 7 (July 1960), pp. 31-35.

Specialized Agencies] not only do not guarantee peace between States, but themselves frequently reflect and experience the impact of contradictions and conflicts between States, which became particularly acute when capitalism entered its imperialist stage. It should also be borne in mind that many of these organizations are dominated by monopoly capital, which has secured control over the bourgeois state machine and directs and guides its activities."[23]

Soviet jurists take pains to delimit the scope of the Specialized Agencies. Holding that the Agencies do not possess a legal capacity comparable to that of a government, the jurists insist that they be restricted to the specific purposes for which they were established, subject always to the limitations imposed by their creators. Not only do the Specialized Agencies not have a supra-governmental capacity, but they cannot "pretend to a position of equality with the governments who are the sovereign subjects of international law."[24]

The need to provide Soviet scholars with factual information led to the publication in 1960 of what is the most comprehensive Soviet reference book on International Economic Organizations. In 1962 an expanded second edition was published—a testament to its value for scholars and officials.[25] Containing background information and brief accounts of the activities of approximately 440 intergovernmental, governmental, and nongovernmental organizations, the book devotes less than one-fifth of its 1,108 pages to UN bodies and the Specialized Agencies. It deals mostly with non-UN economic, social, professional, and quasi-political groups, both Commu-

[23] F. I. Kozhevnikov (editor), *International Law* (Moscow: Foreign Languages Publishing House, 1961), p. 348.

[24] S. A. Malinin, "Juridical Nature and Legal Status of the United Nations Specialized Agencies," *Sovetskoe gosudarstvo i pravo* (November 1958), p. 89.

[25] V. G. Solodovnikov (chief editor), *Mezhdunarodnye ekonomicheskie organizatsii* (Moscow: USSR Academy of Sciences Publishing House, 1962. Second Edition).

nist and non-Communist. Nonetheless, the handbook does bring together valuable factual data on international organizations for Soviet research workers. Capsule commentaries on the Specialized Agencies and regional economic commissions provide handy recapitulations of the Soviet stand in these organizations. They also explain that the Soviet Government has not joined the World Bank, the International Monetary Fund, or the International Finance Corporation because they are "under the control of the United States governmental-monopolistic circles, which have converted the Bank into a weapon of their reactionary foreign policy and have used it for the creation of favorable conditions for the export of American capital"; [26] nor has it become a member of FAO because the imperialist powers pre-empted all the key posts in the organization. There is no section devoted to WFUNA, though it is listed in the Appendix.

Brief reports on the economic and social activities of international organizations occasionally appear in *Pravda* and *Izvestiia* at the time of annual meetings or visits by UN officials. *Kommunist,* the official Party journal, rarely mentions UN affairs, and never the Specialized Agencies—another pragmatic gauge of the lack of interest in UN affairs which prevails among the power elite of the USSR. The two most important journals devoted to international affairs—the monthly *International Affairs,* and the weekly *New Times,* both published in various languages—devote less than 1 per cent of their coverage to developments in international organizations. Such articles as appear on the UN invariably deal with the Soviet position on disarmament, anti-colonialism, or the troika proposal.

Since the establishment of the International Atomic Energy Agency in 1956, and the start of operations in July 1957, Soviet scholars have carefully followed its developments and have

[26] *Ibid.,* p. 166.

written more fully on its activities than on those of any Specialized Agency.[27] Indeed, more articles have appeared in *International Affairs* and *New Times* on IAEA than on all the Specialized Agencies put together. Soviet writers blame the United States for the Agency's failure to take any giant steps toward promoting the uses of nuclear energy in underdeveloped countries and ridicule American "largesse": "At the first General Conference in Vienna in 1957, Admiral Strauss presented the Agency with a token gift of a slab of black graphite, and announced that his government would make a further gift of five tons of U-235. The presentation ceremony was duly photographed and filmed, and the Western press was loud in its praise of American magnaminity. But months and years have passed and the five tons of U-235 have not been delivered."[28] Stating that American insistence upon a stringent system of inspection is designed "to give Western monopolies control over the national atomic industries developing in countries that are assisted by the Agency,"[29] one writer declared that such a system of controls would, in fact, serve as a cloak for espionage "under the flag of an international organization."[30] The chief Soviet delegate to IAEA observed in *New Times* that American representatives are trying "to convince their colleagues from countries receiving IAEA assistance that control will facilitate scientific progress. In reality, America's efforts are concentrated on hampering scientific progress in other countries and keeping track of scientific developments there through the proposed control system. At Geneva the

[27] The best Soviet account of the negotiations preceding the establishment of IAEA is the monograph by V. Larin, a leading commentator on the Agency's activities, *Mezhdunarodnoe agenstvo po atomnoi energii* (Moscow: State Publishing House for Juridical Literature, 1957).

[28] Vasily Emelyanov, "Americans and the Atom," *New Times,* No. 43 (October 1960), p. 16.

[29] *Izvestiia,* June 18, 1959.

[30] F. Polomsky, "International Atomic Energy Agency: Espionage Under a New Guise," *International Affairs,* No. 8 (August 1960), p. 89.

American delegates are trying to build up a military intelligence system; at Vienna they are working for a scientific and technical intelligence system."[31]

In general, the academic community has failed to be attracted to international organization as a field for investigation. The priorities of government interests, the neglect of the scholars, and the paucity of adequate documentation have evidently influenced graduate students, few of whom elect to do their dissertations in this field. Though exact data is difficult to obtain, the information that is available indicates that approximately the same number of dissertations were written (for the Soviet equivalent of the Ph.D. degree) on UN affairs during the 1945-1953 period as during the 1954-1962 period. That is to say, no greater interest in international organizations was evident among advanced students in the social sciences during the first eight years of the post-Stalin period than in the Stalin period. This is an imperfect standard by which to measure the interest of scholars, but it does have validity, since graduate students in the Soviet Union are also influenced by their mentors, as well as by the government need for specialists, to orient their research toward particular fields. Fewer dissertations are written on the UN and international organizations than on any other aspect of international relations and international law. In the catalogue of dissertations in Moscow's Lenin Library, there is no section or sub-section devoted to UN affairs. Those that are written in the UN field are classified under one of the established categories, e.g. international law. During the Stalin period, one student wrote on the Specialized Agencies (the World Bank and International Monetary Fund); in 1960, another student dealt with UNESCO. No other dissertations have covered the Specialized Agencies, and none has treated any of the regional economic commissions. No dissertation has investigated the UN's

[31] Vasily Emelyanov, "Atomic Energy Politics," *New Times*, no. 23 (June 6, 1962), p. 13.

role in promoting economic growth in underdeveloped areas. Finally, though the total number of dissertations written in the international field has increased in recent years, the number devoted to UN affairs remains the same two or three a year as during the Stalin period. International organization is clearly not regarded by graduate students as a promising field for research.

Scholarship bears the imprimatur of Party fiat. It supplies the Kremlin with the necessary information and analyses required for its mushrooming diplomatic activities. It helps to cultivate a favorable image of the Soviet Union abroad, particularly in the underdeveloped countries among the intellectual elites who, the Kremlin hopes, will accept Marxism-Leninism as *the Weltanschauung* shaping their attitudes and policies. Recent efforts to improve the quality of Soviet scholarship may also be seen as part of Moscow's desire to become the political-scientific-cultural capital of the world.

Soviet writers of contemporary international affairs present their interpretations in accordance with the tightly circumscribed body of official dicta. Research is conducted along officially approved paths, always responsive to the shifting boundaries of the politically permissible. There are no incentives to explore controversial areas or to subject official policy to searching evaluations. Add to this the traditional ambivalence of the Party with its expressions of encouragement, on the one hand, and extensive proscriptions on the other, plus the occasional use of Soviet scholars as scapegoats, and it is not surprising that Soviet scholarship, though constantly improving, has not yet produced the quality of analyses of contemporary developments called for repeatedly by the Party.

Since scholarly writing in the social sciences tends to respond to pressure from above and to reflect the primary interests of the leaders, the marginal attention devoted to the functioning of the UN and international organizations may be regarded as symptomatic of their lack of status in the policy-making echelons of the Soviet Government. This relative dis-regard is a consequence of the Soviet conviction that the UN is incapable of affecting the alignment of international power, of the residue of slowly changing underestimation by Soviet leaders of the ways in which the United Nations can help to advance their objectives, of the bipolarity inherent in Soviet ideology which views international organizations as capitalist creations, and of the antipathy and outright hostility toward any competitor institution which might lay claim to the alle-giance of the Soviet people.

Prospects are bleak for a change in the Kremlin's attitude toward the United Nations. Implicit in this assumption is the view that Soviet leaders will continue to regard international organizations as legitimate battlegrounds for advancing Soviet objectives, rather than as possible instrumentalities for bridg-ing national rivalries and promoting cooperation within an international framework. Nevertheless, we should seek the reasons for those Soviet policy changes that did occur in inter-national organizations since Stalin's death and establish, within the limits of prudence and probability, the likelihood for their continuation and the conditions under which they might be influenced to move in the direction of increased Soviet involvement in the activities of international organiza-tions. We therefore need to examine the relationship between Soviet policy and Soviet perception of the non-Communist world, to determine how Soviet policy in international organ-izations has been influenced by ideological considerations.

VIII ✣━━━━

Ideology and Behavior

NONE of the determinants of Soviet policy in international organizations is as elusive and as subject to conflicting interpretation as ideology. Yet any analysis of the forces behind Soviet policy and behavior must come to grips with it. Since Soviet policy in international organizations is a facet of overall Soviet foreign policy, before venturing to evaluate the impact of Marxism-Leninism on Moscow's behavior in these organizations, it is first necessary to examine the broader question of what role ideology plays in the formulation of Soviet foreign policy.[1]

The relationship between ideology and behavior is neither constant, consistent, readily apparent, nor easily measured. But it would be folly to assume, therefore, that the relationship is not meaningful and operative, that ideology does not function as a forceful and creative guide to Soviet conduct. George Kennan has cautioned against the tendency to dismiss

[1] Literature on the subject is not abundant. Several key articles are: Zbigniew K. Brzezinski, "Communist Ideology and International Affairs," *Journal of Conflict Resolution* (September 1960), which is also included in his stimulating collection of essays on *Ideology and Power in Soviet Politics* (New York: Frederick A. Praeger, 1962); George F. Kennan, "The Sources of Soviet Conduct," *Foreign Affairs*, Vol. 25 (July 1947), pp. 566-582; and Adam B. Ulam, "Soviet Ideology and Soviet Foreign Policy," *World Politics*, Vol. XI (January 1959), pp. 153-172. In addition, see Chapters I-III, XII in Alexander Dallin, *The Soviet Union at the United Nations* (New York: Frederick A. Praeger, 1962); the useful articles compiled by Professor Dallin in *Soviet Conduct in World Affairs* (New York: Columbia University Press, 1960); and Chapters 16-18 in Barrington Moore, Jr., *Soviet Politics: The Dilemma of Power* (Cambridge: Harvard University Press, 1950); Bertram D. Wolfe, "Communist Ideology and Soviet Foreign Policy," *Foreign Affairs*, Vol. 41 (October 1962), pp. 152-170.

Marxist-Leninist thought "as mere window dressing, to ignore its political content and implications, and to see behind it nothing more than a primitive lust for military conquest— usually envisaged as a determination to overrun Western Europe, in particular, by force of arms, as soon as military conditions might prove favorable."[2] Zbigniew Brzezinski has drawn attention to the rationality implicit in the behavior that stems from the ideology: "There is a tendency in the West to view ideology as something irrational and to counterpoise it against pragmatism and empiricism. . . . It would appear that ideology is not incompatible with rational behavior, once the basic assumptions are granted. While these assumptions may or may not be rational, they are at least so far removed from immediate concerns that they do not produce a conflict between the ideology and a rational approach to reality."[3]

The dichotomies between theory and practice, between what Soviet leaders purport to believe and the factors that actually determine their courses of action, complicate any attempt at understanding. There is a danger of giving disproportionate weight to ideology and of distorting its true role in the appraisals of the decision-makers. All that one can hope to achieve is an approximation of its real operational significance. Obviously, this cannot be adduced by stringing together a series of quotations from the canonical writings of Marx, Lenin, Stalin, and Khrushchev. Complex and changing behavior cannot be explained by a mechanistic application of doctrine to conduct. Khrushchev himself, in a speech at the Third Congress of the Rumanian Workers' Party on June 21, 1960, referring to the conflicting interpretations expounded by Chinese Communist leaders, berated the quote-gatherers who repeated what Lenin had said decades ago about the inevitability of war, revolution, etc., and who applied these views

[2] George F. Kennan, *Russia, the Atom and the West* (New York: Harper and Brothers, 1957), p. 17.
[3] Brzezinski, *op. cit.*, pp. 110-111.

unimaginatively to the contemporary era. While accepting the fundamental doctrinal tenet that "the nature of capitalism, of imperialism does not change," he dubbed it unwise "to repeat, without due account of the concrete situation, without due account of the changed balance of world forces, what the great Lenin said in entirely different historical circumstances . . . :

"We live at a time when Marx, Engels and Lenin are no longer with us. If we act like children learning to read, who compose words letter by letter, we are not going to get very far. Marx, Engels and Lenin created immortal works that will live down the ages. They showed mankind the way to communism. And we are following it firmly. Taking Marxist-Leninist theory as a basis, we must think for ourselves, and study life thoroughly, analyze the contemporary situation and draw conclusions of benefit to our common communist cause.

"One must not only know how to read, but must also understand correctly what one reads, and know how to apply it to the concrete conditions of our time, to take account of the existing situation, of the actual balance of forces. A political leader who does so shows that he is not only able to read, but also to creatively apply revolutionary theory. If he does not, he is like the man of whom the people say that 'he reads books with his eyes shut.'"[4]

Since each set of Soviet leaders assumes that its interpretations of Marxism-Leninism are creative and correct, some non-Communist observers are inclined to dismiss ideology, and the ideological pronouncements of the leadership, as mere "propaganda," as a "prop for mass manipulation."[5] Soviet

[4] N. S. Khrushchev, *On Peaceful Coexistence* (Moscow: Foreign Languages Publishing House, 1961), p. 247.

[5] Herbert Marcuse, *Soviet Marxism* (New York: Columbia University Press, 1958), p. 39.

leaders, they contend, are opportunistic, cynical, and concerned with the preservation and maximization of their power. But this does not negate the fact that the assumptions upon which they formulate policy, and the normative ends to which they aspire, are conditioned by the corporate body of Marxist-Leninist thought;[6] by their selection and ordering of events from reality, as they perceive it through their distinctive ideological kaleidoscope; by the manner in which the ideology is interpreted and applied in specific situations; and by their personal predispositions toward certain aspects of the ideology. One recent study points out that to interpret Soviet policy "in traditional terms of 'national interest' and deny that ideology plays any real role today in its direction," is to overlook or underestimate "the worldwide scope of Soviet activities or its preoccupation with revolutionary change throughout the world." Only the commitment to ideology "can explain Soviet dedication to transforming by force the social and economic structure of Eastern Europe, which only creates increased hostility toward the U.S.S.R."[7]

[6] See Moore, *op. cit.*, p. 415. "Students of languages have pointed out how the structure of a language may make it difficult to understand—that is, to make the desired responses to—concepts that have originated in another language and culture. To realize these difficulties, one has only to think of the obstacles involved in understanding a problem in long division with the use of Roman numerals alone. On these grounds, it is at least a reasonable hypothesis that a set of ideas, or a system of political notation, such as Marxism-Leninism, would make certain types of political responses difficult, or perhaps even impossible, whereas it would make others relatively easy. Although the limits of a system of political notation are probably not as definite as those in the linguistic and mathematical symbol systems, it seems a very probable inference that such limits do exist."

[7] "Ideology and Foreign Affairs," U. S. Senate, Committee on Foreign Relations, 86th Congress, 2nd Session (January 17, 1960), pp. 13-14. The Harvard study group maintained that "the notion of 'national interest' can be ambiguous when applied to Communist regimes. If 'national interest' means whatever the Communist rulers say, the question still remains as to how far Communist conceptions distort the analysis of the Communist leaders even in assessing national interest."

The Integrative and Interpretative Function of Ideology

Soviet ideology is a systematic body of goals, ideas, and assumptions shared by the elite and affecting their attitudes and behavior. It helps to shape the mode of their response to social, economic, and political phenomena; it conditions their perception of reality, and provides the terminology and the methodological tools for a "scientific" interpretation of history, as well as the categories for dialectically viewing, assessing, and rationalizing events. Facts—that is, propositions of known, accepted, or verifiable character—are selected and ordered according to the leadership's evaluation of any particular situation, and developments are related one to another within a rationalistic system. Soviet practitioners have never pretended that ideology could mark each path, crossroad, or detour on the international landscape, but the general direction of history is allegedly revealed through the time-telescope that Marxism-Leninism gives "with which to look into the future and see the outlines of impending historical changes."[8]

This set of immutable norms combined with an interdependent superstructure of assumptions and beliefs, this ideology "then becomes part of the reality and an autonomously existing factor, conditioning behavior through the selection of the various policy alternatives that exist at any particular moment."[9] The decision to discard an old policy and undertake a new course of action, which is then ideologically rationalized, does not weaken belief in the innate validity or dialectical well-springs of the ideology itself. For an ideology to exert a continuing and cohesive hold on its followers, it must "be at least in part above and beyond rational criticism."[10]

[8] *Fundamentals of Marxism-Leninism* (Moscow: Foreign Languages Publishing House, 1960), p. 18.

[9] See Brzezinski, *op. cit.*, pp. 101-102.

[10] Moore, *op. cit.*, pp. 409-410.

322

The doctrine of Party infallibility serves as the bond between what can be posited as scientific evidence and what must be accepted unquestioningly as an article of faith. Marxism-Leninism, as interpreted by Soviet leaders throughout the years, has always sanctioned flexibility (or opportunism, depending on one's attitude) in tactical, short-term situations. This has often led Western observers to regard the Soviets as practitioners par excellence of an unregenerate Machiavellianism. But even the tactical shifts are chosen from a range of alternatives determined by the ideology and do not vitiate the fundamental image of the event induced by the ideology. For example, in the Soviet decision to participate in the UN program of aiding underdeveloped areas, Moscow acted as a consequence of a modified assessment of how best to advance Soviet policy in the underdeveloped countries, which it was then extensively overhauling, and not out of a changed assessment of the character of international organizations. Similarly, Moscow's decision to initiate a program of foreign aid stemmed from its belated recognition of the importance to Soviet interests of encouraging diversity in the underdeveloped world, and not from any essentially changed ideological appraisal of the bourgeois-nationalist regimes being supported.

During the pre-1945 period, when the USSR was weak and exposed, its leaders showed a capacity to adapt in the face of danger, notwithstanding certain ideological assumptions which might have precluded such action. Thus, in the early years of the Bolshevik regime, the belief was widely held that all capitalist countries were committed to the overthrow by force of the Soviet State and that world revolution was both imminent and necessary for its preservation. It was the ability to avoid a paralyzing adherence to this concept, to take advantage of the differences among the capitalist states, and to come to terms with many of them (for example, the 1922 Rapallo accord with Germany) that helped to assure the survival of the new regime. From the blunders that were made, e.g. in China in the 1920's and Germany in the early 1930's, we can find the evidence that enables us to reconstruct roughly the determinants of policy, and among these, distortions shaped by ideology loom large as compelling factors.[11] Even after an unsuccessful policy was adopted, there is no evidence that ideology henceforth assumed a less important role in the thinking of the decision-makers.

But the Soviet Union is now a super-power and need no longer adapt to the international environment out of weakness. How this will affect its reliance on ideology is a key question. Are not the achievements of Soviet foreign policy over the past two decades, indeed, since 1917, more than adequate to reinforce the confidence of increasingly militarily powerful Soviet leaders in the basic beliefs of their ideology?[12] May not success be expected to have a revitalizing effect on the ideology and stimulate this generation of leaders to place even greater reliance upon it? Vernon Aspaturian asks the question: "When we ruminate on the rise of the Soviet Union from a shattered pariah state to world power in less than four decades, can it be validly maintained that dialectic had nothing to do with it?" And he offers this answer: "Really, the Soviet leaders had little more than this map of reality called dialectic as a surrogate for experience, wealth, and power, and they parlayed it into the most fabulous returns, against virtually impossible odds, within the span of a single generation. . . . Since the Soviet dialectic has been so effective dur-

[11] The contrary has frequently been argued; namely, that in following balance of power policy during the interwar period, Soviet leaders dispensed with or minimized ideological considerations.

[12] For an authoritative treatment of Moscow's design for a Communist world order and its opposition to all integrative efforts in the non-Communist world, see Elliot R. Goodman, *The Soviet Design for the World State* (New York: Columbia University Press, 1960). Professor Goodman concludes that Soviet doctrine maintains a consistent and continued belief in the inevitability of a Communist world, notwithstanding the important ideological modifications of recent years.

ing moments of weakness in Soviet history, is it any wonder that Soviet leaders remain even more convinced of its 'scientific' character, now that the psychological and political balance of power seems to be shifting in their favour, just as the dialectic had unerringly predicted?"[13]

The Core of Beliefs

The elements of the ideology that have particular relevance for the formulation of foreign policy are the preoccupation with change, the bipolarity of political reality, and the inevitability of communism. Marxism-Leninism predicates constant change and seeks to assign order and direction to the inner contradictions that impel it. History is carried forward, say the Marxists, as is all change, through the clash of antagonistic forces, specifically through the class struggle. It is a self-perpetuating struggle between the "progressive" and the "reactionary" forces, which occurs not merely between nation-states, but within them, between classes and groups. To obtain an accurate picture of the pattern of internal and international developments upon which to base policy, Soviet leaders "seek to establish the correlation of the various forces that are dynamically coexisting within a given society [as well as between societies] and chart their likely pattern of behavior as well as their likely influence in the future."[14] It is this attention to the major social and economic forces dynamically interacting in a society, rather than to individuals or the wealth-and-power possessing few, that frequently gives the Soviets an advantage in anticipating and exploiting the political opportunities afforded by revolutionary convulsions. Above all, conflict, which is both a cause and an effect of change, is viewed as a continuing phenomenon. When coupled with

[13] Vernon V. Aspaturian, "Diplomacy in the Mirror of Soviet Scholarship" (MS), pp. 23-24.
[14] See Brzezinski, *op. cit.*, p. 105.

325

the fundamental belief in the inherently aggressive character of capitalism, it precludes the possibility of any durable accommodation between the two systems.

Second, Marxism-Leninism sets the categories which it uses to define the interaction of competing forces—classes, groups, and nations—within a system of thought that polarizes the antagonistic forces of any particular epoch. This system conditions Soviet analysts to perceive and present the world as divided into two competing camps, the "socialist" and the "capitalist." Invidious comparisons are made between the predatory character of "capitalist" policies, methods, and purposes, and the peace-loving ones of the "socialist" camp. The Soviets reaffirm the incompatibility of the two systems even on issues that would seem to offer a prospect for cooperation. For example, in the ILO, the Soviet Government refused to support a resolution calling for a program to promote cooperation between workers and management groups, on the ideological assumption that such cooperation was impossible: "To talk of harmony between class interests . . . is an attempt to evade reality."[15] Though emphasizing the hostility between the two systems, in international organizations they maintain that the two can coexist peacefully. This contradiction has been explained away many times by Soviet leaders. In a report to the Supreme Soviet, Premier Khrushchev noted that: ". . . reciprocal concessions for the benefit of the peaceful coexistence of countries must not be confused with concessions on principle, on what affects the very nature of our socialist system and our ideology. There can be no question of any concessions or adaptation in this respect. Any concessions on matters of principle, on ideological points, would mean a shifting to the standpoint of our opponents. They would amount to a qualitative change of policy and would constitute a betrayal of the cause of the working class. Who-

[15] ILO, *Provisional Records*, 45th Session (June 1961), p. 149.

ever took that path would betray the socialist cause and should, of course, be criticized without mercy."[16]

Since 1956, neutralists have been accorded a special status in the Soviet conceptualization of the world. Though this has been interpreted by some observers as a shelving of the "two-camp" thesis, it seems more probable that it is only a temporary refinement, designed for a transitional phase of the present epoch, and that it in no way contradicts the ideological assessment of the bipolarity of camps and forces. It assuredly does not sanction cooperation with the "capitalist" countries on issues endowed with ideological significance, even though the common objective of both is ostensibly the improvement of conditions in the underdeveloped countries.

The 1961 Program of the Communist Party of the Soviet Union states that "capitalism is the last exploiting system," that "the basic contradiction of the contemporary world [is] that between socialism and imperialism," and that "a grim struggle is going on between two ideologies—Communist and bourgeois." Clearly the bipolar image of world alignments continues to dominate Soviet doctrinal evaluations and pronouncements of the shifting balance of world forces.[17] The Program acknowledges that the neutralist countries are "sweeping away the colonial system and undermining the foundations of imperialism," "establishing and developing national democracies," and "objectively" functioning as "a progressive, revolutionary, and anti-imperialist force." But nowhere is it stated that neutralist countries, and the so-called "zone of peace" which they comprise, are a permanent feature

---

[16] N. S. Khrushchev, *World Without Arms—World Without Wars*, Vol. 2 (Moscow: Foreign Languages Publishing House, n.d.), pp. 383-384.

[17] For example, the bipolar view of the world is stated explicitly in the speeches of recent Party Congresses, the Declaration of the 81 Communist and Workers' Parties (November 1960), and the major Khrushchev report of January 6, 1961—"For New Victories of the World Communist Movement."

in the evolutionary historical process. Indeed, Khrushchev has frequently intimated that, in the long run, they have no choice but to turn to the socialist camp. In a radio broadcast in Moscow, on October 20, 1960, he observed:

"The peoples of noncommited countries face an historic choice. The imperialist camp is attempting to involve them in the arms race, to place the manpower and material resources of these countries at the service of war. Imperialism does not offer them anything for doing away with the economic backwardness they have inherited from the colonial past. Imperialism does not desist from attempts to interfere in their internal affairs with a view to imposing a new colonial yoke upon them.

"The socialist community of peoples offers the young states a different path—the path of nonparticipation in the arms race, of developing their economy and culture, of tolerating no interference in their internal affairs. Need one say what will be the choice of the peoples?"[18]

Speaking of the neutralists to the Fifth Congress of the World Federation of Trade Unions in Moscow in December 1961, he put their choice more militantly: "If today you are against communism, tomorrow you will have nowhere else to go, tomorrow you will come to communism."[19] Thus the "national democracies"—the latest term used to describe the most "progressive" neutralist countries—are called upon to choose between the socialist or capitalist camps because neutrality is impossible in the long run.

Can we assume that such commitment does not help to shape policy formulation? Alexander Dallin describes the implications for international organizations in the following manner:

[18] "Soviet Affairs Note," No. 252 (Washington, D. C., May 5, 1961), p. 8.

[19] Quoted from Alexander Dallin, "The Soviet View of the United Nations," *International Organization*, Vol. xvi (Winter 1962), p. 21.

"The area of uniqueness lies above all in the Soviet view of the historical process and its translation into action. The profound conviction that in the long run neutrality and impartiality are impossible or nonexistent vitiates the fundamental assumption on which international organizations such as the United Nations are built. The communist image of the United Nations as an arena of struggle is not a reluctant recognition of a tragic fact but an exhilarating ride on the wave of the future.

"The Soviet view, in sum, combines a revolutionary outlook with a conservative pursuit of its security and a pragmatic effort to make the most of the complex and shifting United Nations scene."[20]

The token contributions of Soviet leaders to international organizations bespeak their rejection of and contempt for the approach of UN programs seeking to overcome economic backwardness and inequities in underdeveloped countries. The strategy of conflict diplomacy in international organizations expresses their conviction that minimal accommodation to UN programs is necessary in order to enable them to play the power-game and simultaneously to prove to the underdeveloped countries that this Western instrument has little to offer them in their search for economic development and security. The enlargement of the socialist camp, the weakening of world capitalism, and the emergence of colonial areas which are sympathetic toward "socialism," have only encouraged the Soviets to pursue their goals unrelentingly; these developments certainly have done nothing to discourage them from retaining a tenacious commitment to Marxism-Leninism.

Third, the steadily growing military power of the Soviet Union and the extension of Soviet global influence buttress the Soviet belief in the inevitability of communism as the dominant social system, and the correctness of their policies and

[20] *Ibid.,* p. 30.

the assumptions which underlie them. The conviction of communism's coming triumph pervades the demeanor and utterances of Soviet leaders. Khrushchev's statements are many and well known; to a Japanese correspondent on June 18, 1957: "We are convinced that sooner or later capitalism will perish, just as feudalism perished earlier. The socialist nations are advancing towards communism. All the world will come to communism. History does not ask whether you want it or not." He told the Rumanian Workers' Party on June 21, 1960, that "the development of world history has been such that there are now on our planet two social systems—the socialist and the capitalist. These social systems are antagonistic. We people of the socialist camp are sure that the hour of capitalism has struck, that capitalism is living its last. The apologists of capitalism are trying to lengthen its life by primping and dressing it up. You may recall that in the United States I was all but accused of wanting to bury every capitalist physically. The communists know that capitalism will inevitably go under and are glad that its end will come . . . capitalism is digging its own grave. . . . The future belongs to the working class, to its ideas, which are embodied in Marxism-Leninism." In an interview over a radio network in New York on October 13, 1960, he said: "The development of communism in society is governed by its own specific laws. . . . There was the feudal system, and it was succeeded by capitalism. A new epoch has come now. Socialism and communism, the highest phase in the development of society, is coming to replace capitalism. Such is the objective law of the historical progress of society." He carried this idea further in the significant January 6, 1961 speech to high-ranking Party members:

"Our epoch is the epoch of the triumph of Marxism-Leninism.

"The analysis of the world situation at the beginning of the sixties can only evoke in every fighter in the great Communist movement feelings of profound satisfaction and legitimate pride. Indeed, comrades, life has greatly surpassed even the boldest and most optimistic predictions and expectations. Once it was customary to say that history was working for socialism; at the same time, one remembered that mankind would dump capitalism and that socialism would be victorious. Today, it is possible to assert that socialism is working for history, for the basic content of the contemporary historical process constitutes the establishment and consolidation of socialism on an international scale.

"The guarantee of all our future victories lies in faithfulness to Marxism-Leninism. The path of the Communist movement has been difficult and thorny. No other party has had to go through so many trials and so many sacrifices. Numerous reactionaries have been trying to destroy communism, yet communism has emerged from all these trials ever stronger and has become a mighty force today. You have all seen beautiful giant trees rooted in the soil. Such trees fear no storms or hurricanes. A storm may pass and break brittle trees, while the giant tree remains standing unshakable. Its crown becomes even thicker and rises higher toward the sun. The same occurs in the Communist movement. Imperialist reaction has sent one storm after another upon it, but the Communist movement remains steadfast; it is growing and is becoming stronger."

This study reflects the view that Marxism-Leninism has been and currently is an important determinant in shaping the Soviet attitude toward international organizations and Moscow's policy in them. We have made use of a number of Khrushchev's remarks which we believe to be accurate reflections of his faith in the essentials of the Communist creed, in full awareness that quoting Soviet leaders to "prove" a thesis too often is carried to such extremes that it becomes a barren exercise in scholasticism. This risk was taken because the total information as to whether, and to what extent, ideology affects the thinking, motivations, and actions of Soviet decision-makers is so fragmentary that no shred of relevant data should be overlooked.

Ideology and Soviet Decision-Makers

Those who sustain the view that ideology is losing its relevance for Soviet leaders as a determinant of foreign policy take three general lines of approach: the historical, the sociological, and the political. Since the contentions of these groups affect their assessment of Soviet policies and of the alternatives which Moscow is most likely to adopt in a given situation, they require close examination.

Proponents of the historical approach draw an analogy between the past history of Islam and the present condition of communism. They note that Islamic doctrine considers it the sacred duty of Moslems to conquer all non-Moslem countries in order to spread the gospel of Mohammed, in much the same way as Marxism-Leninism calls upon its adherents to communize the world. Islamic doctrine has never been officially repudiated, the historically minded observe, but there is no current threat of military danger from the Moslems. So too, they contend, Marxism-Leninism may in time, if indeed it has not already reached such a stage, undergo a mellowing process which will diminish the threat of Soviet military expansion, even though it remains officially established as the ideology of the Soviet state. Another frequently cited example is the missionizing absolutism of the Roman Catholic Church several centuries ago, and the seemingly irreconcilable ideological hostility between Roman Catholics and Protestants, wherein each group viewed the other as *the* threat to its existence, in much the same way that the Soviet and Western camps view each other today. Again, doctrine remains intact, though time has diminished the militancy. Here the historical analogies must end, for in both these examples neither of the ideologies commands sufficient military power, nor do the great bulk of their adherents have the will to seek fulfillment of their faith by force.

The historians derive support from the studies of sociology and social psychology. With an ironic reliance on materialist determinism, the sociologically inclined contend that the new Soviet social groups—the technicians, scientists, administrators, and managers—who have come into prominence as a consequence of industrialization and modernization, function as a stablizing, moderating influence. This "new class," eager to safeguard the prerogatives and affluence which are now theirs, is assumed to be capable of influencing the formulation of foreign policy and thought to be counseling the leadership to follow an increasingly cautious and conservative path. Consequently, preservation of the *status quo* transcends the revolutionary content of the ideology and, with the further professionalization and bureaucratization of Soviet society, reliance upon ideology is expected to become even more ritualistic. Perpetuation of the empire will replace the revolutionary drive to transform the international order.

These two interpretations indicate that ideology will be used to justify, not determine, policy. The historians and sociologists believe that administration of a complex, industrial society requires Soviet leaders to act with regard for the wishes of the new social classes upon whom they depend for production and management. They argue further that the management of a modern society imposes upon the rulers a need for a pragmatic rather than an ideological outlook, and that in coping with the infinite complexity of specific situations, Soviet leaders are unconsciously acquiring a nonideological orientation.

The third group, the politicians and political analysts, builds on the interpretations of the historian and the sociologist. Cognizant of the contradictions which emerge from the efforts of Soviet ideologues to square doctrine with reality and theory with practice, many political figures assume that the erosion of ideology as a factor in policy formulation is already far advanced. One official stated that Communist ideology, whether in the fields of "propaganda, political action, subversion or foreign aid . . . is often proving either an ineffective servant of Soviet foreign policy or an actual handicap to its operations; and that as Soviet experience has made this or that manoeuvre or adjustment to reality, the ideology itself has become increasingly twisted and confused or outright ignored."[21]

These analyses all have much to commend them: Soviet practice has not conformed to pre-1917 expectations; one can list numerous instances where behavior contradicted the tenets of Marxism-Leninism; to the outsider, "the rationality of Soviet realism appears as utterly irrational, as terroristic conformity."[22] But this writer questions the transference of observations about history or the internal ordering and operation of Soviet society to the area of contemporary Soviet foreign policy formulation. Expectations based on historical analogy can be misleading; they cavalierly dispose of time, as if the

[21] Chester Bowles, "Is Communist Ideology Becoming Irrelevant?," *Foreign Affairs*, Vol. 40 (July 1962), p. 564.

[22] See Marcuse, *op. cit.*, p. 86. Professor Marcuse goes on to state that "the key propositions of Soviet Marxism have been the function of announcing and commanding a definite practice, apt to create the facts which the propositions stipulate. They claim no truth-value of their own but proclaim a pre-established truth which is to be realized through a certain attitude and behavior. They are pragmatic directives for action. For example, Soviet Marxism is built around a small number of constantly recurring and rigidly canonized statements to the effect that Soviet society is a socialist society without exploitation, a full democracy in which the constitutional rights of all citizens are guaranteed and enforced; or, on the other side, that present-day capitalism exists in a state of sharpening class struggle, depressed living standards, unemployment, and so forth. Thus formulated and taken by themselves, these statements are obviously false—according to the Marxian as well as non-Marxian criteria. But within the context in which they appear, their falsity does not invalidate them, for, to Soviet Marxism, their verification is not in the given facts, but in "tendencies," in a historical process in which the commanded political practice will *bring about* the desired facts."

dangers of today can be dismissed by assurances from other times and other situations. The effective military power of the Moslem rulers did wane—but slowly! Islam continued to expand for decades and remained a major danger to its neighbors for generations, during which time belief in the doctrine persisted. The subsequent decline of Islam, and the fraticidal, nearly suicidal, civil wars of Christian Europe, offer scant solace to those who are concerned with the present Soviet threat and see no indications that the Soviet imperium is in imminent likelihood of experiencing a comparable decline. History does not repeat itself, and Soviet expansionism, driven by a dynamic ideology and powered by an ever-growing military capability, may continue its expansion for decades to come. If the erosion of ideology proceeds in part from a decline in military prowess or in the expansionist vigor of the ruling elite, the day when the Soviet Union will be the scene of such a development seems far distant.

To the outsider, the Soviet manipulation of doctrinal matters may seem cynical, particularly when associated with internal struggles for power. But even if the leaders are cynical about their egalitarian goals, we cannot assume that they have a similarly corrupted attitude toward the elements of their ideology which relate to international affairs and the formulation of foreign policy.

Militant ideologies do not erode merely because they are confronted with a reality which contradicts them. According to Adam Ulam, "the most fundamental objection to the postulating of an erosion of the ideology by contact with reality is that this ideology [Marxism-Leninism] is propagated within a totaliarian system. If the rulers of this system see in the ideology . . . not only the rationale of their absolute power but a source of their inner security and effectiveness, then the doctrine will not be soon or easily repudiated." Ulam continues: "Furthermore, while the Soviet citizen, including the indoctrinated Party member, has numerous occasions to discover the contradictions or irrelevancies of Marxism in his daily life, he enjoys no such tangible experiences insofar as the world outside the USSR is concerned. And to the Soviet leaders, the field of foreign relations offers the best opportunity to attempt to demonstrate the viability of Marxism, conscious as they are of the necessity of preserving and developing the ideological *élan* of the Communist Party and of the regime."[23] Faith is durable and resilient. When merged with patriotism, it becomes a force to be watched.

From what we know of political infighting in the Soviet hierarchy, it is clear that the engineers of the Soviet state are not rigid determinists. Their sharing of a Marxist-Leninist heritage does not signify unanimity on all major policy questions. Though all Soviet leaders may agree at a given time in their evaluation of "objective" conditions existing in the ever-shifting pattern of world forces, they may legitimately disagree on which of several policy alternatives to adopt. A common perception of reality does not necessarily produce uniform answers to specific policy problems. Debate and discord in the inner circles of the Party are probably as intense as that found in the decision-making circles of any government, though they are not aired publicly. The range of possible alternatives is limited by ideology, but we do not know how stringently or how loosely any faction adheres to accepted doctrine to formulate its position, or to what degree naked power considerations alter these calculations. The alternative chosen brings into play the motivations and predispositions of the individual leader. At this point our most diligent research reaches an impasse, for the fact is that we know virtually nothing of the degree to which doctrine affects the actual thinking of individual Soviet decision-makers. Once a course of action is adopted, it is rationalized in ideological terms and accorded the sanction of scientific truth. The policy of the

[23] See Ulam, *op. cit.,* p. 159.

leader in power is the unquestioned truth of the moment, though a truth that may change overnight.[24]

The present generation of Soviet leaders are capable and confident of the superiority of their system. They need not believe in the imminence of world revolution or the necessity of using force to bring about the eventual downfall of capitalism to share a belief in the inevitability of communism, the growing ascendancy of Soviet power, and the essential validity of their analysis of developments in the non-Communist world. By any standards, their achievements are impressive. Commenting on the "new confidence . . . of the new group of Soviet diplomats," one respected foreign correspondent described this generation in the following way: "The new men of Soviet diplomacy have all the deceit, all the resolution, all the patience of their predecessors. But they have something else; they know the world and they are convinced the world is going their way."[25] Furthermore, these Soviets firmly believe the view of the world "that has been implanted in their minds by years of propaganda."

The Khrushchev era has witnessed many changes in Soviet society, but not in the institutionalized basis of Communist Party rule or in the fundamentals of ideology applicable to the outside world. The constancy with which the basic tenets of Marxism-Leninism have been adhered to by the decision-makers has been remarkable, especially in the field of international affairs. Khrushchev's doctrinal pronouncements modifying certain former assumptions do not connote a departure from the fundamentals of doctrine set forth earlier in this section; rather, they place Soviet analyses of international developments on a plane of perception that more accurately reflects current international reality. They are revisions made

[24] George F. Kennan (Mr. "X"), "The Sources of Soviet Conduct," *op. cit.*, p. 573.

[25] See Drew Middleton, "The New Soviet Man in Diplomacy," *The New York Times Magazine* (December 7, 1958).

in response to developments which are considered favorable to Soviet interests. Thus, such doctrinal modifications as the noninevitability of war, the "zone of peace," and the end of "capitalist encirclement," reflect the oft-repeated conviction that the balance of world forces is shifting to the "socialist" camp. The Khrushchev announcement in 1958 that the "capitalist" states were no longer encircling the "socialist" states, but that the reverse was true, can only be interpreted as a sign of growing self-assurance in the military power of the Soviet bloc and as an expression of confidence in the continued expansionist drive of international communism.

Essentially, this generation of Soviet leaders holds the same ideological views as their progenitors; it sees the world as they did and shares their expectation of the ultimate triumph of communism. It also suffers from a similar incapacity to assess accurately many of the creative and regenerative aspects of Western economic trends. In Max Frankel's revealing portrait of Anatoly F. Dobrynin, he reported that the Soviet Ambassador admitted difficulty in understanding the operation of the United States economy:

"From his questions, Americans all over town have discovered that despite Dobrynin's long training and familiarity with this country's idiom, he is also still the prisoner of his own. The role and political meaning of wealth baffle him; the incompatibility of a Rockefeller and a Kennedy eludes him. The differences between the capitalist titans of yore and the managers of capital of today are new to him. The evidence that here rich can strike at rich and poor at poor rattles him.

"He is a measure not only of how far the Bolsheviks have come in understanding the West and its ways, but also of how far they still have to go."[26]

An elderly Indian economist, a convinced Marxist and long-

---

[26] See Max Frankel, "Moscow's Man Intrigues Washington," *The New York Times Magazine* (July 29, 1962).

time Sino-Soviet sympathizer, dolefully observed that he found it impossible to establish sound, meaningful contacts, or engage in scholarly exchanges with Soviet and Chinese economists: "We could never engage in open and objective discussions because they were incapable of criticism of official policy. They are hostile to Western ideas, bound by official interpretations, and under questioning adopt a rigid, inflexible position." Diplomats have similar experiences. One former British diplomat is of the opinion "that no Soviet negotiator (Khrushchev may prove to be an exception) can ever persuade himself of the sincerity of his *bourgeois* interlocutor. The latter must *ex hypothesi* be hostile to the Soviet system and must try to destroy it. Consequently, it is useless and a waste of time to try to persuade or convince him by rational argument."[27] Concerning the innate suspicion of Soviet officials toward foreign diplomats, George Kennan once wrote during the Stalin era that ". . . the foreign representative cannot hope that his words will make any impression on them. The most that he can hope is that they will be transmitted to those at the top, who are capable of changing the Party line. But even those are not likely to be swayed by any normal logic in the words of the bourgeois representative. Since there can be no appeal to common purposes, there can be no appeal to common mental approaches. For this reason, facts speak louder than words to the ears of the Kremlin; and words carry greatest weight when they have the ring of reflecting, or being backed up by, facts of unchallengable validity."[28] Despite changes in the style of post-Stalinist diplomacy, there is every reason to believe that Mr. Kennan's observations are equally true today.

In discussions of Soviet behavior in international organizations with Western and neutralist nationals who have had the

[27] Sir William Hayter, *The Diplomacy of the Great Powers* (New York: The Macmillan Company, 1961), p. 29.
[28] Kennan, "The Sources of Soviet Conduct," p. 574.

opportunity to observe and deal with the Soviets at conferences, the view was almost invariably expressed that there
are no signs that Soviet officials have reservations about the
correctness of Soviet policy, the assumptions upon which it
is based, or the aims which it seeks; certainly, none were expressed to non-Communists. On occasion, ostensibly because
of merit in a Western view, Soviet diplomats may, to exploit
intra-Western differences, privately intimate the willingness
of the Kremlin to make some concessions and hint that unless
they are accepted by the West, the extremist factions in the
Party may gain the upper hand.[29] Closer investigation of these
intimations invariably has shown that there is no shift in
Soviet position and no greater understanding of the West's
policy. Non-Communist officials agree there is nothing to
indicate any current erosion in ideological commitment. The
time is not yet in sight when Marxism-Leninism may lose its
dynamism, may no longer impel Soviet leaders to strive for
a radical transformation of the international order, and become
transformed into a creed which operates solely to perpetuate
the rule of a national elite.

Some Inferences Concerning Ideology and Policy

Disillusionment with ideology results from prolonged, personal contact with those contrasts between theory and practice which are both embittering and enduring. No such cor-
rosive inroads have yet affected the leadership's level of
expectations in the field of foreign policy. The postwar extension of Soviet power and influence has, on the contrary,
reinforced their belief in the relevance and reliability of their
ideological heritage, particularly in the efficacy of doctrine

[29] For an illuminating discussion of this gambit by a Western specialist experienced in negotiating with the Soviets, see Philip E. Mosley,
"Soviet Myths and Realities," *Foreign Affairs*, Vol. 39 (April 1961), p.
344.

as a guide to conduct in the international area. One Western specialist maintains that not only is the expansion of Soviet power tangible "proof" of the correctness of ideology, but conversely, "the international aspect of Communism, its continued expansion, thus becomes a crucial point in the preservation of the ideological motivation of the Russian Communists."[30] He continues: "*Somehow* the ideology has to be shown to be important, dynamic, and capable of expansion and conquest. If it is not shown to be so, then even the most rapid growth in the material welfare of the citizens of the USSR will not enhance, but most likely will decrease the ideological appeal of Communism, with which is bound up the preservation of the leading role of the party and of totalitarianism itself. It is this restlessness in the search for a justification of the ideology, a rationale for continued totalitarianism, which opens up incalculable dangers for world peace. Being intelligent men, desirous of learning about the outside world, genuinely interested in improving the lot of their people, the Soviet leaders cannot desire a world conflict. But at the same time, they are driven by an ideological compulsion much more complex than the now obsolete dream of world revolution, to adventurous and aggressive foreign policies."[31]

The influence of ideology on the makers of foreign policy can perhaps be visualized in terms of a series of concentric circles. The inner circle represents fundamental security considerations and identification of the main enemy, the capitalist camp. Containing the core beliefs of the ideology, and tempered by past struggle with the capitalist powers, it is most resistant to outside influence and change. It induces in the leadership a state of anxiety over security and gives rise to policies which are, in turn, deemed threatening by the objects of these policies, the capitalist nations, who then react in

[30] Adam B. Ulam, *The Unfinished Revolution* (New York: Random House, 1960), p. 278.
[31] *Ibid.*, p. 281.

341

such a way that the resulting tension creates the very situation originally forecast by the ideology. Though often producing an effect contrary to that desired or intended, the behavior of Soviet leaders may be the result of a conditioning which leaves them no other choice, despite their awareness that by their actions they are jeopardizing the attainment of their objectives. When, during his visit to England, Khrushchev was told that his anti-British attitude was defeating his own purpose, he remarked: "I know this is true, but I cannot stop myself. We Russians have lived surrounded by dangers in a state of siege for a generation. So we are apt to be afraid, and to say and do the wrong things."[32]

The outer circles, which include Soviet policy in international organizations, are amenable to modification and experimentation because they are further removed from the behavioral imperatives that are considered vital to the preservation and perpetuation of the elite and the ideology. For example, in the drive to improve relations with the neutralists, Moscow finds it useful to give them full support on issues in which they are intensely involved, and to contribute to UN programs of aid for underdeveloped countries. By contrast, no accomodation is deemed possible on so central a problem as German unification, where a basic threat to the integrity of the inner circle is involved. One would expect that uncritical application of Marxist-Leninist categories and assumptions to underdeveloped countries (outer circles in our schematic design) would result in grievous and frequent miscalculations because the social, political, and economic environment in these countries differs radically from the environment with which the ideology was originally concerned and to which it has periodically been adapted. And often it does. But, to the Soviet advantage, the political climate and the prevailing attitudes found among

[32] See Lord Taylor, "Deep Analysis of the Russian Mind," *The New York Times Magazine* (January 7, 1962).

key social and political elites in underdeveloped countries—
the desire for change, the suspicion of the West, the instability
of a transitional society—are remarkably receptive to Soviet
ideological prescriptions and prognostications which are often
borne out, though for reasons not originally anticipated by the
Soviets. Soviet ideology "starts with certain advantages: it has
a revolutionary theory, it can play upon social discontents
and post-colonialist frustrations, it offers a myth of accelerated
industrial development."[33]

That Moscow's image of the West is conditioned by the Soviet
ideological position on the irreconcilability of capitalism and
socialism, and in its turn conditions policy, may be seen in the
essentially unchanged character of the Soviet assessment of the
problems of Western Europe. The treatment of Western Europe by Soviet leaders and scholars is a convincing manifestation of continuity in Soviet policy and ideology from Stalin
to Khrushchev; opposition to NATO, to the remilitarization
of West Germany, to American bases in Europe, and to all
moves designed to promote European unity remain constants
of Soviet analyses and reflect the doctrinal assumption of the
insolubility of the "contradictions" of capitalism. As long as
Moscow has an obvious stake in a divided and weak Europe,
and as long as there are sufficient indications of Western
differences and rifts, i.e. the "contradictions" of capitalism,
Soviet leaders will continue to act as if these are permanent,
pervasive, and controlling features of intra-Western political
and economic relationships. The Soviets view the Western
world as rent by strife, desperately seeking to salvage what it
can and to postpone the progressive deterioration of its once
unchallenged prestige and power. What we have is a situation
in which the ideological assumptions are reinforced by observable political phenomena, and political phenomena are

[33] Leopold Labedz, "Introduction," *Survey*, No. 43 (August 1962),
p. 4.

categorized and evaluated in the light of the assumptions.

Bertram Wolfe has written: "What reason does a man looking with Khrushchev's eyes have for abandoning the view that 'capitalism-imperialism' is decadent when it is losing all its colonies, did not show the resolution to protect Hungary's freedom or complete the unification of Korea, failed to make the military moves to prepare its sort of peace during World War II, thereby letting maimed and bleeding Russia pick up all of Eastern Europe, half of Germany, win powerful allies and partners in Asia, expand the 'Camp of Communism' from one-sixth of the earth to one-fourth, with one-third of the earth's population? We may offer our explanations of all this. None of them would seem to him to refute his simple explanation of 'decadence' and 'progress.' "[34]

However, in their approach to the changing conditions of underdeveloped countries, Soviet leaders have demonstrated a much greater readiness to revise matters of doctrine. Thus, Stalin's rigid "two-camp" thesis has been superseded by the more flexible "zone of peace" concept, and his limited view of "peaceful coexistence" has been transformed into a dynamic and bold challenge to Western influence on traditional Western camping grounds. Considering colonialism and imperialism historically doomed, Soviet leaders regard the attainment of political independence by underdeveloped countries as a major step in undermining the "rear" of capitalism, and as evidence that the presence and policies of the socialist camp can be instrumental in bringing about a rollback of Western influence. The "objective" forces, the societal developments and the direction and tempo of change within the "zone of peace" are favorable to the triumph there of communism. For the first time, they foresee Communist Parties coming to power without the use of armed force and believe that, because of threats from the former ruling Western states and

[34] Wolfe, *op. cit.*, p. 167.

from "reactionary" elements within their own countries, the neutralist nations will inevitably be drawn closer to the socialist camp.

The Soviets are capable of readily revising assumptions and policies relating to developments in areas which neither threaten vital security interests nor involve revision of core beliefs, or else are moving in a direction favorable to the extension of Soviet influence. This capacity for revising outmoded doctrinal assumptions, and always within the broad framework of Marxism-Leninism, testifies to the continuing belief in the ability of ideology to explain contemporary developments. For example, Lenin's thesis that imperialist nations must come into conflict over the division of the spoils of colonialism has been viewed as largely outdated by events since 1945. Moscow no longer considers it likely that capitalist countries will fight among themselves for control of the remaining colonial areas. The pattern of evolving independence for underdeveloped countries has gone too far. However the Soviets contend that though *political* independence has been largely achieved, many underdeveloped countries are still the *economic* vassals of the Western Powers. The term "collective colonialism" has recently appeared in the Soviet lexicon to describe the situation whereby the Western Powers cooperate to maintain their influence.[35] Since, say the Soviets, the imperialist powers can no longer individually suppress the national-liberation move-

[35] The term first came to my attention in an article denouncing SEATO's efforts to compel member Asian countries to embark on a program of armaments which were beyond their economic means. See K. Vladimirov and A. Yefremov, "An Instrument of Military Gambles and Provocation," *International Affairs*, No. 9 (September 1959), p. 33. Though they did not elaborate on the term, its meaning was clear.

The term next appeared in Khrushchev's February 26, 1960 speech, delivered during his visit to Indonesia, in which he noted that "the various forms of collective colonialism represent a special danger for the peoples of Asia, Africa, and Latin America." Since then, it has received increasing usage and elaboration.

ments in underdeveloped countries, they have pooled their power to protect their shrinking political and economic interests. Under the lure of cooperation in building up these backward lands, they entice the newly independent former colonies into economic, military, and political alliances which are, by their very nature, dominated by the West. One Soviet writer described collective colonialism as follows: "This policy signifies *joint* participation of the imperialist countries in suppressing the liberation movement (Algeria, the Congo, etc.), *joint* exploitation of the natural wealth of the Asian and African countries (activities of international companies), *joint* action of the colonialists in the United Nations and other international organizations against the legitimate demands of the Asian, African, and Latin American peoples."[36] Economically, the former colonial powers, no longer confident that their investments are safe, have established joint investment enterprises to safeguard their holdings. Militarily, the Western Powers seek to preserve a foothold abroad by drawing the nominally independent underdeveloped countries into military alliances under the guise of a "defense" against communism. Politically, the collective colonialism of the Western countries finds expression in the United Nations and other international organizations where the West tries to maintain a united policy on the question of abolishing colonialism and to squash the efforts of the new nations to obtain a greater voice in the operation and policies of these organizations.

International organizations hold a marginal place in the Soviet design for security and expansion. Bourgeois in origin, and dominated by the West, they are regarded as useful but minor arenas for conflict diplomacy. Soviet policy in them is predicated on the assumption of an unrelenting Western hostility, a view unfortunately strengthened by Western behavior in international organizations. Shifts in Soviet position have

[36] V. Bogoslovsky, "The Essence of Collective Colonialism," *International Affairs,* No. 12 (December 1960), p. 20.

occurred as part of the post-1953 change in approach toward neutralist countries, and participation and politiking in international organizations have increased as the Kremlin has moved to a far-ranging policy of competitive coexistence. This policy arose from a desire to minimize the possibility of nuclear war or any uncontrollable escalation of brushfire wars, and from confidence that in the ideological, economic, political, and cultural struggle, the international position of the Soviet Union will continue to improve, and to deprive the West of its waning influence in underdeveloped countries.

The Soviet attitude toward international organizations derives from Soviet *perceptions* of the motivations, policies, and objectives of the Western Powers who dominate them. These perceptions, which are significantly fashioned by the ideology, forestall any sympathetic Soviet evaluation of international organizations; they determine the selection and interpretation of information which in turn undergoes distortion in a manner tending to reinforce the elite's interests and outlook on the world. The result is that the Soviets see international organizations (just as they do Western actions and motivations) in the worst possible light.

Soviet writers postulate the inevitable continued "ideological struggle" of the camp of communism and the camp of capitalism until communism triumphs, though, at the same time, they call for an end to the Cold War. They distinguish sharply between the Cold War and the inevitability of "ideological struggle": ". . . to regard the 'Cold War' as a species of ideological struggle, to place an equal sign between these phenomena, and even more to put forward a demand for the cessation of the ideological struggle in order to achieve a relaxation of international tension—this is theoretically unfounded and politically injurious."[37] The Soviets consider that

[37] G. Frantsov, "What Lies Behind the Slogan Ideological Disarmament," *Kommunist*, No. 13 (September 1962), pp. 110-111.

"as long as there exist antagonistic classes with opposing ideologies and world outlooks, it will be impossible not to have 'ideological struggle.'" They do not recognize that the resolution of political tensions is seriously complicated by the intensification of ideological conflict, that their perception of political problems and institutions is distorted by their a priori views and assumptions.

This does not mean that the Soviet Union has not on occasion played a constructive role in international organizations, or that it may not be induced to assume an even more important one. Moscow may participate actively in international organizations, but it does so for reasons unrelated to the long-range purposes of these institutions; it continues to regard them as capitalist creations, as inimical to the attainment of Soviet goals. This fundamental ideological antipathy is at the heart of what distinguishes Soviet behavior from that of non-Communist countries. Other countries may oppose the strengthening of international organizations: some because they resent the dominance of a few powers; others because they are not convinced of the value of international organizations for them; a few because they see threats to their newly won independence. But the dissatisfactions and uncertainties of these non-Communist countries are not rooted in a systematic body of thought and a mode of analysis which fundamentally militate against greater commitment to international organizations. For Moscow, on the other hand, as long as ideology functions as an active and pervasive catalyst and conditioner of political perception, analysis, and value-orientation, international organizations will remain convenient institutions for maneuver and manipulation.

IX ◈⸱⸻

Prospects and Proposals

A NUMBER of years ago, Walter Lippmann called attention to the political significance of the underdeveloped countries by referring to them as "the middle world"—the region between the Western and Soviet blocs. Appreciating their importance, Moscow has devoted increasing attention to the economic and social activities of international organizations concerned with their welfare. Concomitantly, she has succeeded in making her programs of bilateral assistance to Afro-Asia respectable and coveted. Soviet prestige is growing, as accommodation replaces intransigence, and isolation gives way to participation. The new approach is a response not only to Moscow's reevaluation of the role of underdeveloped countries in the struggle with the West, but also to the qualitative transformation of international organizations: the influx of Afro-Asian states has ended the unchallenged dominance of the West and opened opportunities for political maneuvers hitherto unavailable to the Soviet Union.

Soviet policy in international organizations may be classified into three periods: 1945-1953; 1953-1960; 1960-present. During the Stalin period, political and security considerations were so narrowly construed that membership in the United Nations was maintained almost exclusively to forestall the formation of anti-Soviet coalitions. The veto power in the Security Council enabled Moscow to block adverse political decisions. Participation in international organizations was politically ineffectual, and, in the Specialized Agencies, limited to those with technical, nonpolitical functions, such as the ITU and UPU. The second period, initiated by the decision to contribute to the UN Expanded Program of Technical Assistance, was dominated by a drive to achieve respectability among

349

neutralist countries. Moscow realized that international organizations could serve her interests with minimum financial outlay and no risk to the preservation of the Soviet empire, and that political differentiation in the underdeveloped world held great potential for the extension of Soviet influence. Thus, it grouped underdeveloped countries into three general categories, based on the degree of their affinity for close relations with the Soviet bloc and their potential for eventual communization: the most "progressive" group includes Cuba, Ghana, Indonesia, and Mali; also capable of playing a positive role in opposing Western "imperialism" are the "peace-loving" bourgeois-democratic regimes such as India, Egypt, and Morocco; the third group, which is allied with and controlled by the Western Powers, includes underdeveloped countries such as Pakistan, Iran, and Thailand. Moscow understood that the antagonisms among these groups and between them and the West could redound to its benefit.

Khrushchev's troika proposal of September 1960 signified Moscow's entrance into a third phase in which it aspired to bend international organizations to Soviet purposes. This development is an outcome of the increasing estrangement between neutralist and Western nations, the growth of Soviet confidence in its military prowess, and the strong dissonances in the Western camp. Through tacit alliance with the neutralists, Moscow seeks to overcome its position of perpetual electoral inferiority and tó end Western domination of international organizations. It has terminated the isolation which was its lot during the Stalin period and forged the outlines of a coalescing anti-Western voting alliance.

International organizations have become useful to Soviet diplomacy, a reflection of the widening range of the concerns of foreign policy. Though the Soviet Union is still interested predominantly in the political aspects of UN activities, participation in the economic and social activities has become necessary because of the inseparability of political and nonpolitical issues and the all-encompassing nature of the Cold War. International organizations have become indispensable for establishing contacts with neutralist officials, demonstrating Soviet support for neutralist policies, and gaining a wide audience for Moscow's views. They are tailor-made for Soviet conflict diplomacy. The Soviet pattern is readily observable in international organizations in which underdeveloped countries figure prominently: Moscow makes proposals for drastic and rapid changes with little regard for their feasibility and with little apparent interest in actually seeing them realized; it adopts an extremist position on anticolonialism and anti-imperialism and, under the banner of "democracy" and "progress," is making its bid for leadership of the neutralist countries; it condemns the most liberal proposals of the Western countries as inadequate, but embraces those of the moderate neutralists as contructive. Support is offered as evidence of Moscow's desire to help underdeveloped countries preserve their independence and develop their economies; by demanding prompt action Moscow seeks to place itself in the forefront of movements for change. When opposed by the Western countries, Moscow charges them with indifference and domination. It keeps carefully attuned to neutralist sentiment. No area of neutralist interest is too insignificant for Soviet attention; no problem is to trivial to be raised if it holds the promise of a shred of political gain.

The position on the SUNFED question is illustrative of Soviet style in international organizations. A proposal favored by underdeveloped countries, but rejected by the West as untimely and unrealistic, was championed belatedly by the USSR. As long as it is debated with continued regularity, under various labels, the Soviets have the propaganda initiative. Should a watered-down variant be suggested by the neutralists, they are quick to support it, partly because it does not commit them to extend much tangible aid, and partly because they can then attack the West for inadequate attention to the problems of underdeveloped areas, a theme many neutralists are receptive to. On the SUNFED issue, as on so many others, the Soviet Union seeks to nurture an image of energetic concern for underdeveloped countries and to dominate the proceedings of international organizations with its proposals and resolutions. By preempting so much of the time of the working committees, Moscow, under the guise of wanting to help underdeveloped countries, prevents constructive action from being taken and suffuses the atmosphere with apathy and disillusionment which encourage the cynical view neutralists hold of international organizations and further dispose them toward bilateral aid programs. It thus contributes to the prevailing image that international organizations are useful only as forums for political controversy and for whatever a nation can extract from UN operational programs. As interpreted by the Soviets, this means that the level of constructive activities is to be kept at a minimum, far below the organizations' untried and rich potentialities.

The United Nations, as the international organization dealing with the major political controversies, receives most of the Soviets' attention. This focus on political issues is neither surprising nor unusual, being characteristic also of Western and neutralist nations. Now that the new nations have affected the balance of voting power, Moscow envisages a more activist role for itself. According to one group of Soviet writers: "In the struggle for peace and the diminution of international tension, the actions of the USSR and the other socialist countries in the United Nations play a serious role. The socialist governments resolutely expose the attempts of the imperialist powers to utilize the UNO for aggressive purposes, they courageously criticize and reject the decisions of the General Assembly which were taken under pressures of the USA's 'mechanistic majority' by those who are dependent upon it. . . ."[1] One Soviet commentator attributed the importance

[1] I. F. Ivashin, V. P. Nikhamin, and F. G. Zyev (eds.), *Mezhduna-*

of the UN to the fact that it "is an international forum conducted openly before all the peoples. . . . The existence of such a forum makes it to a certain extent harder for the aggressive forces to prepare and carry out military gambles. Whoever mounts the United Nations rostrum ultimately has to let the world public know his position, whether he wants to or not."[2] The peace-promoting function of the UN is handicapped by American control: "In order to serve as an important instrument in solving international problems the United Nations must be an international organization and not a branch of the State Department."[3] This is a criticism they apply to all international organizations. Post-Stalinist attention to the welfare functions of international organizations has been a necessary adjunct to Moscow's courtship of underdeveloped countries, but it does not reflect a change in the Soviet view of the

---

rodnye otnosheniia i vneshniaia politika SSSR (Moscow: Publishing House of the Higher Party School of the Central Committee of the CPSU, 1961), p. 403.

[2] O. Nakropin, "The United Nations Must Be An Instrument Of Peace," International Affairs, No. 11 (November 1957), p. 115. See also L. Fituni, "The United Nations Organizations and the Security of Peoples," Mirovaia ekonomika i mezhdunarodnye otnosheniia, No. 5 (November 1957), pp. 31-37.

One Soviet commentator maintained that, despite its obvious shortcomings, the UN serves a positive function: "It facilitates to a certain extent the establishment and development of ties and intercourse between states and in this way provides some prerequisites for an extension of international cooperation in various fields—political, economic, social, and others. The consideration of numerous international problems by UN bodies contributes to the clarification of the views of various states on this or that issue, brings the most important international questions to the notice of a broad public and helps to mobilize the progressive forces of various social groups for the preservation and consolidation of peace and for the peaceful settlement of outstanding international issues. In certain instances, UN consideration of international disputes has facilitated their settlement in the interests of world peace and security." A. Vorobyov, "The Tenth Anniversary of the United Nations Organization," International Affairs, No. 6 (June 1955), p. 44.

[3] Nakropin, op. cit., p. 116.

Western-controlled character of these organizations or their peripheral role in the mainstream of international affairs.

As far as many neutralists are concerned, Western and Soviet policies in international organizations bear a striking similarity: each bloc is more preoccupied with thwarting the policies of the other than with advancing the purposes of the organizations; each hopes to win the neutralists to its position; each contributes to the economic and social activities of international organizations but a pittance compared to the amount it extends on a bilateral basis. Though the Western countries contribute more generously than the Soviet bloc, the neutralists see the difference as one of degree, not of kind. They have adapted quickly to the structure of international organizations and to the power-oriented behavior of member nations. In pursuit of their own interests, they have come into more frequent and open clashes with the Western countries whom they regard with a suspicion stemming from centuries of colonial control. Resentful of their continued economic dependence, many neutralists believe they have more to fear from the West than from the Soviet Union.

For its part, the West is disturbed by what it regards as the immaturity of many neutralist nations: specifically, with their pronounced sympathy for Soviet proposals, particularly those designed to embarrass the West, and their obsessive concern with anticolonialism. Western uneasiness is the outgrowth of the continuing shift in effective power in the UN and other international organizations. By exaggerating the radicalism of the neutralists, by underestimating, out of its own anxiety, the growing sense of realism and maturity of many of the new nations, and by giving only weak support to the international organizations it created, the West is paving the way for the progressive intrusion of Soviet influence.

Moscow benefits from the derangement of Western purpose and policy in international organizations. It thrives on the neutralists' resentment of the paternalistic manner assumed by the West wherever questions of communism are involved. By exploiting Western-neutralist tensions, by attacking the West, and by lending support to extremist views among the neutralists, the Soviets have politicized the atmosphere, with the result that developmental functions are kept to a minimum. This has the effect of demonstrating the impotence of international organizations to underdeveloped countries and encouraging them to look elsewhere for assistance.

The Specialized Agencies and regional economic commissions are now committed almost completely to the task of promoting the economic, social, educational, and scientific development of underdeveloped areas. But, though they do constructive work, they have not received the kind of support from the Great Powers that is needed for a truly significant impact in the field of economic development. This stems from the belief among the "have" nations that they can derive greater political benefits from aid given through bilateral channels; competitive foreign aid programs have become key factors in Cold War diplomacy. That the Soviet Union relegates international organizations to a minor place in the structure of political concerns is evident from its position on organizational questions and from its minimal financial contributions. Under the cover of defending national sovereignty, Moscow has consistently opposed increases in the authority of international organizations. It contends that they were established for limited purposes and ought not be pressed to develop into something for which they were not originally conceived. Moscow's interest in international organizations is narrowly directed: to persuade the neutralists that they have common cause with the Soviet bloc against domination by the West.

Given the present state of affairs, Western attempts to convince the Soviet Union that strengthened international organizations are to its interest are politically and ideologically foredoomed to failure. *Only Moscow's conviction that in-*

355

creased participation would facilitate closer relationships with the neutralists, indeed that it was necessary for such a development, might bring about a modification of Soviet attitude and behavior; for whatever the current position of Moscow might be on international organizations, conditioned as it is by Soviet perspectives on the West and Western policies, a growing commitment by the politically important underdeveloped countries could prove a trend too strong for the Soviet Union long to withstand. And in this reconstitution of the institutions and environment of the world beyond the Soviet orbit lie the most promising hopes for the consequent erosion of Soviet ideology.

It is with this long-run objective in mind that a number of moves should be tried; they will at least clear the atmosphere and show the neutralists that the West does not seek to manipulate these organizations to advance its own interests, but desires to work with underdeveloped countries in a genuine partnership for economic progress and international stability. The problem can be approached in two ways, each of which would, it is hoped, reinforce the other: first, associate the USSR more intimately and intensively in the planning and programming of activities; and second, improve the cooperation between the Western and neutralist countries.

For more than a decade and a half, the Soviet Union has been kept on the periphery of policy-making and administration in international organizations—initially through its own choice, and later as a consequence of Western control which barred the Soviets from positions of authority. In its criticisms of Western high-handedness and anti-Soviet attitudes, Moscow has ground for grievance. That it has contributed to the present state of affairs by its own actions and attitudes goes without saying. But this is not the place to review or assess responsibility for the genesis and generation of Cold War politics; it is our purpose here to suggest ways of diminishing negativism in international organizations. The Soviet Union has not been accorded responsibility or status commensurate with its position as a Great Power and should be brought more directly into the decision-making levels of international organizations. There is no guarantee, and perhaps little likelihood, that greater responsibility for policy would lead to extensive Soviet commitments, any more than the long Western preeminence resulted in full-fledged Western support. But as a Great Power, the Soviet Union has legitimate claims to such treatment, and it can be hoped that increased responsibility may moderate some of its unjustified criticisms of international organizations.

First, a Soviet citizen should be made the head of one of the Specialized Agencies. At present, all the Directors-General are Westerners, with the exception of Dr. Sen (of the FAO) who is an Indian. The time is overdue for an "internationalization" of the top executive posts. The changing composition of these organizations should be reflected in the decision-making levels. Though no rigid, troika-type arrangement should be adopted, a redressing of national representation is needed. The danger that an organization headed by a Soviet citizen might become subservient to Soviet interests, or be turned into a Soviet-front organization, is remote, because the membership of each organization is the ultimate judge of the Director-General's competence and impartiality, and has the authority and means to remove unfit officials. We cannot a priori assume that a Soviet Director-General would not function in a way satisfactory to the great majority of the member nations. For its part, Moscow would stand to lose considerable prestige among the neutralists if it sought to use a Soviet Director-General to promote Soviet interests.

Second, Moscow should be made the headquarters of one of the Specialized Agencies. Though most of them are now engaged principally in activities pertaining to underdeveloped countries, their headquarters are all located in Western European countries. Whereas, at the time the Agencies were originally established, the overwhelming majority of members came from the Western world and the activities were Western-oriented, there is no longer any justification for the geographic concentration of the Agencies. It would be thoroughly appropriate for some of those Agencies which are most active in underdeveloped countries, e.g. FAO, WHO, ILO, UNESCO, to relocate in other parts of the world. In the decentralizing process, one of the new centers could be Moscow or Leningrad. The Soviets currently use the forums of international organizations to reach the opinion-molding elite, as well as the mass audiences, of other countries. Establishment of the site of a Specialized Agency in Moscow would provide non-Communist officials with an opportunity to reach more of the Soviet public. Working in the Soviet Union, either as governmental representatives or as members of the Agency Secretariat, would give neutralist officials new insights into the nature of Soviet society and the operation of Soviet "socialism." The West should make the proposal in conjunction with several of the leading neutralist countries, or encourage the neutralists to make it alone. The Soviet Government might well reject a proposal to establish the headquarters of an international organization in the USSR, but the responsibility and the onus should be theirs.

Third, consideration could be given to holding alternate sessions of the General Assembly in New York and Moscow. This might entail impossible administrative problems for the Secretariat, but not until they have been carefully explored should the idea be rejected. The Soviet Government has occasionally suggested that UN headquarters be transferred from New York to West Berlin, Vienna, Geneva, or some other city, in order to lessen Western control over the UN. Dissatisfaction with New York as the site of General Assembly sessions also exists among some neutralists. Again, it is highly questionable whether Moscow would agree to such a proposal, but if it did, unknown and unforeseen are the salutary effects this might have on the future of the UN.

358

Fourth, the West is wasting a unique opportunity by failing to challenge the Soviet Union to enter into a joint program of helping underdeveloped countries within the framework of international organizations. Secretary-General U Thant called on member nations to make this "the decade of development." The Soviets have indicated their support for SUNFED but have never stated how much they would be prepared to contribute; also, they persistently hold that an agreement on disarmament must be reached before more money can be diverted to the needs of underdeveloped countries, a view generally shared by the Western countries. The West should reverse its position and offer to match any contribution made by the Soviet bloc. By stating its willingness to contribute to SUNFED, or to any other program for aiding underdeveloped countries, an amount equal to that which the Soviet bloc is prepared to give, the West would do much to wrest the initiative on this issue from Moscow. The more money that the USSR can be induced to direct into economic development through international channels, the better will be the prospects for political stability in underdeveloped countries. So far, the Soviets have reaped impressive political harvests from meager contributions to UN programs. It is to the advantage of the West and the neutralists that Moscow increase its contribution. To wait for a disarmament agreement before expanding aid to neutralist countries is to play into Moscow's hands. Walter Lippmann has framed the dilemma as follows: "We cannot compete with communism in Asia, Africa, or Latin America if we go on doing what we have done so often and so widely—which is to place the weak countries in a dilemma where they must stand still with us and our client rulers or start moving with the Communists. This dilemma cannot be dissolved unless it is our central and persistent and unswerving policy to offer these unhappy countries a third option, which is economic development and social improvement without the totalitarian discipline of Communism."[4] Disarmament is one pressing problem; economic development is another. We cannot do much about the first, but we can significantly attack the second. Aid channeled through international organizations offers potential political and economic returns that are far greater than those currently received from the massive bilateral programs. It could place developmental activities on a more economically rational basis and do much to take the Cold War out of programs for helping needy nations. Suitably presented, such a program of development would be one challenge that the Soviets could not afford to ignore.

Fifth, the West has been remiss in squandering prospects for strengthening international organizations in the interest of temporary political triumphs of dubious merit. Its preoccupation with winning minor parliamentary skirmishes with the Soviet Union is endangering its opportunities for cooperation with the neutralist nations. For example, whether the Communist-controlled World Federation of Trade Unions is accredited to the International Atomic Energy Agency is a matter of no importance. Yet, by debating this issue with the Soviets, the West serves the Soviet objective of publicizing the organization and intensifies the politicization of IAEA. To involve organizations in circular political debate prevents useful work from being accomplished and engenders among neutralists a bitterness that is directed primarily against the West as the bloc responsible for setting the tone of the proceedings. Accreditation can be granted all non-governmental organizations which desire it, without in the least adversely affecting the operations of the Specialized Agencies. It would merely provide an opportunity for officials of, let us say, the WFTU to make a few speeches, reiterating views that have already been stated by Soviet delegates. The Agencies' work is far too important to be impeded by endless, parliamentary

4 Walter Lippmann, *The Coming Tests With Russia* (Boston: Little, Brown & Co., 1961), pp. 36-37.

wrangling. Since the West still dominates the proceedings of the Specialized Agencies, it must be held largely responsible for the lamentable waste of time and effort afflicting the Agencies.

These suggestions, even collectively, would seem inadequate to the task of stimulating an expanding Soviet interest in international organizations, particularly when they are juxtaposed to the general Soviet repugnance toward engaging in meaningful cooperation with capitalist countries, and the marginal role assigned to international organizations in the Soviet approach to international affairs. However, in the context of the growing importance of underdeveloped countries to Soviet policy, it is possible that Soviet leaders would increase their commitment to the so-called "nonpolitical" activities if they thought it necessary for the advancement of their influence among the neutralists. Certainly, the Soviets now support in principle any economic and social program which is strongly favored by neutralist countries. But it is also true that they have shown a continued illiberality toward new programs, even when the money was intended for underdeveloped countries. This, however, is not damaging to them for several reasons. First, as long as bilateral aid remains the major source of foreign assistance for neutralist countries, the "token" contributions of the USSR to international organizations is not critical in view of their considerable bilateral aid programs. Second, the neutralists do not regard Western contributions as significantly greater than those of the Soviet bloc, since the bulk of Western aid to underdeveloped countries is given to those who are allied with the West and is also channeled bilaterally. Accordingly, the difference between the amounts of Western and Soviet support for the economic and social programs of international organizations is not significant, in view of the difference between the amounts of foreign aid rendered through international and bilateral channels. Third, the neutralists share the Soviet view that Western concepts dominate the allocation of resources available to international organizations and that this acts as a legitimate deterrent to larger Soviet commitments. Finally, seeing that international organizations show no promise of developing as major sources of capital, the neutralists have no stake in making a political issue of strengthening them.

One clear fact emerges from an examination of international organizations: namely, that the combination of Western and neutralist cooperation is sufficient to make any economic and social proposal a reality; further, the Soviet Union, for political reasons, will not oppose a proposal enjoying neutralist approval and will participate and contribute, though often only minimally. Cooperation between the neutralist and Western nations is essential for the future of international organizations; when the two conflict, the Soviets are afforded the opportunity for political mischief. If they work in concert, each can advance its own interests: the West can improve its relations with underdeveloped countries, retain an important measure of influence in international organizations in which it no longer commands a voting majority, and strengthen institutions through which economic progress and orderly international change might be channeled; the neutralists will find international organizations indispensable for obtaining serious consideration for their views, for developing closer ties with other underdeveloped countries through cooperation rather than competition, and for encouraging the wealthy nations to devote more of their resources to the well-being of the poor nations. The neutralist nations have within their reach an opportunity to convince the Western nations that they are not out to get whatever they can for themselves by playing on the Cold War rivalry. By evidencing a readiness to cooperate within an international framework, the neutralists may encourage greater support from the Western countries; by attributing political value to international organizations, they may also induce Moscow to increase its commitment.

Such developments will not end the Cold War. Nor, in the short run, should they be expected to decrease international tension. But they could conceivably result in greater Soviet cooperation in the task of helping the poor countries, and then, inadvertently but inevitably, in strengthening international organizations as a consequence of greater Western-neutralist cooperation and growing Soviet participation. "In the long run," Inis Claude has written, "it may be that the economic and social work will prove to be one of the means of developing a system whereby man can control his political climate."[5]

In the past, the United States supported international organizations because they supported the United States. The introduction of numerous neutralist nations has complicated the operation of these organizations and the possibilities of obtaining a consensus which would permit the continuation and expansion of their established purposes.[6] The West's preoccupation with the efforts of the Soviet Union to exploit these organizations for the furtherance of Soviet objectives, coupled with its excessive concern that the newly independent countries, inexperienced and impatient, will be used as pawns against the West, has given rise to suspicions on both sides that forestall the mutual benefits that the West and the neutralists stand to gain from an effectively functioning system of international organizations. The tendency of the neutralists to support psychologically satisfying Soviet proposals, to devote inordinate attention to the fading issue of colonialism, is

[5] Inis L. Claude, Jr., *Swords Into Plowshares* (New York: Random House, 1956), p. 402.

[6] At the June 1963 annual conference of the International Labor Organization, 32 African members walked out in protest against the continued participation of the South African delegation. Premier Ben Bella of Algeria has urged that the boycott be extended to other Specialized Agencies, and even to the UN General Assembly. Should the African nations adopt such a radical and divisive course, they would undoubtedly be supported by the bulk of neutralists from other regions, and by the Soviet bloc. Another step in the emasculation of international organizations would then have been taken.

a burden the West must be prepared to assume for the next few years, a minor, though irritating, legacy from the past.

The time has come for the United States, as the leading Western Power, to act in a manner that leaves no doubt of its wholehearted commitment to international organizations, to the task of promoting economic and social development in concert with underdeveloped countries. International organizations can serve as valuable bridges between the West and the new nations, over which can pass not merely goods, but knowledge and understanding. By transforming them into Cold War arenas, the West demeans the very institutions that it created and that are capable of playing an important role in promoting international stability. Let Western delegates, led by the United States, devote themselves to the problems in which the underdeveloped countries have a vital interest; let them seek to resolve differences, to negotiate genuinely, and to concentrate on the goals that are mutually shared. For the West, the dialogue with the underdeveloped countries is the only one worth pursuing in international organizations. Efforts to dominate, to dictate policy, to bend these organizations to narrowly conceived political objectives, will result only in widening the gulf between Western and neutralist nations, and in emasculating international organizations, an end which Moscow devoutly desires and from which it alone stands to gain.

Selected Bibliography

The principal published materials used in this study consisted of the records and documents of the Economic and Social Council, the Technical Assistance Committee, the International Labor Organization, the International Atomic Energy Agency, the Economic Commission for Asia and the Far East, and their respective subsidiary bodies. Where pertinent, the records of the General Assembly and the World Health Organization were also examined.

It is not my intention to compile a list of all the books and articles already cited in footnote references. Most of the Soviet sources are presented in my bibliographic article in the *American Political Science Review* of December 1960. Mention may be made, however, of a few of the works which are particularly relevant to this study.

BOOKS

Dallin, Alexander. *The Soviet Union at the United Nations.* New York: Frederick A. Praeger, 1962.

Jacobson, Harold K. *The USSR and the UN's Economic and Social Activities.* Notre Dame: University of Notre Dame Press, 1963.

Lie, Trygve. *In The Cause of Peace.* New York: The Macmillan Company, 1954.

Sharp, Walter R. *Field Administration in the United Nations System.* New York: Frederick A. Praeger, 1961.

Wightman, David. *Toward Economic Cooperation in Asia: The United Nations Economic Commission for Asia and the Far East.* New Haven: Yale University Press, 1963.

ARTICLES

Allen, Robert Loring. "United Nations Technical Assistance: Soviet and East European Participation," *International Organization*, Vol. xi, No. 4 (Autumn 1957), pp. 615-634.

Armstrong, John A. "The Soviet Attitude Toward UNESCO," *International Organization*, Vol. viii, No. 2 (May 1954), pp. 217-233.

Asher, Robert E. "Multilateral versus Bilateral Aid: An Old Controversy Revisited," *International Organization*, Vol. xvi, No. 4 (Autumn 1962), pp. 697-719.

Ginsburgs, George. "Soviet Atomic Energy Agreements," *International Organization*, Vol. xv, No. 1 (Winter 1961), pp. 49-65.

Goodrich, Leland M. "Geographical Distribution of the Staff of the UN Secretariat," *International Organization*, Vol. xvi, No. 3 (Summer 1962), pp. 465-482.

Jacobson, Harold K. "Labor, the UN and the Cold War," *International Organization*, Vol. xi, No. 1 (Winter 1957), pp. 55-67.

———. "The Soviet Union, the UN and World Trade," *The Western Political Quarterly*, Vol. xi, No. 3 (September 1958), pp. 673-688.

———. "The USSR and ILO," *International Organization*, Vol. xiv, No. 3 (Summer 1960), pp. 402-428.

Malinowski, W. R. "Centralization and Decentralization in the United Nations Economic and Social Activities," *International Organization*, Vol. xvi, No. 3 (Summer 1962), pp. 521-541.

Masters, Roger. "The Emperor's Old Clothes: Russia and the United Nations," *The Yale Review*, Vol. lii, No. 2 (December 1962), pp. 176-187.

Rubinstein, Alvin Z. "Soviet Policy Toward Underdeveloped Areas in the Economic and Social Council," *Interna-*

tional Organization, Vol. IX, No. 2 (May 1955), pp. 232-243.

――――. "Soviet Policy in ECAFE: A Case Study of Soviet Behavior in International Economic Organization," *International Organization,* Vol. XII, No. 4 (Autumn 1958), pp. 459-472.

――――. "The U.S.S.R. and the I.M.C.O.: Some Preliminary Observations," United States Naval Institute *Proceedings,* Vol. LXXXV, No. 10 (October 1959), pp. 75-79.

――――. "Selected Bibliography of Soviet Works on the United Nations, 1946-1959," *The American Political Science Review,* Vol. LIV, No. 4 (December 1960), pp. 985-991.

Schaaf, Hart C. "The United Nations Economic Commission for Asia and the Far East," *International Organization,* Vol. VII, No. 4 (November 1953), pp. 463-481.

Wightman, David. "Efforts for Economic Cooperation in Asia and the Far East: The Experience of ECAFE," *The World Today,* Vol. 18, No. 1 (January 1962), pp. 30-42.

Index

AAUN. *See* American Association for the United Nations

Abdel-Ghani, Mr., 117

ACABQ. *See* Advisory Committee on Administrative and Budgetary Questions

Academy of Construction and Architecture (of USSR), 293

Academy of Sciences (of USSR), 292-93, 301

Adenauer, Konrad, 174

Advisory Committee on Administrative and Budgetary Questions (ACABQ), 80, 125-26

Afghanistan: economic and technical assistance to, 46, 161, 163, 233, 236; view of foreign aid, 52, 54; feud with Pakistan, 91, 182; Soviet policy in regard to, 91, 138, 157; attitude toward volunteer workers, 115, 116, 118, 120; Soviet loan offer to, 159; wisdom of close Soviet ties, 188

Africa, 8, 164, 171, 188-89, 212, 249, 251, 272

Albania, 103

Algeria, 346, 363n.

All Union Council of Trade Unions, 293

All Union Society for the Dissemination of Political and Scientific Knowledge, 291, 293ff.

Allen, Robert Loring, 37n.

American Association for the United Nations (AAUN), 294

Argentina, 239

Arkadev, Georgi F., 281n.

Arutiunian, Amazasp A., xiii, 32, 34, 93

Arzumanyan, A., 174n.

ASA. *See* Association for Southeast Asia

Asher, Robert E., 56n.

Asia, 8, 11, 13, 212, 249, 251

Asian Institute for Economic Development, 189

Asian Planners Conference (1961), 174

Aspaturian, Vernon, 324-25

Association for Southeast Asia (ASA), 175

Aswan Dam, Egypt, 45

atomic power, 191-253. *See also* International Atomic Energy Agency

Australia, 142, 194

Austria, 237

Bagdad Pact, 40

Bailey, Sydney D., 269n., 277n.

Bao Dai, 143

Belgium, 194

Belorussia, 104, 266

Ben Bella, Premier, 363n.

Bhabha, Homi, 210, 211, 215, 221ff.

Bhilai steel plant, India, 39, 44, 48, 161

Board of Governors (of IAEA), 196, 198ff.

Bogoslovsky, V., 346n.

Bombay Institute of Technology, 41ff., 48, 64

Bombay University, 41

Borovskii, V., 163n.

Bowles, Chester, 334n.

Brazil, 194, 226, 238, 239

Brynielsson, Harry, 197ff.

Brzezinski, Zbigniew K., 318n., 319n., 322n., 325n.